THE ART OF BEING BLACK

The Art of Being Black
The Creation of Black British Youth Identities

CLAIRE E. ALEXANDER

CLARENDON PRESS · OXFORD
1996

Oxford University Press, Walton Street, Oxford OX2 6DP

Oxford New York
Athens Auckland Bangkok Bombay
Calcutta Cape Town Dar es Salaam Delhi
Florence Hong Kong Istanbul Karachi
Kuala Lumpur Madras Madrid Melbourne
Mexico City Nairobi Paris Singapore
Taipei Tokyo Toronto
and associated companies in
Berlin Ibadan

Oxford is a trade mark of Oxford University Press

Published in the United States
by Oxford University Press Inc., New York

British Library Cataloguing in Publication Data
Data available

Library of Congress Cataloging in Publication Data
Data available

ISBN 0-19-827982-5

1 3 5 7 9 10 8 6 4 2

Typeset by Graphicraft Typesetters Ltd., Hong Kong
Printed in Great Britain
on acid-free paper by
Bookcraft (Bath) Ltd
Midsomer Norton, Avon

FOREWORD

STUART HALL

Professor of Sociology, Open University

QUESTIONS of cultural identity have become central to the agenda of contemporary social and anthropological research. As the waves of forced and unplanned migrations transform the hitherto well-defined and apparently stable cultural formations of the globe, so the issues of how, and with what groups, do peoples on the move identify themselves—and how this is influencing the self-identifications of people from the indigenous, native, or 'host' societies—has come to constitute a subject of enormous public interest and debate.

Are the cultural identities of social groups constituted primarily by stable, structural features of social organization, such that the vicissitudes of movement, dispersal, and displacement cannot deeply influence or disturb them? Has ethnicity acquired something of the permanence of shared genetic dispositions? Do we bear our cultural identities, the signs and symbols of our 'belongingness', like (as some would argue) indelible number-plates on our backs? And does the process of political and cultural representation operate, so to speak, with subjects who possess already fully formed identities? Or are the unities that cultural identities appear to constitute the result of what we might call a 'practice of narration', the invention of the cultural self, producing a fixed belongingness in rather the way we construct, after the event, a persuasive, consistent biographical 'story' about who we are and where we came from? To put this question another way, are cultural identities fixed, given, and unified, or are they shifting, subject to the 'play' of history and representation, plural and diverse if not actually divided, and unified only by those retrospective processes which *narrate* them as unified, those narratives of the cultural self whose function is indeed to stitch up or suture diversity and difference into something we can experience as unified? Is ethnicity moving from a matter of 'descent' to 'assent'—not the rediscovery of our 'roots' in the past but a tracking of our 'routes' to the present? Is cultural identity those imperatives we obey or that which we perform?

These are some of the critical questions which underpin and give a wide, general significance to Claire Alexander's fascinating ethnographic study of how the identity commonly known as 'black' is being produced, performed in the British urban context today. Much of the debate that flows from the questions identified above has been pursued on a very broad and general canvas —one that is too wide to capture the complex and subject interweaving of practices and meanings which now constitute the taking-on of this identity amongst young British 'black' people. Claire Alexander, however, has gone back to the detailed 'microphysics' of power and meaning which alone offers a sufficiently fine-grained analysis to show the mechanisms of identity construction and 'performance' at work in all the rich detail we require if these more abstract theoretical questions are to be adequately addressed. She is working in the distinguished ethnographic tradition of *Tally's Corner* and *Street Corner Society*, but with a new sensitivity to the complexities of the practices of negotiation, and a new set of questions born of a new and later historical situation—that presented by the new, multicultural cities of the 'First World' after the Great Migrations of the post-war era. She is working with an acute sensitivity to the way questions of cultural identity are cross-cut and often displaced through other dimensions—especially class, gender, sexuality, and generation. She settles for neither of the two fashionable extremes: neither a celebration of performativity and creativity nor a return to images of ethnic absolutism and exclusion. Instead, she weaves through her narrative a sense of both the symbolic constraints and symbolic resources which 'tradition' provides for cultural-identity construction, and a respect for the profound 'work' which goes into the symbolic production of cultural identification, combined with a rich understanding of its necessarily contingent and open-ended character.

This is work which enriches us in its blend of empirical 'thick descriptiveness' and subtle theorizing. It suggests how diverse, how complex the self-ascription 'Black British' now is; how the performance of identity is not a simple repetition of what was already there, but a 'performativity' which is always conducted within situational, normative, historical, and material constraints.

It suggests why 'being black' is a kind of discursive accomplishment, a practice rather than a reflection. It invites us to rethink identity *through* difference. In doing so, it takes us to the heart of what lies behind the urgent but so often too empty question of our times: 'what is it like for displaced people to become something, someone?' And it reminds us that the question of cultural identity, as Michel Foucault so poignantly reminded us, is not in fact 'Who are you?' but 'What can you become?' It gives flesh to the theoretical abstraction that cultural identity involves, not discovering the subject you *really are*, but the more perplexing process of the production—and self-production—of new subjects.

ACKNOWLEDGEMENTS

THERE are many people to whom I am indebted for their support, advice, and assistance during the writing of both this book and the thesis on which it is based. First, I must express my deepest thanks to my supervisors, Terence Ranger and Colin Clarke, for their continued guidance—and for always giving me the freedom to do what I really wanted—and to my examiners, Stuart Hall and Marcus Banks, for their encouragement during this project. I am grateful to St Hugh's College, Somerville College, and the Institute for Social and Cultural Anthropology, Oxford University, which were my bases during the research and the preparation of the book. I would also like to thank the ESRC, which funded the initial study, for their tolerance and support, and the staff of Oxford University Press, for their help in the preparation of this material. I am particularly grateful to Peter Momtchiloff for his enthusiastic support of the project and his willingness to take a chance on me.

Most of all, I would like to express my love and thanks to those people who allowed me into their lives: to 'the boys'—Ricky, Clive, Frank, Nathan, Arif, Malcolm, Satish, Shane, and Dion—and to Angelina, Darnell, Rommell, Eleanor, and Fenella. Without their help, their patience, and their friendship, the research would have been impossible. I also extend my appreciation to the co-ordinator, staff and members of the Community Centre, and to the many other men and women whom I encountered during my time in London. I would especially like to thank Angela and Ann-Marie for their support and understanding in some difficult times.

In Oxford, I was lucky enough to receive the support and advice of a number of people. Foremost amongst these are Ossie Stuart and Yunas Samad, whose belief in me has been a crucial source of strength over the past few years and from whose wisdom and good sense I have benefited greatly. I am also grateful for the stimulation and support of all members of, and contributors to, the Ethnic Relations Seminar, St Antony's College—particularly Phyllis Ferguson, Melanie Chait, and Paul Goodwin.

Since this research has been almost an obsession for the past five years, I would thank my friends for putting up with me and helping me through it. To Rachel Wicaksono, who was there from the beginning, to Mark Larrimore, and to Huma Rizvi, especially, I send love and gratitude. Also to Ruth Quinn, Simone Abram, Janet and Rob Hufton, and Clare Twigger: I couldn't have done it without you. Special thanks to Terrence 'Spyder T' Webster, for giving me the courage to start.

Finally, I thank my family for all their support—even when they thought I was crazy—and especially my mother, who waded through my interview tapes, and refused to transcribe only one. And Teferi, who was always there for me, and whose love and friendship remain my source of strength.

This book is dedicated to you all with love.

C.E.A.

London
1995

CONTENTS

Contents

1

Introduction

> So there it is, work it out for yourself,
> Yeah, be selective, be objective,
> Be an asset to the collective,
> 'Cause you know you've got to Get A Life.
>
> (Soul II Soul; *Get A Life*)

IN April 1989, *The Face* heralded the arrival of Soul II Soul as 'The New Funki Face of Black Britain'. In the summer of that year, in the clubs in Oxford, and undoubtedly elsewhere in Britain, their music was playing, and young black men were moving on to the dancefloor with a proprietorial air. *Sky Magazine* wrote, 'This summer has seen the explosion of a new black pride. African pendants, Muslim headgear and militant rap lyrics can be seen and heard in all the trendiest British nightclubs' (Sept. 1989). Soul II Soul were portrayed as the vanguard of what one record producer described to me as 'a black cultural explosion', an assertion of a culture and identity that had been hitherto largely ignored, or positively denied. For Soul II Soul, the emphasis was on creativity and alterity; the expression of black life which demanded to be taken on its own terms:

> Well, take a look up and take a glance
> At the Alternative
> Of what do you have to give
> And put that in the way that you want to live
> Your life
>
> (Soul II Soul; *Feeling Free*)

What Soul II Soul proclaimed was a new identity—the existence of an expression and culture that was Black British; an identity in which 'black' constituted an integral element rather than a qualifying adjective.

For the media, the emphasis was very much on the external style associated with this supposedly 'new' black identity. Thus, Adrian Dannatt wrote of the then new Razor-cut:

the Razor is the ideal cut of an aspirant generation. This is the style of those who want the job, want the position, want the power, but are not prepared to let anyone forget what colour they are (*The Guardian*, 11 Sept. 1989).

What it meant to those wearing it remained largely unconsidered, merely assumed. It was also assumed that because the external trappings had only then reached public attention, the impetus behind them had itself been recently created. As Soul II Soul's doyen Jazzie B. stated in an interview in *The Face* (Apr. 1989), however, both the group and the style were very much part of an evolving identity founded on the experience of growing up black in Britain: 'What I'm doing is a sign of the times. . . . My generation of West Indian origin is the last of its kind, my children will be almost totally English.'

BLACK AND BRITISH?

It is true, however, that the creation of an identity which is both black and British is held by many to be something of an anomaly, if not a travesty. In Eastbourne in 1968, Enoch Powell proclaimed in his infamous speech, 'the West Indian does not, by being born in England, become an Englishman. In law, he becomes a UK citizen by birth; in fact, he is a West Indian or Asian still' (16 Nov. 1968).[1]

Twenty-five years on, the arguments have changed little. In 1978 Margaret Thatcher took up Powell's vision of traditional communities torn apart by black immigration in her 'swamping' statement. The following year, she reasserted, 'Some people have felt swamped by immigrants. They've seen the whole character of their neighbourhood change. . . . They feel their whole way of life has been changed' (*Observer*, 25 Feb. 1979). In 1990 Norman Tebbit again picked up the themes of 'foreign' cultures and questionable citizenship in his evocation of the 'cricket test'[2] for

---

[1] Throughout this section, England and Britain are used interchangeably. This reflects both usage by the authors cited, and also the hegemonic nature of English identity, which defines the limits of Britishness.

[2] Norman Tebbit argued in April 1990 that the loyalty of ethnic minority groups in Britain was in question if they did not cheer for England in test cricket matches (cf. Solomos 1993: 228–9).

Britain's ethnic minorities, insisting on the threat posed to the 'British character' by 'the waves of newcomers intent on importing their nationality to our nation' (*Today*, 21 Apr. 1990).

A recurrent theme throughout is the equation of the black communities with a 'culture' that is alien to, and unassimilable with, the British 'way of life'. Both Powell and Thatcher insisted on the incompatibility of black cultures with British culture, and point to an inherent danger posed by people who are 'in fact. . .still' outsiders and whose very presence threatens the national landscape and character. Tebbit's statement similarly, while insisting on the need for an 'assimilation' that can be observed and quantified, simultaneously reasserts the impossibility of achieving such a position. The equation of Britain's black communities with the 'foreigner' and the denial of nationhood found in Powell's speech is also made by Tebbit, who explicitly conflates 'nationality' with 'culture', and with an attack on British national identity.

The 'Britain' at the centre of each of these statements is envisioned as an idealized and harmonious whole, where the individual, community, and nation become interchangeable and inseparable. As Benedict Anderson has argued (1983), the emergence of modern national identities involves the creation of political communities which are 'imagined' by its members as finite and internally coherent entities. The creation of national boundaries thus necessitates both processes of inclusion and of exclusion, along with an incumbent ideology which defines and embraces those who belong and rejects those who do not. A primary source of distinction is 'culture', in which 'Native' identity is preserved through the erection of 'cultural fences' (Baumann 1988), which are portrayed as fixed, closed to 'the Other' and exclusionary. The perception of essential cultural 'difference' forms the basis of what Martin Barker has termed 'The New Racism' (1981) that builds on the belief in 'natural' bounded units—such as Thatcher's imagined Britain—which are distinguished from others through the possession of an in-built cultural knowledge, visioned as primordial and inviolable. 'Culture' then becomes a primary source and symbol of differentiation and boundary maintenance, in which 'nationhood' and 'way of life' are indistinguishable: as Martin Barker writes, 'The Nation is its "way of life"' (1981: 17).

It is the perception of a 'way of life' under threat which forms the basis of Powell's vision, Thatcher's 'swamping' speeches, and Tebbit's 'cricket test'. 'Culture' is, moreover, inescapably equated with 'race' in what Barker calls 'pseudo-biological culturalism' (ibid. 23). Phenotype thus becomes the primary signifier of the outsider; of an inalienable cultural 'strangeness' (Baumann 1988), and hence of a perceived threat to national integrity. 'Culture', 'ethnicity', and 'race' are collapsed in a discourse of community and nation that continues to deny the place of Britain's black communities within the realm of national culture and belonging. Ironically, this view of culture as the birthright of bounded holistic 'communities' informs not only far right political discourses around nationality and immigration, but has also been taken up in the liberal and left-wing celebration of cultural diversity and multiculturalism (Gilroy 1992: 56). Multicultural discourses in education, for example, have led to the reification of cultural difference characterized by the 'saris, samosas and steelband syndrome' (Donald and Rattansi 1992: 2).

Where nations are imagined as conterminous with ethnic, racial, or religious homogeneity, such an ideology imposes notions of absolute identities—an individual is either part of the imagined community, or is 'the Other': hyphenated or 'hybrid' identities transcend national boundaries and threaten the social order. The 'reimagination' of English identity in the post-war period has thus defined itself against the presence of minority groups and placed them outside its bounds (CCCS 1982: 80–5). To be black and British, then, constitutes something of a paradox. As Paul Gilroy notes, the idea of the black community in Britain as irrevocably alien has a long and firmly entrenched history. He writes, 'The enemy within, the unarmed invasion, alien encampments, alien territory, and New Commonwealth occupation have all been used to describe the black presence' (1987: 45). Black people in Britain have been consistently portrayed as outside the realm of the national culture and, moreover, incompatible with it. Indeed, the stigma of 'race' has become a symbol of internal crises at a state level, 'what is seen to be at stake in the arena of race is the survival of the existing order of things' (CCCS 1982: 27). Gilroy has thus argued for the centrality of 'race' to an understanding of British politics, in which racism is not epiphenomenal—the 'coat-of-paint' on British society—but a defining and legitimating characteristic (1992: 52).

The perceived threat of the black Other—the 'alien', the 'stranger' —forms a common theme in both the construction of the Black British communities and state responses to them. The reworking of the concepts of 'nation' and 'citizen' in continued immigration legislation has increasingly placed the black communities outside the realm of 'national culture' (Solomos 1992), while internally, an emphasis on the 'deep social problems' of black people, both economic and cultural, has rendered their presence illegitimate and 'strange'. A series of moral panics around mugging (Hall *et al.* 1978), immigration (Solomos 1992), the Rushdie affair and the rise of religious fundamentalism (Samad 1992), and the growth of 'Yardie'[3] drug gangs (Popham 1993) has served to objectify and criminalize black communities, to legitimate increased social control, and to reinscribe political and social marginalization (Hall *et al.* 1978; Solomos 1988).

Black youth in particular have been typecast into a role of almost pathological dislocation—culturally confused, alienated from both their parents and society at large, and implacably hostile. The image of rioters at the Notting Hill Carnival of 1976 remains very much the epitome of society's view of black youth; symbolic either of the 'enemy within' or of society's failure to meet the needs of its most vulnerable members, depending on one's perspective. In 1967 Ken Pryce wrote in *Endless Pressure* of black youth's 'psychic and cultural confusion and lack of confidence in dealing with the stress of racial rejection' (1967: 112*a*): twenty-five years on, when this youth has matured and has family of its own, the spectre remains unchanged, with the added threat of violent, if futile, retaliation. Thus, in 1985, Enoch Powell was *still* saying:

What sort of country will England be when its capital, other cities and areas of England consist of a population of which at least one-third is of African and Asian descent? My answer . . . is that it will be a Britain unimaginably wrecked by dissension and violent disorder, not recognisable as the same nation it has been, or perhaps as a nation at all (cited by Jones 1988: 1).

---

[3] 'Yardies' are, supposedly, gangsters, born and bred in the slums of Jamaica, who are intimately connected with the supply and sale of drugs—especially crack cocaine—in both the UK and USA. The construction of Yardie gangs pays particular attention to the high levels of violence attached to these groups (cf. Victor Headley's novel *Yardie* (1992), London: X-Press).

Gilroy notes, 'The idea that blacks comprise a problem or, more accurately, a series of problems, is today expressed at the core of racist reasoning' (1987: 11). The view of the black communities as forever migrants, the 'supreme and ultimate stranger(s)' (Patterson 1965: 209), has denied any historical dimension to black life and expression and ignored their contribution to contemporary British life—as if Britain could be understood as a culturally separate and racially inviolate entity.

What ideas of cultural separation and marginalization deny is the constant challenge of:

the activities of blacks who pass through the cultural and ideological net which is supposed to screen Englishness from them and from the complex organic process which renders black Britons partially soluble in the national culture which their presence helps transform (Gilroy 1987: 61).

Despite imagination to the contrary, the British 'nation', 'community', or 'culture' does not remain impervious to the 'strangers'. Its boundaries have been altered and reshaped to create a new identity; a hybrid, perhaps, but no more imagined and no less real than any other.

A PORTRAIT OF BLACK YOUTH: CONSTRUCTIONS OF A RACIALIZED OTHER

On 22 June 1948, the *Empire Windrush* docked at Tilbury with 492 Jamaican migrants, signalling the beginning of large-scale post-war immigration from the Caribbean. In the ten years following, it is estimated that about 125,000 Caribbean immigrants entered the country (Fryer 1984: 372). By the mid-1970s, over two-fifths of the black population of Britain was British-born (ibid.) while in the mid-1980s it was estimated that African-Caribbeans and their descendants numbered a quarter of a million people, of whom over half were born in the United Kingdom (Peach 1986). In the four and a half decades since the first significant arrivals, studies of the black communities in Britain have proliferated: yet the majority have been strikingly similar both in their approach and in their findings, and have been echoed and re-echoed by the popular press. The predominant view is of the black communities as eternal migrants, outside society and thereby constituting a problem. Theories of 'alienness' have been merely transformed into theories of 'alienation'.

The following section does not attempt an exhaustive account of the construction of the black presence in Britain, which has been comprehensively documented and persuasively critiqued elsewhere.[4] What follows represents rather a thumbnail sketch of black youth, which contends that what marks out their portrayal is a process of racialization (Small 1991, 1994), that has consistently objectified and pathologized black culture and experience. Indeed, it can be argued that it is not only the so-called 'new racism' which has incorporated ideas about cultural purity and essentialism into the arena of race and ethnic relations: such notions have long formed part of mainstream academic discussion. By failing to deal adequately with the idea of black culture, and retreating to theoretical notions of 'race', research on Black British youth has largely consigned them to the margins, cast and miscast as a series of folk devils and policy problems.

In *There Ain't No Black in the Union Jack*, Gilroy writes, 'West Indians . . . are seen as a bastard people occupying an indeterminate space between the Britishness which is their colonial legacy and an amorphous ahistorical relationship with the dark continent' (1987: 45). The portrayal of the African-Caribbean community in Britain as riven by cultural doubt, dislocation, and inauthenticity can be traced to some of the earliest studies of the migrants. Patterson's picture, in *Dark Strangers* (1965), of a mutilated slave culture, with weak matriarchal family structure and a high incidence of single-parent families and illegitimate children, provides a representative baseline of cultural and social pathologies that are reflected and replayed in most subsequent studies (Pryce 1967; Cashmore 1979; Troyna 1979; Cashmore and Troyna 1982). As late as 1988, Alastair Hennessy contrasts the 'authentic' cultures of the Asian subcontinent with the cultural deprivations of the Caribbean migrants:

all Asians . . . have cultures which are not European-derived as well as their own languages, which provide a sense of identity and can be a source of defiance and pride. Nor do Asians have to struggle against the

---

[4] Cf. Hall *et al.* 1978; Gaskell and Smith 1981; CCCS 1982; Fryer 1984; Gilroy 1987; Solomos 1988.

legacies of a slave past, or the hangovers from Victorian preconceptions about 'darkest Africa' (1988: 50).

For Hennessy, Caribbean culture is 'derived' from Europe, transmitted and maintained through a language that is not 'their own', and defined through a historical past centred solely in British imperialism. By implication, ownership of these cultures is brought into question, creating a distorted and inauthentic set of traditions, which are a source of dislocation, confusion, and rejection. Hardly surprising then, according to Hennessy, if black youth 'began to develop lifestyles of resistance and defiance, or to turn to nihilistic destruction or to crime' (ibid. 44).

The problematization and criminalization of black culture receives one of its fullest expositions in Pryce's 1967 study, *Endless Pressure*. Coupled with the deprivation of legitimate access to the material symbols of success, the possession of a mutilated culture leads to the formation of a marginalized and criminal subculture, focused around coping strategies involving pimping and prostitution, illegal dance-halls, gambling, drinking, and hustling in all its manifestations. Pryce divides the community along a stable/law-abiding–hustling axis; with hustlers at one end of the continuum and 'mainliners' at the other. The work is mainly concerned, however, with the deviant/hustler orientation in which the values of mainstream society are grotesquely distorted and enacted.[5]

In this atmosphere of cultural deviance, black youth grows and defines itself. The social deprivations of the St Paul's area:

inhibit the smooth adjustment of the West Indian youth in Bristol and are part of the complex of causes responsible for his inability to establish a firm, rooted sense of identity necessary to resist the demoralizing effects of discrimination (ibid. 108).

These youth are 'unemployed, homeless and in conflict with their parents' (ibid. 35), pressured by 'unrealistic' educational demands, and develop, it seems inevitably, 'psychic and cultural confusion

---

[5] Pryce's division is also to be found in work by Troyna (1979) and the CRE (Gaskell and Smith 1981). Interestingly enough, the distinction between 'respectable', 'decent', and 'mainstream' black families—who share the values of the dominant culture—and the 'alienated', 'street' individuals—usually young men— is also to be found even in recent work in the United States, such as Elijah Anderson's *Streetwise* (1990), an article 'The Code of the Streets' in *Atlantic Monthly* (May 1994), and Mitchell Duneier's *Slim's Table* (1992).

and lack of confidence in coping with the stress of racial rejection' (ibid. 112*a*). Amongst older youth, this alienation leads to the rejection of white social values in favour of what Pryce regards as spurious roots ideologies, most notable of which is Rastafari.

Pryce's view is of a generation rootless, culturally adrift, unable either to adapt to society or accept marginality. These images are re-created and replayed with the creation of successive folk devils—the black mugger, the Rastafarian drug dealer, the rioter, and most recently, the Yardie. Hall *et al.* (1978) have noted how these already familiar indexes of alienness and dislocation facilitated the construction of the black mugger in the mid-1970s. The same images have consistently informed accounts of black life and experience, notably in the work by Cashmore (1979) and Troyna (1979), on Rastafari and youth culture and, more recently, by Abner Cohen (1993), on the Notting Hill Carnival. Black youth in particular are portrayed as consumed by culture conflict and alienation, divided from both their own community and wider society. The pathology attributed to the black community as 'strangers' is sharply focused with regard to youth, who in turn have become emblematic of the perceived ills of the wider collectivity.

At the same time, it can be seen that the issues surrounding youth have become a major site for confrontation and struggle by the whole black community (Hall *et al.* 1978; Sivanandan 1981/ 2; CCCS 1982; Gilroy 1987). It has been argued, moreover, that the isolation and construction of black youth as a problem category in the mid-1970s was a direct response to the increasing activism of the black community, particularly around the issue of police malpractice (Sivanandan 1981/2; Howe 1982; Gutzmore 1983; Ramdin 1987). This social category became 'the central yardstick' by which to measure race relations and immigration policies (Ramdin 1987) and the central focus for debates around social control (Solomos 1988). As Fisher and Joshua note, the term 'black youth' came specifically to denote a problem category:

that special class of West Indian youngsters, usually in conflict with their parents' generation, 'often kicked out of their homes', 'who do not register for work, who are aimless, rootless drifters concerned with hustling for a living' (Cross 1979); 'cultural conflict', 'alienated' and 'adrift from society' and from the 'instruments of law and order' (1982; 135 references in original).

John Solomos similarly argues, 'The term "alienated generation" carried with it the image of a whole group of young blacks
becoming separated from the main institutions of society and
withdrawing into their "racial" identities' (1988: 129; emphasis added).
What is significant here is the way in which notions of 'race'
have consistently informed approaches to black culture, reifying
and transfixing cultural expression into a cycle of imputed
pathology and cultural anomie (CCCS 1982: 95–142). As early as
1963, in the United States, Glazer and Moynihan distinguished
between ethnic groups and African-Americans, who were perceived as a 'racial' category defined through a process of malad-
justed acculturation to the dominant American norms and beliefs
(1963). Meanwhile in Britain, the 'race relations' school of thought
focused attention on the conflictual nature of encounters between
racialized 'quasi-groups', defined by power inequality and economic subordination (Rex 1986: 84), at the expense of the cultural
—or 'ethnic'—dimensions of interaction. The problem-oriented
accounts that proliferated tended to portray black communities
as victims of overarching structural constraints, through which
alone their experiences were defined and enacted. 'Race', then,
becomes the sole definitional characteristic of the black communities; 'culture', if considered at all, can only be understood as
the response to victimization and discrimination. Hence the 'culture of poverty' thesis which informs studies on both sides of the
Atlantic (Anderson 1990, 1994; Jencks 1992; Cashmore and Troyna
1982; Cohen 1993).[6] As Lawrence notes, 'Blacks are pathologized
once via their association with the "cultures of deprivation" of
the decaying "inner cities" and again, as the bearers of specifically *black* cultures' (1982*a*: 56; emphasis in original).

CULTURE WARS I: 'RACE', ETHNICITY, AND THE STRUGGLE FOR AUTHENTICITY

In a forthcoming paper, 'Asians Have Culture, West Indians Have
Problems: Discourses on Race Inside and Outside Anthropology',[7]

---

[6] I have selected here examples of only some of the more recent studies, which
have remained more popular in the United States than in Britain.

[7] This paper, along with papers by John Eade and Stuart Hall, are due to be
published in a forthcoming collection, *Culture, Identity and Politics*, ed. Y. Samad,
O. Stuart, and T. O. Ranger (Avebury Press).

Sue Benson argues that the conflation of black cultures with 'race', and their subsequent separation from the sphere of ethnicity, has rendered academic approaches to the African-Caribbean community in Britain deeply ambivalent. Where, as Hennessy makes clear, Asians are attributed with 'authentic' cultural features, black Britons are assumed to be defined and circumscribed solely by 'racial' positioning. Marion Fitzgerald thus writes in 1988:

Afro-Caribbeans have repeatedly been shown to have a much stronger sense of *racial* injustice than Asians . . . this consciousness derives significantly from the initial shock of being perceived as *different* and rejected as unfit for equal treatment *simply because of the colour of their skin* (1988: 263; emphasis added).

Over twenty years earlier, Patterson wrote of the shock of black immigrants in not being accepted as British and of the 'preoccupation with colour' (1965: 203), leading to a 'frustrated, hypersensitive, chip-on-the-shoulder attitude' (ibid.). Two decades on, the arguments remain strikingly similar. Black people are seen as defined primarily by the colour of their skin, which is the sole 'simple' justification for unequal treatment. Difference is ascribed in racial, rather than cultural terms: it therefore becomes 'natural', unalterable, and inescapable in significance and effect.

The racialization of the black community has, Benson argues, resulted in an academic division of labour, wherein the 'cultural' differences of Asians are seen as the field of anthropologists, leaving the 'racial' arena, with the issues of power, domination, and discrimination, to the sociologists. The notion of 'black culture' has thus been either largely ignored or engendered a problematized rehearsal of distorted mainstream values and practices. Benson contends that the absence of the small-scale bounded communities replete with standard structural-functionalist institutions, which form the basis of traditional anthropology—what she terms the 'tribal paradigm'—have rendered ethnographic accounts of the black community problematic. Moreover, the concept of 'race' has proved difficult to encompass within the bounds of ethnographic study, because it remains outside and transcends the vision of social and collective organization. Anthropology has, then, remained largely silent on questions of inequality, racism, and domination: such subjects being considered, Benson claims, 'not a proper subject for anthropology'. Early studies of black migrant communities in Britain (Patterson 1965; Rex and Moore 1967) reflect such uncertainty, focusing primarily on the 'problems' of, and prospects for, cultural assimilation, while denying structural constraints within the host community.

It can be argued, then, extending Benson's paradigm, that where Asians have 'ethnicity', African-Caribbeans have 'race', a formulation consolidated by the long-standing belief in the cultural vacuity of black life. This has served both to obscure the racialized structured positioning of British Asian communities (Eade, forthcoming) and to deny the contribution, continuities, and resilience of Black British expressive cultures (CCCS 1982). The equation of black culture with 'racial' identity, which attributes 'blackness' a fixed and permanent status, precludes the possibility of internal definition or of individual negotiation. It is significant, for example, that even later accounts of white ethnic groups in the United States have explicitly excluded African-American groups from the symbolic and conscious construction and manipulation of ethnic identification (Waters 1990). For the latter, ethnic identity—or rather, 'race'—becomes compulsory and is held to be somehow more 'real' than for whites; an integral and essential part of being 'the other', of being black. Mary Waters thus argues:

white ethnics have a lot more choice and room for maneuvre than they themselves think they do. The situation is very different for members of *racial* minorities, whose lives are strongly influenced by *their race* or national origin, regardless of how much they may choose not to identify themselves in racial or ethnic terms (1990: 157; emphasis added).

Waters's point is very much that whites have a choice in the creation of their identity, and that blacks, by virtue of their 'race', do not. Black people are denied any element of choice, and hence of creativity, in the construction of black identity; they cannot and do not make use of the forces of symbolic ethnicity to manipulate their identity; they can only reflect and re-create the dominant ascriptions of what 'blackness' is. This forms the essence of labelling theory; that minority groups cannot but become subject to dominant definitions and perforce re-create them; the 'translation of fantasy into reality' (Young, cited in Hall *et al.* 1978: 42). Minority culture is thus neither more nor less than the dominant culture prescribes; there is no space for resistance or alternative definitions.

It is the disjunction between external 'them' categorization and internal 'us' definition which has been seen as the basic distinction between 'race' and ethnicity (Rex 1986: 18–22; Jenkins 1986: 176–7). Sandra Wallman notes that 'race' 'continues to connote difference that seems to be immutable' (1986: 229), whereas ethnicity 'signifies allegiance to the culture of origin and implies a degree of choice and a possibility of change which 'race' precludes' (ibid.). Approaches to ethnicity, particularly in social anthropology, have thus moved towards a focus on internal identifications in which 'Culture' becomes the primary definitional characteristic. 'Culture' constitutes a category of classification and interaction, encapsulating ways of knowing which can be transposed onto discrete social units and which achieves significance at the boundary, where difference is perceived and evaluated (Barth 1969; Ardener 1987). In perhaps the most influential of such studies, Frederick Barth argues that ethnicity should be understood as the conscious maintenance of difference between groups through the symbolic construction of boundaries. Cultural content becomes an implication of boundary construction— a *symbol* of difference as well as its primary source. Nevertheless, as Wallman makes clear (1986: 230), culture remains as the 'vessel' from which boundary markers are selected and wielded, a latent natural resource of difference.

However, by positing the crucial element of ethnicity as self-identification, such work writes 'across' race (Miles 1982; Wallman 1986; Benson, forthcoming). Barth's analysis thus hinges upon the freedom and ability of the individual to move across boundaries, take advantage of alternatives or freely ally himself to another group, by learning its cultural codes. This in turn assumes an equality of status and consensus within the power structure, which has rarely, if ever, been achieved (Rex 1983, 1986). In the majority of situations, ethnic ascription takes place amid the unequal distribution of power and the assignment of minority status which 'carries with it exclusion from full participation in the life of the society' (Wirth, cited by Rex 1983: 25). Membership of a perceived group will be ascribed both internally and externally, particularly in the case of physical boundary markers such as skin colour; what Ulf Hannerz calls the 'burden of ethnicity' (1974).

Ironically, moreover, a traditional organicist approach to culture leads ultimately to the reification of absolutist notions of

cultural authenticity, which in turn reinscribe new racist ideologies of essential cultural difference. The equation of ethnicity
with the possession of a primordial identity structured upon
religion, language, custom, history, and, most significantly,
'blood'/origins (Barth 1969; Isaacs 1975), serves to naturalize
culture, leading to a 'biological culturalism' (Stolcke 1993: 27), in
which 'race' becomes the immutable signifier of 'ethnicity', and
'ethnicity' the attribute of 'race'. 'Culture' thus becomes 'a pseudo-
biological property of communal life' (Gilroy 1993: 24). James
Clifford writes:

A powerful structure of feeling continues to see culture, wherever it is
found, as a coherent *body* that lives and dies. Culture is enduring, traditional, structural. . . . Culture is a process of ordering, not of disruption. It changes and develops like a living organism. It does not normally
'survive' abrupt alterations (1988: 235).

Moreover, as Gilroy points out, the conflation of 'race' with 'ethnicity', and of both with an essentialized cultural difference, has
formed as much a part of anti-racist as New Right ideologies.
Thus, he argues:

the commonsense ideology of anti-racism has also drifted towards a
belief in the absolute nature of ethnic categories and a strong sense of
the insurmountable cultural and experiential divisions which, it is
argued, are a feature of racial difference (1992: 50).

If, then, ' "ethnic group" is very like "race" without the biology'
(Tonkin, McDonald, and Chapman 1989: 14), for social anthropologists, 'ethnicity' has constructed and essentialized the notion
of difference. Tonkin *et al.* argue that discussions of ethnicity
'have a strong and familiar bias towards "difference" and "other-
ness"' (ibid. 15). More critically, they assert:

It is . . . not surprising that social anthropology should have found 'ethnicity' consonant with its ambitions and wishes, since an appetite for
significant difference has always been present in the anthropological
project, even when this has been disavowed (ibid.).

As Henry Louis Gates has recently warned, the underlying assumption of 'ethnicity', whether as an internal 'cultural' or an
external 'racial' phenomenon, is the assertion of homogeneous
bounded entities—what he has referred to as the 'bubble theory

of culture'.[8] Ethnicity thus becomes, he claims, 'a master-code for human difference'.

By retreating to a 'natural' racialized foundation to culture, most approaches to black identity and expression have failed to recognize that discussions of 'race', 'ethnicity', and 'culture' are themselves social and cultural constructs (Miles 1982) and therefore open to interaction, negotiation, and subversion. As Stephen Small has commented, 'even where authors still say. . . that "race" is a social construct, they continue to write as if it were not' (1991: 11). Assumptions of the absolute powerlessness of black people in the face of overarching structural constraints, on the one hand, and of cultural deprivation and racial alienation, on the other, have rendered black cultural expression and resistance invisible, if not absolutely inconceivable. It is significant that even proponents of subcultural theory, who assert the power of cultural resistance to hegemonic ideologies (Hall and Jefferson 1976; Mungham and Pearson 1976), have largely fought shy of attributing these qualities to black communities. Conveniently ignoring the changing and innovative face of black youth expression —and its constant incursions and inclusions into mainstream white youth culture (Gilroy 1987; Jones 1988)—Brake, for example, writes, 'What many whites forget is that for black people, their primary identity... is mediated by their colour, and the oppression that brings' (1980: 115).

Nevertheless, it is within the realm of subcultural theory that the origins of a less organicist approach to culture can be found. Moving away from the reification of hermetically sealed cultural bubbles which form the basis of both New Right admonitions of 'difference', and liberal anti-racist celebrations of 'cultural diversity', 'culture' becomes a primary site for the creation and enactment of alternatives. Hall and Jefferson thus define 'culture' as:

> that level at which social groups develop distinctive patterns of life, and give expressive form to their social and material life-experience. Culture is the way, the forms, in which groups 'handle' the raw material of their social and material existence (1976: 10).

Culture objectivizes group life in meaningful shape or form to provide 'maps of meaning' which are used to experience and

---

[8] These remarks are taken from Gates's series of Clarendon lectures at Oxford University, titled 'The Limits of Identity: Narratives of Contingency' (Dec. 1992).

interpret social relations. It is also ranked along lines of dominance and subordination according to the power relations of society, and will enter into struggle with the dominant order in order
to overthrow its hegemony. It thus becomes a force of engagement rather than distinction.

Subcultural theory has itself been accused of the reification of
separate homogeneous and oppositional cultural groups, and of
the imagination of a static and absolute social structure by which
they are ultimately subordinated (Hall and Jefferson 1976; Willis
1977, 1978). However, its acknowledgement of both the determining force of a hegemonic order and of the ideological space
which is contested by subordinated groups remains a crucial
recognition of the role of culture as a site of struggle. Thus, Roger
Hewitt (1986), in a notable exception to the problem-oriented
accounts of Black British youth, notes that although external
overdefinitions of black youth form a type of rhetorical closure
which lessens cultural significance at a societal level, at a street
level, black culture reigns supreme: 'the distinctive voice of black
adolescents is "I am strong" and the "I am weak" audible in the
wider public area remains unheard' (1986: 205). The boundaries
between these arenas are not discrete and impermeable, however, as Hewitt seems to suggest, and black street culture does
mediate events in the public arena, and vice versa. The challenge
remains then of how to figure cultural expression as a dynamic
relation between the structural features which determine and
overdetermine it, and the actions and experiences of those who
are so defined and circumscribed.

Work has already been done in this area, notably by the 1982
CCCS volume *The Empire Strikes Back*, and the subsequent work
particularly of Paul Gilroy (1987, 1993). These have attempted to
break the cycle of imputed pathology which envelops the black
community and renders their collective struggles and cultures
illegitimate. Seeking to reinstate the role of cultural expression in
the development of black struggle in Britain, these writers have
asserted both the unifying strength of Black British cultures and
a historical dimension which has generally been denied or subsumed in the aura of 'racial' categorization.

Gilroy thus attacks the portrayal of the black community as
'forever victims, objects rather than subjects, beings that feel, yet
lack the ability to think and remain incapable of considered behaviour' (1987: 11). This perspective, which Goulbourne terms

the 'zoological' view,[9] denies the continuing struggles of the black community, in which youth play a crucial role, and the dynamic nature of identity construction. As Gilroy writes, 'racial subordination is not the sole factor shaping the choices and actions of Britain's black settlers and their British-born children' (1987: 153). For Gilroy, black culture is more than oppositional; it offers the creation of positive cultural alternatives, 'Black expressive cultures affirm while they protest' (ibid. 155).

What black cultures affirm, especially with regard to youth, has not been clearly established. As Winston James writes in 'A Long Way from Home: On Black Identity in Britain':

when it comes to the study of the culture, ideology and life-styles of youths of Afro-Caribbean descent, platitudes, and more often, negative stereotypes abound . . . at present, despite (and because of?) the amount of ink spilt on the subject of Afro-Caribbean youth, we know relatively little about the culture and ideology of youths of Afro-Caribbean descent in Britain (1986: 269).

Discussion has, he continues, 'generated a lot of heat and virtually no light' (ibid.); the best work being involved with 'ground-clearing' rather than 'building'.

It is with 'building' that this study is concerned. It takes as its foundation the work of Hall, the CCCS collective, Gilroy and others, who have argued for the creativity of Black British culture; who see youth as an integral and essential part of the struggles of the black community; and who see black identity as a dynamic, positive, and creative process. Much has already been done to deconstruct the 'black youth folk devil' and the reified cultural pathologies of popular and academic imagination. It is hoped that this study will not so much address these arguments directly as constitute a critique in itself, by shedding some light amongst the heat.

THE AIM OF THIS BOOK

In this book I hope to examine the creation of Black British youth identities. I am concerned not with generalized external pronouncements about the 'problems' or 'crises' of black identity,

[9] Paper presented to the Ethnic Relations Seminar, St Antony's College, Oxford, 15 Feb. 1990.

but with its form and content as it is lived in everyday experience. I thus move away from a predominantly macro-structural approach, in which black youth constitutes a social category considered only in its relation to—or confrontation with—institutions, to consider the experiences of individual black youths at a micro-level. Far from constituting a culture of despair and nihilism, I hope to show that black youths are concerned with the construction of new cultural alternatives, in which identity is created and re-created as part of an ongoing and dynamic process. By focusing on a small group of black 'actors', I am hoping to portray an alternative vision of black youth; not as a unified and homogeneous, externally defined and structurally constrained entity, but a collection of individual lives, choices and experiences.

My study, then, is of 'culture'; not an essentialized, fixed, and traditional heritage but a continually created and 'invented' tradition, which reimagines itself in each mind and life. In this re-definition, I believe that the collective struggles of black youth are not weakened; indeed, they can only be strengthened by the resistance to any imposed definition of 'blackness' and the recognition of the cultural battle for the ideological space to be 'black'—whatever that may mean:

> Whatever you claim to be
> Yours,
> That's the nature of this Game.
>
>   (Soul II Soul; *Feeling Free*)

STARTING-POINTS

The aim here then, is to provide an in-depth, 'street-level' account of the creation and manipulation of identity by a group of Black British youths. In moving away from wide-reaching, quantitative generalizations, I am hoping that a clearer idea of Black British experience will emerge, which takes account of the qualitative aspects of black life. The intensity of the fieldwork, together with limitations upon time and resources, therefore dictated that the scope of the study remain small-scale and sharply focused.

My research was concerned with youths mainly, though not exclusively, of African-Caribbean origin. As my study was concerned with the creation of 'Black British' identity, it also involved black youths of African descent, and one of Asian origin, who insisted in defining himself as part of a black group—with mixed success. I was not concerned generally with youths of Asian origin, who have been defined in a different way, and who construct their identity from a different cultural and historical environment. All my informants were born in Britain and, although some had spent time in their parents' country of origin, all had grown up here. They were, therefore, part of the second generation living in Britain. Not all would define themselves as 'Black British'; this constitutes more an external definition for the purposes of limiting the research. Internal definitions of identity will be discussed later.

My informants were predominantly male, partly because the category 'black youth', which was the focus of my research, is usually imagined as an exclusively male domain, partly because black expressive culture remains one dominated by men, but largely because it was young men that I first met. During the course of my research, I did, however, meet and get to know a number of black women, who provided a valuable insight into their experience both as a comparison with, and contrast to, the experience of black men. The creation of identity amongst black women is not, however, a primary focus of my study, and merits separate consideration.

The age of my informants ranged from 18 to 24 years. Although 'youth' usually serves to denote a younger age range, it is felt to remain appropriate to the groups I studied, who were all single and who all took an active part in the public expressive arena in which identity is created and negotiated. The group is thus consistent with a view of youth culture as redefining social categories in the public leisure sphere, where the influence of the male peer group is paramount (Hall and Jefferson 1976; Mungham and Pearson 1976).

The fieldwork was carried out in London in the twelve months beginning in July 1990. The initial work was centred around three groups: a group of nine or ten men, aged 22–24, living mainly in East London; a mixed group of men and women, aged 18–23, living in North-West London; and thirdly, a group of men who were members of a black community centre in West London. As the fieldwork progressed, it became necessary to drop the last group as a major focus of the study; partly through lack of time and partly through problems of access, which will be discussed later.

My study therefore dealt with a relatively small number of informants—a number which decreased as the fieldwork progressed. It was, then, a rather detailed and very personal study of a group of individuals than a wide-scale, representative sample. This was partly due to the time and resources available to the study, but also—and primarily—a conscious decision on my part. It was, and remains, my feeling that there is missing from the majority of work on ethnic groups in Britain any sense of the subjects as 'real' people, in all their complexity of experience and attitudes. Larger studies tend by their very nature to quote statistics and cite generalizations, with little sense of how these relate—or don't—to the lives of the very subjects they claim to represent. A study of identity cannot afford to make generalizations, and this study makes no such claims. Identity creation is too personal and too complex to sustain such an approach.

My work thus constitutes a study of a small number of people in a geographically dispersed area. It was, therefore, unable to adopt a classic anthropological approach (Cohen 1974): it was not concerned with an organized group with discrete social and geographic boundaries, but with an urban population which is highly mobile and elastic in its boundary creation and maintenance. Because of this, I adopted a network approach, beginning with one or two personal contacts and spreading from there as the occasion arose and circumstances permitted. Admittedly, such an approach makes it almost impossible to achieve a uniform perception of the research subjects or a consistent level of acceptance (Bott 1971: 49), which inevitably limits knowledge of certain members. This was certainly true in my case, where the core group was defined largely by the extent of my knowledge of them, while other members remained more distant and less known. Given the personal depth of the study, such inconsistencies were inevitable, but not particularly damaging to my purpose, which was never intended to be 'scientific'.

In defence, I would claim that my informants were studied as examples of black youth, not as representatives. Benson writes in a similar vein about her study of interracial marriages in Brixton: 'It is, inevitably, a study of individuals and of individual atti-tudes, of individual problems and the way in which individuals regard those problems' (1981: preface, vii). Benson notes, more-over, a dissatisfaction with 'the inappropriate nature of imper-sonal survey techniques' (ibid.) in dealing with her chosen subject and area. Given the highly politicized and sensitive nature of work produced in the field of race and ethnic relations, she found a high degree of suspicion of research amongst her potential informants. For my study, nearly fifteen years after Benson's original fieldwork, the problem of access and acceptance were even greater. It is possible that it is these problems that account for the dearth of qualitative studies of black youth. In the case of the two groups I finally made the foci of my study, these were overcome—or at least negotiated—through the use of personal contacts. In the case of the third group, a number of factors made such negotiation impossible within the limits of the study.

It is the all-male group from East London with which I achieved the closest and most sustained contact, and which forms the major focus of the study. Access to its members was gained through a friend, who introduced me to Ricky. Ricky was looking for some-one to share his flat in East London, and I moved in at the be-ginning of July 1990. Meeting the other members of the group then became something of a matter of course, and I was able to observe them at a uniquely informal and personal level. All the group knew my intentions, but because I was first and foremost Ricky's new flatmate, my academic purpose became less intru-sive and less constraining. This was undoubtedly aided by my age, gender, and ethnic origin. As a young person, of about the same age as my informants, I was able to fit into their social life without difficulty and without any concessions or awkwardness on their behalf. As a woman, I presented no threat to the internal structure of the group and could be 'carried with' the group to most places as something of an ornament. Also, because I was a woman, my intellectual purpose was largely ignored: I suspect that had I been a man, the group would have felt the need to compete. As an Asian woman, particularly, I was regarded as something of an asset to the group's image. Had I been white, the level of acceptance and assistance I received would have been withheld: there would have been a number of places to

which I would not have been allowed to go and a range of attitudes and practices I would not have witnessed. Had I been
black, I may have been spared some of the more overtly sexist
assumptions I was confronted with, but I think that the group
would have felt threatened by my presence. Most of the boys
were intimidated by black women—and they were especially
fearful of intelligent black women, who, they felt, undermined
their control over situations. I was, however, 'black enough'.

There were, of course, a number of negative aspects to my
position. As a woman, there were places I was not expected to
attend—notably on the boys' nights out, which had a primary
purpose of meeting women. This was circumvented to some
extent by constant pressure on my part and through my relationship with Ricky, who already had a steady girlfriend who accompanied him on these occasions. I was therefore allowed to 'tag
along' with them. As a woman, also, there were strict limits
imposed on the people to whom the group would introduce me.
I found it almost impossible to meet any of the women associated with the group, because the boys were concerned that I
would give away their secrets—for example, stories about other
women. When I did become friendly with the girlfriend of one
of them, the entire group felt threatened by the association. Gaps
in my direct experience were to a large extent filled through my
friendship with some members of the group, who took great
delight in recounting stories of themselves and others at every
opportunity. My friends and I came to think of this group as 'the
boys', partly because of its all-male, overtly macho nature and
partly because they insisted, as a typical in-joke, on calling me
'one of the boys'—when it suited them.

I met the second group also through informal personal contacts. I was introduced to Angelina, my 'gatekeeper', in March
1990, through her tutor at university whom I was consulting
about my research. After lunch, when I explained my intentions,
we swapped telephone numbers, and I contacted her when I
arrived in London. As a sociology undergraduate, Angelina was
very interested in my project and introduced me to a number of
her friends, her family, and her boyfriend, all of whom I got to
know quite well. Most of these had grown up in North-West
London in an area with a large black population and something
of a reputation for violence. The people I met through Angelina

therefore provided an interesting and revealing contrast to both the area of East London in which I lived, where the notion of 'black community' is less clearly defined, and to the stereotyped notions of youth growing up in areas of dense black population.

My relationship with this group was in some ways less personal than with the first, and certainly less problematic. Because I lived some distance away from their homes, I was not able to have such unlimited access to them or the opportunity for informal observation. I was, therefore, limited on the whole to prearranged times and invitations to specific social events. Nevertheless, I spent a considerable amount of time with them, a relationship which was made both easier and more rewarding by my friendship with Angelina. This made my meetings with her friends and family less awkward and less formal. I was, first and foremost, a friend of Angelina's; because Angelina knew and trusted me, her family and friends did likewise.[10] Had my entrance been more 'official', I suspect the results would have been different. As a woman, I was readily accepted by Angelina and her female friends; more than this, I was accepted as a 'black woman', with its incumbent feelings of solidarity. Angelina herself told me recently that had I been white, I would have achieved little co-operation 'because there would have been no trust'; her brother Darnell told me that he would not have even bothered to talk to me. This was in spite of the fact that both had close white friends, and could perhaps be attributed to a suspicion of 'outsiders'. Again, my age lessened feelings of formality and my gender helped to counteract a widely held dislike of Asians by the males of the group, which arose in part from anti-black activity in the area by Asian gangs from Southall. Generally, however, my position in regard to this group was less intimate and less ambiguous than with the first; it functioned less as a collective, more as a loosely connected group of individuals, while the presence of women helped to strengthen my role at a personal level.

The importance of personal contacts for my research was thrown into sharp relief in my dealings with the third group, which was a group of 30–40 men in a community centre in West

---

[10] John Western similarly notes in his recent work on Barbadian families in London that his friendship with relatives of his 'gatekeeper' 'afforded amicable introductions of limited threat to potential respondents' (1992).

London. Here, although I was given permission by the organizer and had much support from the office staff, my entrance was always regarded as 'official' and I found it impossible to move beyond this. I was able to get to know a number of the men, but was unable to move beyond a relatively superficial acquaintance. Given the personal nature of the subjects I was hoping to address in my work, this was obviously unsatisfactory. I did try initially with this group to widen my contact through the use of a questionnaire; however, for a number of reasons, most men were unwilling to answer any personal questions. As a telling example of this problem, when I showed my proposed questionnaire to the Centre's organizer for comment, and asked if there were any unsuitable questions, he replied, 'Well, question 1, what is your name—they won't answer that'. And they didn't.

I did, however, manage to get to know a few individuals well enough to provide an interesting source of comparison with the other groups. The Centre was a wholly black institution, and its members were part of a more clearly defined 'black' environment. I was therefore exposed to some 'typically black' institutions —the barber's shop, blues parties, dominoes. Moreover, the community centre in itself provided an interesting and informative example of how notions of 'community' are created and sustained. It also illustrated how the black community defines its needs and wants—or is defined—at an institutional level.

The study finally, then, focused on the first two groups, with the third used primarily as a means of comparison and contextualization. Although it deals with perhaps less than fifteen individuals in varying degrees of depth, it is felt that the approach of the study precluded more people. The approach adopted in the fieldwork was primarily one of participant observation: this is defined by Paul Rock, quoting Florence Kluckhohm's 1940 statement, as the 'conscious and systematic sharing . . . in the life activities and affects of a group of persons' (1979: 187). The material I gained from this approach was inevitably filtered and mediated by my position within the groups, as discussed above. I was therefore what Margot Ely *et al.* term a 'limited observer' (1991: 44–5), one who has no public role and who builds trust over time with her informants. Most of my material was obtained from time spent with my informants, both individually and in various group situations, either observing or discussing issues that arose. This was consolidated in the latter half of the fieldwork by informal taped interviews, which helped me to explore individual attitudes as well as record stories and viewpoints which were already familiar to me. These covered the areas which seemed to be of most significance: the community; school and work; social life; personal relationships.

THE PLAYERS

Group 1: 'The Boys'

Ricky: 24 years old, and of Jamaican parents, Ricky was born in London, but spent a large part of his childhood with his mother in Jamaica. He came back with his younger brother to live with an aunt when he was 13, but conflict with her and his father led him to leave home at 15. He spent some time in a hostel, then shared a council flat in a tower block in East London with his brother, until the latter moved to Birmingham. Ricky had not worked for two years when I was living with him, and spent a lot of time with his girlfriend, Anne, a student nurse from Malaysia, or weight-training in the gym.

Shane: 23 years old, of Jamaican origin, Shane also claimed to have spent some of his childhood in Jamaica, but grew up mainly in East London with his mother. He had several jobs in the time that I knew him, mainly in the retail clothes business. He also had aspirations to be a singer, and spent a lot of time with some musician friends. He had a girlfriend who was a student nurse, and a friend of Anne's, but was often unfaithful. Shane was a difficult informant because he was prone to exaggeration and fabrication, not only with me but with the whole of the group, who tolerated him but refused to take him seriously.

Clive: 24 years old, Clive is of Nigerian origin, but was born in London and had lived all his life there. At the time I knew him, he still lived at home with his parents and some siblings. He had a girlfriend, Pat, of seven years' standing, and one son, who was 2 years old. Clive had no intention of settling down in this relationship, however, and was very much the partygoer of the group:

he was renowned for the quantity of drink he consumed; the flamboyance of his clothes; and the number of women he picked up. Clive worked as a computer technician for a firm of stock-brokers in the City.

Frank: 24 years old and also of Nigerian origin, Frank was born and grew up in Nottingham, but spent some of his teenage years in Nigeria. He went to polytechnic there, where he trained as a civil engineer. When I knew him, he had recently left an engin-eering job and started work in a designer clothes shop in East London so he could devote more time to his great passion—flying. Frank styled himself very much as the intellectual, father-figure of the group.

Malcolm: 23 years old and of Jamaican origin, Malcolm worked for his father in his grocery store. He lived with his sister and cousins in what used to be the family home, his father having moved elsewhere. He also ran a sound system and was fascin-ated by electronic equipment and 'gadgets'. He was the only person I have ever met who owned two mobile telephones and a message pager. Malcolm was by far the quietest member of the group and extremely difficult to get to know. He lived almost entirely on junk food and had a long-standing girlfriend, Veronica.

Satish: 23 years old, Satish was born in India and only came to Britain when he was 12. He was the only 'non-African' member of the group, but is included because he was always around and generally presented himself as 'black'—to the extent that he would tell others that he was from the Caribbean or had one black parent. Satish was somewhat erratic in his working habits, but was employed for most of my fieldwork in a clothes shop. When younger he had been involved in petty crime and had what the rest of the group considered fairly dubious friends. He had lived with Dion, his Jamaican girlfriend, and their two children for seven years, but still spent most of his time with 'the boys' and had a string of affairs and one-night stands. He and Dion split up and reunited several times during my fieldwork.

Nathan: 24 years old and of Jamaican parents, Nathan lived in South London and worked as a graphic designer for an advertis-ing firm in Covent Garden. Because of the distance between him and other members of the group, I saw Nathan less often than the rest, and was unable to interview him. He was, however, an active member of the group on the social excursions.

Arif: 24 years old and Nathan's flatmate, Arif is of Nigerian origin. Like Nathan, he was distanced from the day to day activities of the group; a factor enhanced by his general unpopularity with the others. Arif was considered to be socially inept and was tolerated primarily as Nathan's flatmate and occasional punchbag. Arif worked with computers.

Edgar: 24 years old and of Ghanaian origin, Edgar was born and grew up in East London. He was an integral part of the group a couple of years earlier, when it was much larger, and now interacted with the others on a more occasional basis. During my fieldwork, Edgar was working part-time in the storeroom of Argos, but was planning on going to polytechnic to study psychology the following year.

Dion: 22 years old and of Jamaican origin, Dion was Satish's girlfriend. Although not officially a member of the group, Dion had known all the boys for many years and was a fascinating source of information on them. Mother of two small children, Dion worked on a part-time basis as a chambermaid for a local agency. I got to know Dion and her family quite well and spent some time with her sisters, Sharon, 28, and Paula, 24. She also introduced me to some peripheral members of the group, and some of the associated women, although I was unable to establish any meaningful contact with them. Dion had aspirations to become an actress, and often displayed a somewhat artistic temperament, notably in her relationship with Satish, which often enveloped everyone around them.

Group 2

Angelina: 22 years old, Angelina was born and brought up in North-West London. Her father was from Grenada and her mother from Jamaica. When I first met Angelina, she was in her second year of her BA degree in Sociology and Social Administration; during my fieldwork, she graduated with a second class degree and started teacher training at the London Institute of Education. She had recently split up from her Jamaican boyfriend of three years' standing, Roland, who was a plumber.

Rommell: 20 years old, and Angelina's brother, also born and brought up in North-West London. During the year of my field-work, Rommell was completing his management training with John Lewis, but having failed to get a management post, left the company and was waiting to begin a BA course in Accounting Studies at the Polytechnic of West London.

Darnell: 18 years old, and the youngest of Angelina's siblings, Darnell had recently finished sixth form college and a temporary job working for Brent Council, and was about to start a BA course in Accounting Studies at the Polytechnic of West London with his brother. Something of a charmer, when I met Darnell, he had just split up with his girlfriend, Julie, because of her conversion to the Black Moslem movement, and was 'involved' with a string of what his sister termed 'girlies'.

Fenella: 22 years old, of Barbadian parents, Fenella was a friend of Angelina's from secondary school. During the time of my fieldwork, she was in her second year of a Humanities course at a polytechnic in Wales.

Eleanor: 22 years old, Eleanor was born in North-West London and, like Fenella, was a friend of Angelina's from secondary school. Her mother was from Dominica and her father from Grenada. Eleanor graduated from Wolverhampton Polytechnic with a BA degree in Biology just after my fieldwork was completed, and had recently started work in a laboratory in London. She had an English boyfriend, Kevin, whom she met at polytechnic.

SUMMARY

What follows will examine the attitudes and experiences of these main individuals, together with material gained less fully and more occasionally from other people. Taking as its point of de-parture the traditional views and stereotypes surrounding black youth, as considered earlier, this book maintains that black youth are involved in the creation of new identities, which are dynamic and allow for negotiation at the level of interaction.

Chapter 2 looks at 'home'; the internal construction of definitions of community and nationhood, and the limits of 'blackness' and belonging. Chapter 3 is concerned with 'work'. Since most of my informants worked in predominantly white environments, the chapter will concentrate on the negotiation of identity and stereotypes within these. It will focus particularly on the construction of images of 'black employment', and their relationship to gender and 'class' identities. Chapter 4 centres on social life; this will consider differences in 'white' and 'black' social environments, and the attitudes, expectations and value systems associated with each. It attempts to tie together the two preceding chapters, because most of my informants moved frequently, and relatively freely, between the two arenas—the 'community' and mainstream spheres—negotiating identity accordingly. Chapters 5 and 6 focus upon the construction of black masculinity. Chapter 5 explores the role of the male peer group and the group's relationship to other men. Chapter 6 will examine the attitudes towards women, and the role conflicts that these encapsulate. Chapter 7 is the conclusion.

2

Home

United we stand and divided we fall,
Black man, know yourself, before your back is against the wall.

(Shabba Ranks)

JUST before completing my fieldwork in London I decided, as a
farewell gesture, to hold a goodbye party for those people I had
been living and working with for the past months. The plan was
to bring all my main informants together to thank them and
wish them well before I disappeared back into 'the country' to
write up my research. I consulted with Ricky, my flatmate, about
the food and the music, and duly invited all 'the boys', together
with Angelina, her brothers, and some of their friends.

Although this was the first time the two groups had been
brought together, individuals from each had met previously at
various stages in my fieldwork, so there was ostensibly little
reason to expect anything other than a fairly relaxed and enjoyable evening. Instead, after initial acknowledgements, the party
divided, with Angelina, her brothers, and their friends in the
kitchen, and the boys occupying the living area. Protagonists of
both groups glared suspiciously at each other, each trying to
situate the other and measure the degree of threat posed to their
own position and sense of control. After an hour or so, Shane
ventured into the kitchen, and approached Darnell, 'So, where
are you chaps from then?' Darnell glared at Shane disdainfully,
sucked his teeth and turned away. He later said to me with some
degree of scorn, 'Where did you find these guys, then? Nobody
says "chaps". He ain't no black man.'

When Angelina informed Shane that they lived in Harlesden,
Shane started to look extremely nervous and retreated into the
living room. The boys, whose self-image was more than a little
shaken by the presence of a group from Harlesden—an area with
a large black population and something of a reputation—and

feeling unable to compete as 'typically black' in the way they felt was expected, turned the music from ragga to American club mixes, closed ranks as a group and started 'busting splits'. Talking loudly about jobs and cars, and posing as upwardly mobile young and sophisticated city blacks, they sought to regain control of the situation, while Darnell, Rommell, and their friends talked as loudly about blues parties and sound systems, perpetuating their image as 'ragamuffins', as 'real blacks', finally disappearing into my bedroom to build spliffs and listen to their own ragga tapes.

This episode centred around two distinct, and in some ways opposed, images of 'being black', which are not related in any simple, unmediated way to external definitions, but to stances within and in relation to 'the black community'. Both groups were concerned to position themselves in relation to the other black group, in such a way as to maintain control of the situation. This was defined entirely in terms of internal images of what 'the black community' represented and their position in relation to it.

Thus, because the boys felt excluded from the 'community' image claimed by Angelina and her brothers, and unable to fulfil its incumbent expectations, the response was to negate this image by bringing in a 'class' element. This attempted to distance them from the more negative elements associated with 'community' images and replace them with an image of wealth and sophistication aimed at undermining the other group. This forced the other group into the role of 'typical blacks', which they in turn upheld by casting the boys as sell-outs, as somehow not 'really black'. The divisions were primarily perceived in territorial terms, to which other images were then attached and which then served to polarize two groups otherwise largely undifferentiated in terms of background, origin, and occupation.

This chapter is concerned with these internal definitions and images of 'the black community'. Where earlier studies have tended to portray black people in Britain as a homogeneous mass, divided only by generational conflict, this chapter will consider the range of positions, attitudes, and images within the bounds of this 'imagined community' (B. Anderson 1983). It will also examine how these attitudes alter and are manipulated by individuals to locate themselves within this community and within wider society. I have deliberately chosen the term 'home' rather than 'community' as the heading for this chapter, because it is concerned with individual conceptions about personal identity and location, rather than external perceptions about the nature of group experience.

SYMBOLS AND IMAGINED COMMUNITIES: THE COMMUNITY CENTRE

In *Imagined Communities*, Anderson writes of the nation as 'an imagined political community' (1983: 6). At a level lower than that of the 'nation', however, it can be seen that the notion of 'community' functions as a highly emotive and potent symbol for both those it envelops and those it excludes. The existence of large numbers of people of African and African-Caribbean origin in Britain has long been imagined as a community within the minds of those it designates and that of the wider imagined 'nation'. The notion of 'the black community' is, however, one that has gone largely unquestioned. Like Anderson's 'nation', the 'community' is 'conceived as a deep, horizontal comradeship' (ibid. 7), and hence one that remains beyond the bounds of analysis: it cannot be understood, it merely exists and is felt. It is thus 'imagined', rather than tangible.

The potency of the idea of 'the black community', for both black people and wider society, depends on its perception as a unified and largely separate entity. From an external perspective this facilitates targeting and labelling processes (S. Cohen 1980), while internally it enables the individual to position himself in relation to these labels and serves as a focus for political and social mobilization. As Gilroy writes:

Community . . . signifies not just a distinctive political ideology but a particular set of values and norms in everyday life: mutuality, co-operation, identification and symbiosis. For black Britain, all these are centrally defined by the need to escape and transform the limits of subordination which bring 'races' into being (1987: 234).

On the whole, projections of 'community' have created the illusion of fixity and absolute identification, premised on the correlation of 'Community' with 'Race'. Crucial to such processes is communication (Anthias and Yuval-Davis 1993: 33), which in turn depends upon the use and manipulation of symbols (S. Cohen 1980: 40). 'Community' becomes a symbol for the presence of black people in Britain, at once both reducing and objectifying the group as a social category, and consolidated through the use of 'markers' (Culler 1988) or symbolic 'border guards' (Anthias and Yuval-Davis 1993: 33).

One of the most obvious and tangible markers of 'the black community' is 'the black community centre', which both testifies to the existence of a 'community', and objectifies and fixes its significant features. As with most symbols, however, the 'community centre' becomes a site for confrontation and struggle in the face of competing definitions of what 'the black community' is. Of most significance to the present study is the way in which the notion of 'community', as symbolized by the community centre, can be seen to incorporate a range of standpoints internal to 'the black community' itself. The notion of community may indeed be imagined within the mind of each black person, but need not be imagined in the same way, nor fixed in its image. 'The Black Community' thus exists on a variety of levels, and the individual's relation to it can be seen to be multi-layered and multi-faceted. For the sake of simplicity, and in the absence of any more suitable label, the study will continue to use the term 'community', although its usage may alter according to the context.

The Community Centre,[1] to which I was a constant visitor in the first six months of my fieldwork, can be seen as an almost archetypal representation of this 'imagined community'. It stands in an area of West London with a large black population and a long-recognized reputation as a locus for black culture and community issues. The Project itself is one of the largest in London, with a programme which has become the envy of, and the model for, many other such centres. It was established about fourteen years ago, and employs fifteen members of staff, who organize a whole range of cultural, educational, and social facilities. It runs a creche, an after-school and supplementary education programme, an employment centre, a mental-health programme, a

[1] The following remarks are based on the situation at the time of my fieldwork, in 1990–1. Towards the end of this time, the Centre suffered some major financial cuts, and it is likely that this has significantly altered the structure and activities of the Project.

music studio, a women's centre, and a computer studies course, which leads to a City and Guilds certificate. It has its own football and cricket team and a kitchen which serves Caribbean food. Most popular is its 'drop-in' facility, which harks back to the Project's origin as a youth centre, although the average age of users has now risen quite significantly.

The Centre is funded almost exclusively by the local Council's Recreation and Leisure Department, with some additional funds under the Local Government Section XI policy to run the employment centre and from the European Social Fund for the computing programme. The relationship with the Council, according to the Centre's co-ordinator, Patrick, is largely cordial, if rather at the mercy of the particular demands of the current political scene. Patrick admits, however, that there is a degree of unwritten conflict between the Council's aims for the Project and those of the Project itself. The Project was established initially only after constant pressure from a black youth group, and was felt to be intended only as a sop to these demands, rather than a serious commitment to the needs of the black community. Its major expansion took place in the early 1980s, just after the disturbances, in which climate it was felt perhaps to be politically advantageous to support—and indeed contain—these needs. In the year of my fieldwork, the Council had just announced a cut of 31 per cent in the Project's budget, compared to an average of 10–15 per cent by other organizations under the same Department; a sign perhaps that the political kudos attached to the notion of 'the black community' was fading. It was widely rumoured that the Chairman of the Leisure and Recreation Committee had said that the Project should revert back to being a drop-in centre for youth, which was its original intention. As Patrick commented:

And when the question was asked 'intended by whom', there was no answer given. So yes, I think there is a conflict in terms of what the Council wants [the Project] to be, and what . . . [the Project] members and users say [the Project] should be (Interview, 30 Jan. 1991).

The Council's intentions are undocumented and so the present study is unable to comment on its viewpoint. From the standpoint of the Project, however, the Council's actions pointed clearly to a policy of containment, rather than advancement, a means of keeping people off the street and out of sight. Patrick's attitude was sceptical:

From the Council's point of view, in one respect, it's good to have [the Project] there, because it's seen as their flagship of what they're doing for the black community; in another respect, when it comes down to the financial commitment, they would like to know it isn't there. . . . I have no doubt that [the Project] is on one day very convenient, and another day may not be so convenient (ibid.).

Patrick and many of the members of the Project felt that the massive cuts would, however, allow reorganization and self-generation of funds which would enable the Project to set its own priorities and explore new areas, away from an external definition of what the community is and the role the Project should play within this. One result of the belief in the black community as a bounded and homogeneous entity is that the Project has been cast as a panacea for all the perceived ills of this community:

[The Project] is expected to fulfil everybody's needs. And in reality, it can't do that. So in some ways, I think the expectations have been too much. Because if you talk to 100 people, 100 people may tell you 100 different things, and I think at some point you have to be rational, and say well, what can we offer and how best we can offer those things and concentrate on that (ibid.).

With regard to the Centre, there existed a number of divisions and standpoints which were manifest at different times and in different situations. Some were indeed built into the very structures and aims of the Project, which inevitably excluded some members of the community, either by choice or by default. The Project, for example, no longer catered for the 13–20-year-old black youths, who had been the original impetus for the Centre; these usually went to other youth centres, perhaps returning to the Project at about the age of 20. It also was not utilized by sectors of the local black population who defined themselves away from the Project's auspices. These are difficult to typify; in general, however, the Centre did not cater for professionals, or those who may consider themselves upwardly mobile:

People have got their own conceptions, or maybe different conceptions of where they fit within the social strata . . . and as far as they will see [the Project] then [the Project] is one which is there for, if you can use the term, the working class (ibid.).

In terms of the wider black community in the area, also, there were a number of divisions and opinions concerning what the

Project was held to represent and what it should be. Patrick told me:

you've got what you might term the elder black community; you've got the younger generation black community. I think it may be fair to say that some in the black community would see the Centre as being positive, some would disagree with that and see it as being negative. Some would see it as not catering for the community as a whole, and [that] it's only catering for a certain section of the community; some would say it could be doing a lot more than it's doing; some would say there's definite elements within the Centre that shouldn't be there. I think you'd have a very wide-ranging view or perception of what the relationship between [the Project] and the wider black community should be (ibid.).

Internal to the Project itself, there were a number of other divisions, which encompassed different standpoints in relation to the 'community'. For example, the Project was divided to a large extent along gender lines. Women were generally more involved with the organized activities offered by the Project: the creche, the after-school activities, the women's programme, the computer course. Men, by contrast, used the Project for more social purposes: the music studio and the sports teams were dominated by men, and the drop-in centre was almost exclusively a male domain. Women that entered this arena were usually on a specific errand or were considered to be looking for a man. Patrick explained that this was because men were more involved in the public arena, whereas women were more involved with family issues and a more private arena for socializing, based around family and a small circle of friends. This is perhaps reflected in the wider black community, where men position themselves within the public arena in relation to their male peers, and women tend to locate themselves more closely around the family and domestic environment.[2]

The most potentially conflictual nature of division was to be seen in the split between those in work and those who were unemployed, often long term. Although this division was rarely expressed or enacted publicly, privately I was made aware of a

---

[2] These observations are undoubtedly an over-simplification of the role of gender in the Centre, and more widely. It is also true that the role of young black women in the public arena has changed considerably since the time of the fieldwork. Gender constructions are considered more fully in later chapters.

certain degree of ambivalence. Maurice the barber, for example, considered some of the more regular unemployed users as 'loafers', who were wasting their time and getting nowhere. He defined himself against the more negative images that the Project attracted, although he had grown up with most of the people, cut their hair, and regularly attended the Project to eat, build a few spliffs, and socialize. Some of those who were unemployed or involved in the 'alternative economy', on the other hand, regarded those who were working as either considering themselves 'above' the rest of the users, or as simply stupid for breaking their backs in a system that was giving them nothing. Which attitude was prevalent depended very much on how the individual himself was doing financially.

A major focus for this hostility was the office staff. Acting as 'gatekeepers' between external society and the different elements of the Project, the staff were often felt to be working against the interests of the community they were supposed to be serving, and, in some cases, protecting. Patrick explained:

The relationship between staff and users is not one which is always very good. Because you've got this area where people feel you're working, right; I'm not working, I'm not getting money, so I'm going to be doing what I want to get *my* money, you understand? And if you say to them, well, and try and show them something else, they see that as a fight, they see that you're fighting against them: it may not be identified as a class situation, but it is an economic situation (ibid.).

Patrick himself was often criticized by some of the regular users for the Centre's strict No Drugs policy. Although Class A drugs were generally felt to have no place within the Centre, some felt that staff should have turned a blind eye to other substances. Patrick had made it generally known that if he learned the names of any dealers, or if any drugs were dealt on the premises, he would inform the police. This led some to claim that Patrick was a 'sell-out', betraying the interests of 'the community' to safeguard his own interests. The position of staff was made more ambiguous by the Project's role as a locally-based centre, working for the needs of the black community. They were loath, therefore, to enforce strict membership criteria, and exclude elements of the community they were supposed to be serving:

As black people, we tend to have this kind of natural instinct not to turn away our own and not to be too rigid in terms of excluding people. . . . So we are open, but that works as a negative force in some cases, because like everything else, you've got good and bad. In our community, you've got good and those who are not so good (ibid.).

As an extension of this inclusive nature, black centres are often held to be representative of, and accountable for, the actions of individual members. Two years before in North-West London, for example, a similar centre had been closed down after a shooting incident.

The role of the community centre as a marker for 'the black community' can therefore be seen to encapsulate a number of differing and sometimes conflictual interpretations. From an external perspective, the Centre symbolizes and fixes a wider societal attitude towards black people, and the role these are seen to play within British society. Within the black community, the attitude towards such centres is more ambiguous: although it is seen as a necessary focus for community interests and rights, it is also associated by some people with the more negative traits ascribed to the black population. Internally to the Project itself, there are also a number of divisions, which centre around the individual's definition of his relation to what he holds the Project to represent. Such a stance brings into question quite what 'community' can mean within such a context, and what its significance is in ascribing black identity.

Nevertheless, the continued existence of the Project, and other such centres, testifies to a high degree of vested interest and belief in the value of 'the community', however 'imagined' and in whatever form. Indeed, at its most abstracted, the symbol of 'the community' remains a primary and formidable instrument of opposition: 'Even if it's from the point of view of being black, I think that in itself is common interest to keep people together' (ibid.).

HOME AND THE WORLD:
ATTITUDES TO NATIONHOOD

A central precept of Anderson's community is the imagination of a finite and enclosed entity. It therefore necessarily creates the idea of boundaries, with the incumbent notion of processes of inclusion, and, more importantly, of exclusion. The way in which the black community has been continuously and systematically excluded from the conceptions of British nationhood was considered in Chapter 1. National boundaries are imagined as absolute and integral; nationhood becomes itself regarded as a primordial and primary identity (Anthias and Yuval-Davis 1993).

The view of black youth as physically and psychologically displaced by their experiences—within Society but not of it—is a common image. As Gilroy notes, however, the absolute nature of nationhood is constantly being questioned and reworked by the activities of black youth who pass through these seemingly intractable barriers as part of 'the complex organic process which renders black Britons partially soluble in the national culture which their presence helps transform' (1987: 61). The position occupied by black British youth in relation to the imagination of nationhood remains somewhat ambiguous; they transcend the boundaries of absolute identity and straddle perceived national/ cultural communities. As Gilroy writes, 'Black Britain defines itself crucially as part of a diaspora' (ibid. 153). As such, the identity black youth ascribes itself tends towards an individual and flexible perception of nationhood rather than an absolute and unquestioned acceptance of group membership.

For the people I knew in London, the question of identity and nationhood was complex and multi-faceted (cf. Western 1992). All, with the exception of Satish, had been born in Britain; all had spent most of their lives here. Only Frank, in fact, had been born outside London. None, however, felt able to describe themselves as 'British', without any further qualification, while 'English' was a label rarely considered appropriate. As Malcolm commented, laughingly, when I asked him if he considered Britain as his 'home', 'No, it's not. Go and tell some skinhead that, he'll kick your head in' (Interview, 12 May 1991). Out of those I met, Malcolm was perhaps the least rooted in his identity; although he did not consider Britain to be his home, he also did not locate himself in relation to his parents' island of origin, Jamaica. He had never visited the island and, although he was planning to visit in 1992, he did not consider this in relation to himself in any significant way, 'If I go back there, I can't say that's my home, 'cos I wasn't even born there . . . I can't miss what I've never had' (ibid.). For Malcolm, the question of nation-hood was one he considered largely irrelevant to his sense of being, of who he is, 'I consider myself a gypsy, just stay any-where' (ibid.).

For the others amongst the boys, the question of 'home' and of belonging was not so straightforward. All considered their fam-ily history and origins important, and all defined themselves in relation to both Britain and either the Caribbean or Nigeria/ Ghana. The history of migration, or indeed of slavery, was an important factor in this consciousness, and one that achieved meaning in a very personal sense. To this extent, to see them as defining themselves as part of a global diaspora is perhaps mis-leading. Those I spoke to rarely related their sense of identity in any pan-African sense to Africa as a whole, or the experiences of black people in the United States. Although Darnell and Rommell talked of the position of black people in Canada, to which I shall return later, this arose from the presence of family there and their recent visit. Only one, Shane, spoke of 'Africa', but this was more the symbolic 'Africa' of the Rastafarians and the black Moslems than an expressed concern with events on the continent itself.

Of all my informants, only Frank, Ricky, and Edgar had spent any significant period of time in their parents' country of origin. Shane claimed to have spent some of his childhood in Jamaica, but this was disputed by the others, and was probably part of his attempt to define and consolidate his stance as a culturally aware and highly politicized black man. There remains a significant amount of kudos attached to living in the Caribbean amongst many black youth in Britain. Shane's attitude was significant in representing this stance, however dubiously grounded in fact.

Both Frank and Ricky felt that having lived in their parental 'homeland' gave them a wider perspective on their position in Britain and that this distinguished them from those of their friends who had always lived in this country. On one occasion, in one of their many arguments, both rounded on Clive—who had never been out of Britain, let alone to Nigeria—claiming that his iden-tity was severely mutilated because he did not know his history, or his 'roots'. However, as the argument progressed, it became clear that the attitude of each was quite different; Frank claiming that Nigeria was his true home, and that he felt a duty to return there to help 'build his country', while Ricky argued that this attitude was naïve and that no one who had lived most of their life in Britain would ever be accepted 'back home' as anything other than a foreigner. Ricky told me later:

I see Jamaica as my country, yes, because basically I'm black, so you've got to look towards your roots like, you've got to look towards your home. Even though not in this world would I go back there and live because it's not—the place is not fit for people to live, not with all the violence that's going on. . . . It's not the sort of place I can say, yeah, I'm going to go home and live back in Jamaica. What, to get killed? It's not worth it, you know (Interview, 12 Dec. 1990).

Ricky had returned to Jamaica when he was 4 with his mother after his parents separated. He and his brother lived there for ten years and were then sent back to Britain to live with their aunt in London. His memories of this time were mixed and somewhat ambiguous. On the one hand, he described it as an 'easy life'; on the other, he remembered the hardships and disadvantages of living in the 'Third World':

A lot of guys who are Jamaican, they've never lived in Jamaica. I have lived in Jamaica for ten years, and no matter how rich you are, unless you can afford your own generator, you have power cuts, which can last for 2 or 3 days, without no light, your fridge is defrosting immediately even if it's packed with food. Which means you have to be running out to buy blocks of ice to keep your food preserved. There's not only that problem, there's also the problem of cutting off the water—or you're suffering from a drought, because it's been too hot—things like that (ibid.).

For Ricky, the prospect of returning seemed both unlikely and undesirable, although he still identified closely with the island. Although many people, young and old, talk of 'return', Ricky was sceptical of both the possibility and the motivation:

Some of them do think they're going back. The more deeper they are into this black thing . . . they feel like they are black militants, then they say, yeah, I must go home. . . . I've seen it happen, you know, all the black people save up, reach the age of 50, 60; they retire and sell their house and are going to go back home. And they do that, go to Jamaica for a little while; people beat down their door, and they get robbed, and everything like goes down (Interview, 9 June 1991).

Ricky claimed that within Jamaica, he and all black people living in Britain would always be regarded as foreigners:

Nobody don't accept them because they don't look on them as West Indian, they look on them as English people. You deserted the country and came and lived over here for how many years, and you go back and you just can't fit in . . . they give you a hard time; as soon as you open your mouth, they call you 'English boy' (ibid.).

Ricky's attitude contrasts interestingly with Frank's experience of Nigeria. Frank returned with his mother at the age of 11, coming back to Britain at the age of 20. Like Ricky, he talked about the hardships of the country:

Life has a different meaning out there; very careless, a very careless attitude to life—any stupid thing, they'll kill you. It's not like here, where you have human rights and that. The wealthy have the say, they control the common people, they're the power—nothing's done unless they say yes (Interview, 24 Feb. 1991).

Unlike Ricky, however, Frank intended to return to Nigeria, and believed himself capable of readapting to the way of life: 'Most of my mature life, I've been brought up a Nigerian and I learned how to behave like a Nigerian. I *had* to learn how to behave as a Nigerian, otherwise I wouldn't be accepted' (ibid.).

Edgar similarly reflects on his experience in Ghana: 'they [his family in Ghana] made sure by the time I left I definitely knew about Ghanaian ways—I knew how to speak it, how to act and so on' (Interview, 17 May 1991). Like Frank, Edgar claimed that he would return to Ghana to live, if he had the money. It is significant, however, that both returned to Britain because they felt restricted by the lack of opportunities in Africa, and that this feeling could be related to their earlier upbringing in Britain: 'There were certain things I wanted, and I couldn't get—the culture couldn't provide it for me. The people weren't relating to me the way I wanted them to relate, and I came back over here' (Frank, 24 Feb. 1991). Such comments would seem to suggest a degree of tension and ambiguity in their approach that they were unwilling to admit. Both Frank and Ricky felt, however, that their experiences had given them an insight into 'their' culture that divided them from the rest of the group. Frank told me:

the way I see life is totally different probably from the person who was born and brought up here, the way they see life. I see life in a more wider perspective; I see that I have achieved something in life . . . because out there in Nigeria, you're no one unless you've done something. . . .

Like people here don't seem to see that; it's all given on a plate—they can't accept, they can't appreciate it. . . . So going back to Nigeria and coming here gives me that zest to do something. It gives you that kick in life (ibid.).

Ricky similarly claimed:

That's why I feel in the group [Frank] and I stand out a little different from the other guys, the rest of them. Our views are different, our characters are more stronger. The rest grew up here and their values are different; it's made their values much more different (Interview, 12 Dec. 1990).

The significance of family origin and culture in establishing a 'true' sense of one's identity, both within and outside Britain, was echoed by my other informants, though it is unlikely that they would have concurred with Ricky's judgement. Although they had spent all their lives in Britain, most had visited their parents' homelands at least once. Their attitude towards these places was at once more idealistic and less ambiguous than that reflected by Ricky and Frank. The visits were considered important in establishing a sense of belonging; as Eleanor told me of her trip to Dominica, her mother's homeland:

To me it was just amazing going out there and seeing my family. It's not a clear picture until you've gone back and you've met them; it's like a bit missing. So when I went back, it sort of completed the picture for me. . . . It's all to do with, I suppose when I say roots, it's sort of like your heritage; it's where you came from (Interview, 2 Apr. 1991).

However, perhaps because these visits were primarily temporary and social in nature, the images of 'home' were necessarily more distanced. Most significantly, those I spoke to did not seem to expect to be fully accepted, nor felt pressured to be so. All went to visit family still living in the Caribbean, and it was this that was considered the most important focus of identity. Angelina, who visited her father's island, Grenada, with her family in 1983, and went to Jamaica with her mother during the period of my fieldwork, told me: 'They called me Miss England, and even though you're black you're still a foreigner: they call you Miss Foreigner or something like that, because you're not from there— not one of them' (Interview, 15 Feb. 1991).

However, because she had family in both places, this gave her some connection with each, which lifted her from the position of mere tourist:

It's a form of respect. They think you've got lots of money, that's what it is, but they treat you different; I'm sure if they could rip you off they would, but if they know you've come to see family, they treat you different than just a normal tourist, because they know you've got commitment and responsibility to your family foremost (ibid.).

Neither Darnell nor Rommell had visited Jamaica, but were planning to go within the next year. For Rommell, these visits were important in redressing the balance against the hostility of British society; they were visits 'home'. 'Home' for Rommell, however, was defined against the role of outsider in a white country, rather than any desire to be accepted into island society:

When I went Grenada, it was just so nice because it didn't have a lot of white people about, so you felt like this sense of relief, because you could go there and do what you want, sort of thing, without bother . . . . When you go to Grenada, you run things there (Interview, 14 Apr. 1991).

Although he claimed to consider retiring to the Caribbean, however, Rommell's primary focus was turned towards Canada, where his father has relatives, and where he and Darnell had spent the summer. This would suggest that Rommell was concerned less with 'belonging' in the Caribbean, than *not* belonging in Britain:

As I said, I don't actually classify England as my home, so that's not saying I don't want to like move from home, because this isn't my home; my home is 14 thousand miles away in the West Indies. So I feel, like, no way about living in Canada or America. . . . My dad wants to go back to the West Indies, my mum most likely in the end will go back and I don't want to be stuck in England (ibid.).

His attitude contrasted significantly with his younger brother Darnell, who can be cast as the eternal tourist. Like Malcolm, Darnell seemed to be happiest as a gypsy; he belonged nowhere, and regarded all about him with amused curiosity, while not identifying himself deeply with any one thing. He described himself simply, and with some emphasis, as 'black'; when I pushed him to define himself further, he added 'Black British'. Although he considered it important to know about his parents' origins, this was secondary to his primary identification, 'because it [family origins] turned me out this colour' (Interview, 22 Mar. 1991). For Darnell, his visit to Grenada made little difference to his sense of self:

I think they liked me. They thought we were different . . . they could tell we weren't from the West Indies, because the way we act, the way we dress. Like we would do things like just go away and come back and feel no way about it; and they would go 'oh, you shouldn't stay out late at night, because this will happen, that will happen', but we didn't realize that, we just went about our business (ibid.).

His views of Jamaica, his mother's island, reflected this sense of separation from his personal experience, 'it doesn't interest me yet. . . . It doesn't seem as if it would be my type of people there —my scene' (ibid.). When I asked him what he expected, he replied, with undoubtedly more reference to a British image of Jamaica than to Jamaica itself, 'Full of people listening to reggae music' (ibid.).

That Darnell's primary identity was not tied to any absolute conception of nationhood, of 'belonging' to a place, was clear in his experiences of Canada. He and Rommell were staying with his father's family, who are from Grenada; the predominant Caribbean group in the area was Jamaican, with something of a reputation for violence. From a Black British perspective, these divisions were seen as meaningless; moreover, for Darnell, the divisions between Canadian blacks and British blacks were equally meaningless:

It was just like, 'where you come from', but it doesn't make a difference where you come from, you're all black, just stick together. . . . They [the Jamaicans] was calling us 'English white' . . . as soon as they heard us talk, they were shouting out 'English boy, English boy', because they were all from Jamaica, and they all thought they were bad man, they were bad—so we just didn't like say nothing, we started playing football . . . and by the end of the night they were going 'yeah, yeah, you lot come party with us, you lot are safe' (ibid.).

It is significant that Darnell did not refer to either his father's or his mother's island identities in recounting this episode. For him, in that situation, being black was enough; although it would be misleading to see Darnell as an exponent of pan-African senti- ments. Indeed, he felt very little sentiment for Africa, or Africans, and when I asked him about African-Americans, he snorted, 'some of them out there are just hard-headed and ignorant' (ibid.).

As mentioned earlier, only one of the boys, Shane, expressed any sentiment towards 'Africa'. Of Jamaican parents, Shane claimed to have lived in Jamaica for several years, but, although he felt accepted 'deep down' as a Jamaican, he claimed to be closer to the idea of 'Africa'. He told me: 'I was born in England but I think I'd prefer if I was born, maybe not in Jamaica, because Jamaica was a slave colony, but I think I'd prefer if I was born in Africa' (Interview, 5 Apr. 1991). This wish was then translated into reality through his assertion 'I am African' (ibid.):

Home, I say is in Africa, although I don't know the land that well. I'm beginning to find out more and more about it, because I am interested in my culture and my roots. I call Africa the motherland; home, that's my real home (ibid.).

The image of Jamaica, grounded in slave history, became sullied by comparison, and Shane's attitude was ambiguous: 'I love Jamaica because my people are there, do you know what I mean? My people, a lot of my roots are still in Jamaica, but still go back to Africa, do you understand? . . . Africa is home for all black man, Africa is home' (ibid.).

Shane's assertion of his African heritage manifested a common tendency that underlay all my informants' responses to 'home' and the world—the ability to choose where to place one's identity. This may be related to life experiences, as with Frank and Ricky, or to family history and origins, as with Angelina and Rommell; or, indeed, it may be unrelated to place or centred upon some belief in a spiritual and mythical homeland. Such attitudes were often ambiguous, sometimes contradictory, and tended to shift on different occasions.

The same can also be said of attitudes towards Britain, and towards British nationhood. It would be tempting—and neat—to imagine that attitudes towards the parental homeland were related inversely to attitudes towards one's position within Britain; that the more one felt alienated from British society, the more one turned to an external source of belonging. It is this belief that has been espoused in the discussions of Rastafari, and that underlies Pryce's belief in 'cultural confusion' and the cultural divide between the first and second generations. The basis for these arguments is the assumption that to achieve nationhood requires an absolute choice. However, for most of my informants, this choice was never made in any absolute sense; they may, like Frank, describe themselves as British, but cheer for a Nigerian football team, or, like Ricky, see themselves as Jamaican, yet cheer for both a football team from Cameroon, and for the black players on the British team.

It is perhaps hardly surprising, then, that attitudes towards Britain were as ambiguous and contradictory as attitudes towards 'the world'. Thus, despite the prolonged contact with their parental homeland, neither Ricky nor Frank felt that this imposed any strain on their position in regard to Britain. When I asked each where they considered to be 'home', both claimed to feel more comfortable and more secure in Britain, and that this was an equally important part of their identity. Frank, for example, told me:

While I was back in Nigeria, I used to fantasize about going back to Nottingham. I had dreams, day in, day out, about what Nottingham was like. When I did go back to Nottingham. . . . I had a different feeling then, like that was home, because that was where I was born and brought up, and there's no place like that. . . . I think Nigeria was the place my parents had to impose on me as my home . . . but it wasn't like I was brought up there. I was just living there (Interview, 24 Feb. 1991).

When I asked him if he therefore considered himself more British, or more Nigerian, he replied: 'I would consider myself being Nigerian in blood—I was born of Nigerian parents—but totally British in upbringing, attitude to life, and so many other things' (ibid.). Ricky similarly described the balance he felt between being Jamaican and being British:

I feel that Britain is my country, but Britain is not where I come from. I am British, just like the same Englishman that walks down the street, but I am not from Britain. I was born in Britain, I grew up in Britain, I like to see Britain do well in things around the world; but then again, you've got to think, I am not from Britain, I am from Jamaica (Interview, 12 Dec. 1991).

Both were aware, however, that, as Edgar put it: 'If you say you're British and you want to be British, that's it: whether or not they decide to accept you as being British is another thing' (Interview, 17 May 1991). The barrier was considered to be primarily one of skin colour, although this in itself was taken to be a symbol of culture, and of 'roots':

Colour is definitely an important issue in this country. It will always be an important issue in this country . . . because blacks for black countries, whites for white countries. It will always, always, always be like that. I mean, it's not an important issue if you live in Jamaica—it's an important issue because you don't live in your own country—you live in a white man's country; you live in England (Ricky, 12 Dec. 1990).

The possession of cultural knowledge was seen as a response to the dispossession of British nationhood. This is not to imply that black youth turn back to illusory roots in the face of racial rejection, or that they are torn between two opposing value systems; rather that this provides alternative standpoints from which to view one's position, either in Britain or outside. The exact balance will be decided upon by the individual, depending on his or her background, cultural knowledge, or individual perception of the situation. When I asked Frank what his Nigerian origins meant to him, he told me: 'It just means I've got a home, I've got roots, I know where I belong. I know my people, I know where my certain class of people come from' (Interview, 24 Feb. 1990). To Frank, and to Edgar, these aspects were complementary parts of the whole person:

It's very important to see where you come from; I think everybody should go back. . . . It made me culturally aware, very, very culturally aware, when I saw where my ancestors were from. . . . It is important, because if you shut that side of you off and say that's it, and say I'm British, I don't care what's happened in my past, you always lose a bit of yourself. I suppose I'm a full person now, I could say (Edgar, 17 May 1991).

This ambivalence was equally true of those of my informants who had spent all their lives in Britain. All expressed a sense of doubt in describing themselves as 'British', perhaps from the knowledge, as expressed by Malcolm, that to be 'black' and 'British' were often seen as mutually exclusive categories. As Clive commented, 'English history doesn't include black people. Black people were only introduced to this country 20 or 30 years ago' (Interview, 12 Feb. 1991). Rommell too expressed a degree of ambivalence towards the idea of Britain as 'home':

Why? Because we're always treated as second-class citizens: always have been and always will be. They only wanted us here in the beginning to do the jobs they didn't want; to run the buses, run the train system, sweep the roads . . . now there's a shortage of jobs, they want to get rid of us (Interview, 14 Apr. 1991).

It is interesting to compare Rommell's response to those of his siblings. Darnell, as mentioned earlier, did, if pushed, perceive himself as British, while Angelina considered herself to have multiple national identities:

all the history they're learning here is *their* history basically, whereas in respect, it should be *my* history as well. But I've also got the fact that I've got another history—I've got the history of the Caribbean, history of slavery and the mother country, Africa, where our roots came from . . . so I've got another history. Maybe that's why we're special— we've got two histories, not just one; or three in my case (Interview, 15 Feb. 1991).

Nationhood became thus very much a matter of perception, both of self and of others. As Clive noted, 'If I go abroad, I'll be called an English lad. If I go back home [Nigeria], I'll be called that white person' (Interview, 12 Feb. 1991). Within Britain, how- ever, his skin colour marked him out as not 'British', and his self- perception was then defined by his family origins and culture, 'It's the centre of belonging, culture, roots, you know' (ibid.). What this meant in terms of actual knowledge about these roots is more questionable: Clive had never been to Nigeria, and he admitted, 'My preconceived view—probably a misconception— is of mud huts in rows, muddy roads, chickens, cows' (ibid.). For Clive, therefore, and for most of my informants, the views of 'home' defined within a British context were based on a primary identity centred around skin colour. Other cultural attributes and signifiers formed a component of this, and could change signifi- cance in certain situations and at different levels, as will be dis- cussed later. However, at its most abstracted, and in opposition to white society, all would defend an identity as 'Black' first, with views of nationhood becoming secondary. As Angelina commented:

I do see myself as British, but I see myself as Black British. There is a difference. You see, I've got my identity and culture about being black. It is very important to me; it's foremost than being British (Interview, 15 Feb. 1991).

'UK BLAK': 'COMMUNITY' AND IDENTITY

In 'The Force of West Indian Island Identity in Britain' (1984), Ceri Peach writes of the emergence of a new 'black' identity amongst African-Caribbean youth, which transcends island or national differences in the face of external pressures and stereotyping. Focusing around the youth symbols of Rastafari and reggae, black youth are seen to be creating a new and distinctive lifestyle which asserts racial unity in the face of a society which had always assumed it, and which was in part responsible for its existence; as Peach writes, 'paradoxically, the early British attitudes that viewed all West Indians as Jamaicans may be becoming true' (1984: 228). He continues: 'The most alienated sections of the Afro-Caribbean youth possess . . . genre-de-vie—a lifestyle complete with distinctive dress, language, music and religion' (ibid.).

Although the symbols of this identity have changed, and dissipated, since the early 1980s, it is nevertheless still true that most black youth would assert the significance of an overarching 'black' identity in opposing white racism. How each would define this at a political level may be open to doubt, however, especially with the emergence of Black Moslem movements in parts of London. For my informants, the existence of a paramount black identity was more a fact of life than a matter of contention. As Clive told me:

I have more in common with black people bar their origins. In today's day and age, it's not a case of who's thinking you're this or that, but black. There's a central sort of way of thinking, acting, doing. . . . I think it's just being black; you can't pick it up, you can't learn it, it's just in you already (Interview, 12 Dec. 1991).

During the first few months of my fieldwork, some of the boys took it upon themselves to initiate me in some of the more tangible aspects of this image: drink Canei wine or Tennants lager, because these were black man's drink; blast your music very loud when driving and nod your head to the beat; never listen to Radio One or Capital Radio, because these catered for white people; never buy your music from HMV. Such examples are facetious, and were meant to be; they do, however, testify to the existence of a widely held image of black identity which all were aware of and, to some extent, conformed to. The basic tenet of this identity was solidarity, to each other as individuals and to the idea of 'the community', and was primarily oppositional in nature. To some extent, at this level, to 'be black' was simply not to 'be white', and was defined against this perceived yardstick. So, for example, Capital Radio and Radio One were seen as 'white' stations; HMV was seen to stock 'white' music. However true— or not—this perception may be, the image was one both of exclusion from the wider bounds of society, and also of particularity: the assertion of a cultural exclusivity which transcends simple opposition.

This sense of solidarity was manifested on a day to day basis in a number of ways, many of which are intangible. They are best captured by the notion of 'respect'. All my male informants considered it important to show 'respect' to other black people within the public arena. Where the other people were strangers, this was usually communicated non-verbally, through a nod of the head or a slight raising of the hand; with friends or acquaintances, this would be replaced by 'touching'.

The arenas for such displays of solidarity were primarily white-dominated; the interplay between strangers in an area of higher black population was considered less important. For example, when the boys were in the West End, they would always acknowledge the presence of other black men in the club or winebar, but this would not happen in a black club, or at other black social events, unless the person were already known to them. Transgressions of these bounds of respect were generally frowned upon.

In one instance, a group of the boys were expelled from Hombres, a club in the West End, after Ricky started a fight. The fight was with a group of white boys, whom Ricky claimed were infringing on his dance space. As we were forced to leave, an African-American man, who obviously felt implicated by the actions of the group, was amongst the loudest in calling for their permanent expulsion; it was against him, rather than the opponents in the fight, that the antagonism of the group was most vehement. All felt that he should have defended them, as black men, against the mainly white staff and clientele of the club. Most of the boys were in favour of waiting outside the club to redress the matter with him, but contented themselves with shouting threats as we drove off. In a similar occurrence, when I met some of the boys in Corks winebar with Angelina and her brother, the bouncer refused entry to Darnell and his friend. Again, the issue centred around the question of 'solidarity'; the bouncer was black, but was denying entry to other black people, while allowing white clientele through the door. After Clive and Frank came up and reasoned with the bouncer, we were allowed in, but both Angelina and Darnell were outraged at the man's behaviour. He was, Angelina complained, a 'sell-out'; someone who had sold his soul and identity to the white establishment.

'Solidarity . . .'

For those I spoke to, the issues of solidarity and community emerged most vividly in the mid-school years. All my male informants claimed to have had almost exclusively black friends at school, although none went to a school that was predominantly black. Clive told me that by the fourth year: 'the black guys were tending to be more noticeable, roamed about in gangs and were renowned for their schoolish violence, so to speak, because they sort of run tings [*sic*] in the school' (Interview, 5 Mar. 1991). Ricky too, who arrived back in Britain at the start of the fourth year, felt drawn to these groups through a desire to 'fit in', and be accepted within a community he recognized. When I asked him what he did at school, he told me, 'Bunk school, run around with the Black guys, hunt skinheads' (Interview, 6 June 1991). Even though Ricky was from Jamaica, he felt that he could relate to the black British groups in a way that simply was not possible with the white groups. For Ricky, the emphasis was on shared experiences, and common ways of thinking and understanding the British experience that inevitably excluded them from their white peers:

I can't really relate to them, know what I mean. You can't 100 per cent be yourself. I mean, if you're used to strolling around and making jokes and all that, you're not on the same sense of humour. There's even a language barrier as well, you know, because if I start blabbing off in Jamaican, and start cracking a few jokes and that, they don't really find it that funny (ibid.).

The element of personal obligation, or sometimes of coercion, in maintaining group boundaries was graphically described to me by Darnell. Darnell attended a Catholic boys' school near his home in North-West London; the school population was mainly Irish, but with a significant number of black pupils. He told me:

all the black people stuck together... even though like people were three years above you, you'd still hang around with them and all the black people in this group.... It was very important, because if you weren't then you were the target of the older black people.... If you were safe with all the older ones, then you were one of them, they aren't going to beat up one of their own; if you weren't, then they'd run after you and beat you up and everything (Interview, 22 Mar. 1991).

Darnell assured me that this element of group activity was by no means serious, 'It was just like a funny game' (ibid.), but it does illustrate both the awareness of group boundaries and of the importance of in-group solidarity. Like Ricky, Darnell saw the maintenance of these not in terms of coercion and sanctions against 'outsiders', but the inevitable result of shared interests:

It's not protection; just like they would do the same things like you wanted to do ... like football; there were like all black people in the sports team, football team, basketball team—even though there was like only ten black people in the year, the whole ten of them would be in the football team, and one white person, and the white person is in goal (ibid.).

Relationships between this group and others were not hostile, and the boundaries remained fluid, assuming more importance in the leisure arena. Out of school, however, the assumed commonality of black experience led to their resurrection, and was consolidated by the geography of the area. Darnell explained:

When the school finished, you went one way; because like the school was on the Harlesden Road—going one way you're going into Harlesden and Stonebridge, go the other way you're going to Willesden and Kilburn. ... So all the white people went that way, and all the black people went the other way (ibid.).

The boundaries of 'the black community' were, however, by no means as fixed and rigid as the above comments would suggest. On the contrary, the perception of these boundaries was very much open to personal interpretation, and both expansion and contraction. Although both Clive and Ricky stressed the significance of these groups in providing a feeling of internal understanding and external difference, both also expressed a degree of ambivalence about these boundaries with regard to their personal position. As Ricky told me: 'OK, fair enough, we were all at school and we were all black guys, and the black guys run the school, but in fairness, while we run school, the white boys were studying in classes' (Interview, 6 June 1991).

'. . . and its limits'

At their widest extent, the boundaries of 'the black community' were expanded to include all non-white minorities. This would seem to underline their oppositional and political nature rather than their cultural delineation, although again the stress was on shared experience in the face of a common enemy. Ricky told me:

For me, I see things in black and white. I see Asians, whether they call themselves Asians, they're still to the black scene, right. The extreme is black, the extreme on the other side is white. There is no need to get caught up in the middle. So, see yourself as black (Interview, 12 Dec. 1990).

Darnell even went so far as to include one of his friends, Rico, who is Portuguese, in the definition of 'black'; this was because he lived near Stonebridge, and had exclusively black friends—he was therefore seen to have a share in the experiences of black life. The boys were generally less expansive in their definitions; the group had no white members, and during the time of my fieldwork I only ever saw one white boy, a friend of Satish's, spend any time with them. He was acceptable, on a short-term basis, because, like Rico, he had grown up around black people and could adapt to their lifestyle and attitude; he would also act on the side of the group in any confrontation with white people. This boy, Danny, was present during the fight at Hombres and was one of the first to get involved with Ricky. The acceptance of such outsiders was, however, tenuous, and the boundaries of the group could contract at any time. Danny, for example, was always regarded with some caution by the boys, who considered him slightly unstable and unpredictable, while Darnell told me that Rico and other such 'honorary blacks' were the first targets for antagonism and exclusion should tensions within the group rise.

The position of Asians within the community definition was equally tenuous. Often Asians were seen as occupying a space between the black and white extremes, and their loyalty could therefore not be guaranteed. In the Harlesden area, tensions between the black and Asian communities were high during the time of my fieldwork; there had been a number of incidents reported of black men being attacked in nearby Southall, and on one occasion, a group of Asian youths had come to Harlesden to engage black youths in battle. Such activities were regarded with some derision by the latter. Darnell told me that the Asian youths had been severely beaten by the black youths and sent back home to Southall in disgrace. In East London, where the black population is less visible and secure, and where National Front activity is a more daily occurrence, the divisions between the two minorities were less pronounced, and more flexible. Shane told me that at school:

I had loads of Asian friends, but they're very hypocritical themselves . . . because you know when they were in trouble, physically being beaten up by a white boy, they come to the black guys . . . because we're supposed to have the strength, we can fight, stuff like that 'we are friends, we're brothers'. And to me it's bullshit . . . because when everything is OK, you were with the white boys talking about us. . . . And when you're with your white friends, you don't know us, it's so painful for you to raise your arm and wave at me (Interview, 5 Apr. 1991).

The position of Satish was very revealing in this regard. Satish was born in India and arrived in Britain at the age of 12. He met Clive about seven years before my fieldwork, while working for Tesco's, at about the time that he met Dion, his Jamaican girlfriend. Publicly, Satish was accepted by the boys as one of the group; he was, however, the first target for insults when the group was in high spirits. These insults were in the majority of cases centred around racial origin; he was often referred to as 'you stupid Paki'—especially by his girlfriend. On a more private level, Satish was considered by the others to be weak—he was felt to be unable to control his relationship with Dion because he was not black. Dion was said to beat Satish quite savagely during their arguments, and this was a source of great amusement to the boys. I suspect if it had been one of the others—a black man—they would not have found it quite so funny, but I was assured that it would never happen to anyone else.

Satish's reaction to his position was continually to reaffirm his 'black' identity to the others and to outsiders. When I first met him, he told me on various occasions that he was a Trinidadian Indian, that his mother was black, that he had been born and brought up in the East End around black people. I only found out the truth from Dion, who said that Satish was ashamed of his origins and avoided any connection with other Asians, outside of his family, as much as possible. Satish often referred to me as 'that Paki girl', as a means of defining himself against the culture he felt me to represent.

'Community' and Language

The presence of community boundaries was both maintained and made more flexible through the use of symbolic boundary markers, such as dress and types of music. Such markers externalized and objectified the internal standards of the group and allowed the manipulation of symbols by the individual in an ongoing process of identity negotiation. Perhaps the most significant of such boundary markers is the use of language. Peach notes that: 'The emergence of a converging black British vernacular reflects that for many of the second and later generations there is a converging black British identity' (1984: 228). Black English, Peach claims, is based on the island creoles of the early migrants, but remains distinct, lying midway along the continuum between Creole and Standard English. Its use, moreover, is not fixed, but assumes significance in interaction, signalling both membership to the group and difference from others. There exists, therefore, an element of choice in its adoption, 'Class, lifestyle and stage of life have an appreciable impact on the extent to which Creole is used' (ibid. 227).

What is of interest to the present work is not the linguistic aspects of language usage, but its symbolic import. Hewitt notes in *White Talk, Black Talk*, that 'the use of patois was the single most persistent feature which bound together the disparate strands of black youth culture' (1986: 114). Its primary significance is, therefore, as an assertion of black unity and community strength, which ties the individual into a group identity—should he so desire.

Much black English vocabulary has become appropriated into

the realm of British popular youth culture. It would be misleading, however, to regard this as weakening the symbolic significance of its usage. Black English is a constant creation and
reworking of language to subvert original meaning and create
new meanings which define black exclusivity. Such meaning
remains largely contextual and is produced through interaction.
One example would be the use of the term 'nigger', which was
a favourite term of both abuse and affection amongst the boys.
The term in its present usage was probably imported from the
more radical hip-hop culture in the United States, where it has
been reclaimed by rap groups such as Public Enemy or NWA
(Niggas with Attitude) and reworked to encapsulate both a positive and negative meaning. Both are related to a particular idea
about 'being black'; it is simultaneously an indictment of the
stereotypical image of black men—loud, aggressive, 'ignorant'—
and an assertion of individual and group strength, which derives
from these same qualities. The term was used by the boys with
both purposes in mind. It was, however, a term they would only
use publicly in reference to themselves, although they did use it
privately in reference to other black groups. It was a term, moreover, that was granted very specific bounds of acceptable usage—
it could only be used by blacks. As Ricky told me, 'It's alright
black guys going around calling each other nigger, but if a white
guy calls you nigger—dead mother fucker!' (Interview, 12 Dec.
1990).

As with most public assertions of community, the use of black
English was a primarily male prerogative. Although some black
women did use it, these were mainly considered to be 'rough'
and unfeminine. Angelina and her female friends told me that
although they could understand some of it, they did not use it
themselves; they did, however, have brothers who used it. All
the boys, except Edgar, claimed to be able to speak black English
with some degree of proficiency. Most were careful, however, to
distinguish it from Patois or pidgin English, which their parents
spoke. As Malcolm told me, 'It's English, but it's like slang sort
of thing' (Interview, 12 May 1991); it was, therefore, to be distinguished from the French-based patois of islands like St Lucia and
Grenada. Darnell described black English as 'just talking fast and
breaking up the words. You just have to be in the right company
and then it just comes out' (Interview, 22 Mar. 1991). The use of

this language was situational and mainly confined to a male peer group; none of the boys would use it to their parents or elders, because this was considered impolite, and none would use it with non-black groups unless they were trying to exclude and intimidate the latter. Frank, who used black English only rarely, told me: 'When I'm with my friends, making a point very clearly and in crude fashion—so basically they understand what I'm talking about—that's when I'd use that style' (Interview, 24 Feb. 1991).

Appropriateness was, then, a crucial part of language usage: the failure to observe these rules, for example, in employment situations or with authority figures, was seen as symptomatic of personal inadequacy. In such cases, black English usage was associated with a negative image of black community, which drew on the popular constructions of wider society. In these situations, therefore, the individual would distance himself from social stereotyping by employing standard English. An example of this distancing can be seen in Edgar, who denied being able to speak black English: 'I always learn the hip words at the wrong time; you know, people stopped saying wicked a long time ago, and I still say it. . . . I just can't be bothered' (Interview, 17 May 1991). Edgar more generally distanced himself from any association with 'the community'; he preferred to see himself as upwardly mobile and set apart from the working-class 'typical' blacks. It was for this reason that he had moved away from the boys in the last two years, and from the identification with any collective image of black youth.

The use of black English illustrates an ambivalence in the notion of 'the community'. On the one hand, it was used as part of an oppositional statement of solidarity; on the other, it was equated with a negative image of what 'community' was held to represent. Floya Anthias and Nira Yuval-Davis similarly point to a dual perception of 'community', as both an 'organic', naturalized whole and as a pathologized and stigmatized repository of cultural disadvantage (1993: 165–7). 'Community' becomes, thus, a source of both strength and weakness; of unity and of differentiation. At a level lower than that of opposition to white society, therefore, the idea of 'community' functions as a more complex and diverse set of identities, as a series of oppositions which come into play in different situations. The farewell party was one example of these oppositions.

'Community and Roots'

One of the factors effectively elided by the assertion of a Black British identity is the consideration of parental background. This is primarily a division between those of African-Caribbean and those of African origin. Amongst the boys, these divisions were a source of amusement and insult, largely directed against the two Nigerians. Clive, especially, was the focus of these jokes; comments were constantly made about his lips and his backside, both considered to be 'typically African', and to the size of his mother's cooking pots, 'Clive's mother cooks rice in a bath.' Clive's general response was to act up to these stereotypes by putting on a heavy Nigerian accent and shouting; he and Frank also traded insults with the others on the image of African-Caribbeans as lazy, dope-smoking Rastas, and would shout 'Rastafari' in a mock Jamaican accent. Although these jokes were an integral part of the group's structure, and were taken in good humour, they did reflect a division that still holds some relevance in the black community. This has been emphasized in the East End by the more recent arrival of significant numbers of West African and North African immigrants, who were not considered part of the Black British identity, nor probably would have wished to be. Clive told me that at school his major source of hostility came from the African-Caribbeans, who would use the term 'African' as a term of abuse:

you silly African used to be a good phrase to describe someone who was stupid or had done something wrong; even if they weren't an African, you'd still say 'you silly African', which is saying that all Africans were silly (Interview, 5 Mar. 1991).

His response was to accuse his taunters of not knowing their roots, of not being 'real' Africans, 'I used to relish the thought that we're all Africans, you are as well, but you're not a *true* African' (Interview, 12 Feb. 1991).

On the 'opposite' side, Ricky told me:

I see Africa as my roots, my deep, deep roots—my ancestors are from Africa. But Africans in a way tend to look down on West Indians, like saying, 'oh, you're mixed, because you went to the West Indies. All my generations are from Africa, but your generations are from here and there and everywhere else, so you're mixed.' But we might be truer to Africa, being mixed, than they are. They are from their country, but

Africans that come here, how much do they see this black and white thing? A lot of them will tend to turn to a white man rather than go to their own black kind (Interview, 12 Dec. 1990).

It is interesting to contrast this with the relative lack of distinction amongst African-Caribbean youth of different island origins. Although amongst their parents' generation this remained a matter of some contention, amongst my informants such issues were more a matter of personal information and family-centred celebration than public debate. Darnell, whose parents are 'mixed'—from Jamaica and Grenada—told me: 'Everyone in this country they think comes from Jamaica, end of story. . . . To us it doesn't make a difference because we were all born in London anyway' (Interview, 22 Mar. 1991).

It would be misleading, however, to place too much emphasis upon the divisions between Black British youth of African and those of African-Caribbean origin. Amongst my informants, this issue was more a source of entertainment than dispute, and only became of relevance in an all-black context, when the oppositional 'Black' identity ceased to be appropriate. In a similar manner, Frank and Clive were heard on several occasions to engage in a further narrowing of the discussion to inter-Nigerian identity, with Frank accusing Yorubas of being stupid, uncultured, and ugly, and Clive accusing Ibos of being the same.

The main issue in this dispute is seen in 'racial' terms, and relates back to the primary black identity—who is the 'truer' black person, or who is the most 'black', together with the question of who defines what this identity should be. It is possible that the salience of the division between African and African-Caribbean youth centres around the symbol of 'Africa' as the spiritual homeland for black people, and the question of 'ownership' of that symbol. The construction of 'blackness' does, however, go beyond this difference of origin to create and mediate other standpoints within the black community. These raise issues concerning some of the ambiguities around stereotypes and images that are held within the bounds of the community, in which 'black' identity becomes a means of differentiation as well as solidarity. These images have both positive and negative connotations and articulate opposing constructions of 'blackness' which are centred around what may be loosely termed perceptions of 'class'.

'Turf Wars': Territory and Identity

One of the most interesting manifestations of these ambiguities is the relationship between territory and black identity. The notion of 'community' itself can be seen to incorporate the idea of territory, and the equation of people to place. Amongst my informants, and more generally, the image of territory and of personal relation to place was strong and at times quite emotive. The 'black community' can therefore be seen to function on two distinct levels: first, at an ideological, non-territorial level; and secondly, at a territorial level, internal to an imagined black community, which is opposed to other perceived 'black' areas. It was this second level that was operating at the farewell party. Both incorporate the idea of 'outsiders' and both operate images and stereotypes to create and maintain boundaries. Integral to these images at this second level is a dual notion of black identity. This was considered earlier in the use of the term 'nigger', and it is the same image of both strength and brute strength which is in operation. As with other standpoints in relation to the black community, these boundaries operated only in specific situations and were elastic in nature. Thus, where the boys had a particular perception about Harlesden, Darnell was able to distinguish parts within this geographical and conceptual area which coincided with particular images.

Again, this division of community, or creation of community at a local level, was more a matter of perception than conflict, although there were rumours of some territorially-based violence between black groups, usually believed to be related to drugs. There were, however, clearly perceived differences between areas within London, which were a source of public comment. At one point in my fieldwork, Frank brought his new girlfriend, Pauline, round to the flat: Pauline lived in Peckham, and Frank and Ricky spent some time teasing her that the area and the people living there were 'rough'. Pauline countered with her own perceptions about East London, saying that the boys lived in 'the country' and had no idea about living in a black area. The intimation was that she was more aware of 'being black' than they were, because she lived in a 'black community', while the boys assumed Pauline was 'more black' in a negative sense, focusing on violence and poverty as the primary markers of this

'community'. Perceptions of other areas were, however, not necessarily negative: the boys often displayed a certain amount of
respect and awe for people from 'black' areas, who were considered to have more cultural resources, while Darnell expressed
respect for East Londoners, who were seen to be more engaged
in everyday conflict against white racist groups.

The complexity of territorial boundaries was illustrated by
Darnell, who gave me his own personal geography of black
London; I will quote this section of the interview at some length
to demonstrate some of the issues and images involved.

D. If you go to Stonebridge, and you're black, you're safe, you don't
   bother, you walk through. If you go to Chalk Hill, now, which is just
   around the corner up in Wembley, they sort of think about it, to mug
   you; like, they know you're black but they'll think about it. But if you
   go to East London, like Hackney, or Brixton, then they want to say
   'we're the best area, we are the badder people, we'll mug you because
   we know you live near Stonebridge, you're from Stonebridge'.

C. They're scared of that area of Harlesden?

D. Yeah, a lot of people are scared of Harlesden and Stonebridge because it's got a bad reputation and the black people that live in
   Harlesden; before they—because it's not a bad place—before they
   put the reputation down there, they boost it up to make other people
   scared of them and then they get respect from the other people, walk
   where they want, go where they want, and nobody will trouble them.

C. And that makes you a target as well?

D. Yes, if you go to the wrong area. But if you just go like Tottenham,
   Dalston; don't touch into mid Hackney and like don't go deep into
   Brixton, then you're safe. People say 'where you from?', if you say
   Harlesden, they do 'Ah, you're safe', and they talk to you really nice
   and all that. But if you go Brixton and go 'yeah, I'm from Harlesden',
   they go 'so, you think you're a bad boy then; come, let me show you
   who's a bad boy' (Interview, 22 Mar. 1991).

Darnell's emphasis is on 'reputation', the perception of what a
particular area is held to represent, and the equation of the individual with this area. Reputation is established in relation to a
series of internal markers of black identity, which are used to
measure how 'black' an area is. This is related not so much to
density of black population, although this is a factor, but to its
conformity to certain internally-held stereotypes. This relates in
turn to the idea of 'community' and what this is held to represent. As mentioned earlier, these stereotypes and images are by

no means unambiguous, and the relationship of the individual to them is similarly ambivalent.

'Community' and the Individual

The contextual and shifting nature of 'community' identification was often manifest in the boys' attitude to other black groups, particularly at an individual level. At this level, 'community' was enacted as a series of roles and codes which altered in different situations, or, indeed, incorporated multiple stances simultaneously. Symbols and images were manipulated by the individual to ally or distance himself from 'the community', which constituted the primary marker of 'blackness', although this was itself open to interpretation. This was clearly illustrated by an incident involving Frank.

For several months, Frank was employed at a clothes shop in East Ham. It was common knowledge that the area was 'worked' by a number of black youths, who entered shops and took what they liked, unhindered by the shop assistants who—rightly or wrongly—feared for their lives. However, when they raided Frank's shop during his lunch hour, Frank felt it was incumbent on him to defend his territory. He therefore rushed out, found one of the thieves and 'warned' him—with a baseball bat—to keep out of his way. The boy, hardly surprisingly, returned the threat. Frank, for the next few days, armed himself with a kitchen knife, ready for the attack, which never happened.

In its most abstract imagination, this incident could be seen to reflect the often documented proclivity of black youths towards violence and criminality. Muggers, drug dealers, rioters—the black raider is just one more construction of black deviance. What is of significance here, however, is not external perceptions, but the way that these stereotypes were brought into play within this event by its protagonists. These provided those involved with a range of beliefs and expectations which were constantly shifting and transforming attitudes and alliances.

The attitude of the raiders themselves is unknown, although they were clearly trading upon one of the most developed stereotypes of black youth as armed and dangerous. The attitude of the boys was, however, complex, and raised a number of questions concerning what 'being black' actually meant within this context.

As black youth themselves, they felt that the incident transgressed unspoken rules of conduct internal to 'the black community'. First, all the boys felt that the raiders should not have entered the shop because it disrespected Frank, who is also black. Secondly, and conversely, it was generally agreed that Frank should not have taken the side of the shop, which was not a black establishment, against the black raiders.

At one level, then, the boys clearly identified closely enough with the thieves as black youth, to assume the existence of shared values and norms—of a 'community'. This identification was, however, subverted by a distinction based upon a different image of 'blackness', which was appropriated both as a self-image and as an attribute of 'the other' as occasion demanded. This drew on a negative image of 'community' constructed around deviance, which fragmented any unified definition and allowed for both processes of individual identification and distinction.

For Frank and the rest of the boys, then, the raiders represented an image of the 'typical' black youth. Frank's confrontation with the raiders can be seen as an attempt to distance himself from this image. For the other boys, however, Frank's action was seen to be merely stupid. The raiders were, after all, violent individuals who in their role as 'typical' blacks were—by definition—better equipped to handle themselves in any confrontation. It is significant that, in choosing to confront the raiders, Frank appropriated for himself the same images: in the days that followed, he constantly asserted to the others that he, as a black man, could handle any attack, and as a symbol of this—as if to complete the image—he started carrying the knife; something he never normally did. The reality behind the image was somewhat anticlimactic, but revealing. Frank, who obviously knew nothing about weapons, put the unsheathed kitchen knife down his sock, cut his leg open running for a bus and had to have nine stitches in his calf.

FAMILY AND 'COMMUNITY'

The relationship between the individual, the family, and the community is one that the present study does not address in great detail. The focus here has been rather on the public enactments of 'community' than on the private domestic relationships of my informants. While acknowledging the significance of family in the creation of individual, personal notions of 'belonging', the scope of this study is unable to explore the variety and affectivity of its expression in the depth it requires and deserves. A few remarks can be made, however, on the relationship of notions of 'family' to 'the community'.

As Gilroy has noted, the black family has been consistently regarded as the 'natural' locus of black culture and identity (1993: 64); it has also been understood in common-sense ideology as the originary and reproducer of black deviance and pathology. Similarly, Errol Lawrence writes:

The 'family' is important not only because it is here that culture is re-produced, but also because it is the principal site where black people are recognized as having a degree of autonomy. This makes it possible to argue that the cultural 'obstructions' to 'fuller participation' in society are reproduced within black families by black people themselves and that like 'original sin' these 'problems' descend from the 'immigrants' to their children, their children's children and all who came after them (1982b: 116).

Images of teenage single motherhood, illegitimacy, matriarchal households, absent fathers, identity crises, gender and inter-generational conflict have all combined to construct the black family as mutilated and dysfunctional.[3] Moreover, by conceiving of the 'community' as the simple accumulation of family units, the perceived pathology of 'the black community' has been equated directly and completely with the inadequacies of black family life. The way in which these images have served to place the black community outside the realm of national life and culture has already been considered (Lawrence 1982a, 1982b; Gilroy 1987, 1993).

Conversely, Gilroy has written more recently of 'the trope of the family' (1993), which substitutes fictive kinship ties for the notion of 'race', and which, he argues, seeks to re-create the patri-archal nuclear family as a resolution of social and political crises.

---

[3] A recent article in *The Guardian*, by Yasmin Alabhai Brown, replays all these images (Monday, 13 June 1994). She writes, 'The black community has been singled out as being out of control. . . . Not many in the black community would deny that there is a problem.'

Although ostensibly opposed to the pathology of the black family, the advocates of its reconstruction make the same equation of assumed dysfunction and crisis, and find the same solution—the reassertion of black masculine control. Moreover, both approaches assume the absolute symmetry of family, 'race', and community boundaries, where, as Gilroy writes, 'Each of these— the familial, the racial, the communal—leads seamlessly into the next' (ibid. 197). 'Family' thus becomes either the smallest element of 'community' or is synonymous with its widest imagination; both naturalizing and reducing the strength and diversity of its expression.

The reification of 'the black family' obscures the breadth and heterogeneity of its lived experience. As 'community' exists in a number of shifting and contextual imaginings, so 'family' is conceptualized and enacted in differing ways, which can either re-create or cross-cut elements of community. Amongst my informants, the idea of 'family' was various in its lived reality and diverse in its affective expression. Rommell and Darnell still lived with their parents in Harlesden, and Angelina returned there when her course ended; both Eleanor and Fenella similarly returned home once their degrees were finished; Frank lived with his sister and saw his mother on regular visits to and from Nottingham; Ricky, who had lived in the flat since he was 16, had not had contact with his mother in Jamaica for several years but saw his father often and was especially close to his paternal grandparents; Malcolm had lived with his cousins in the family home since his mother's death when he was 8, although his father had more recently moved to another house nearby; Clive lived at home with his parents and siblings, as did Edgar; Shane had moved away from home when he was 18 to a flat near his mother's where he spent most of his time; while Nathan and Arif shared a flat but were constant visitors to Nathan's mother's home. Dion and Satish, who were the only members of the group to live in a 'permanent' domestic relationship with their two children, similarly spent large amounts of time with their respective parents and siblings.

What is of interest to the present study is the way in which the idea of 'family' is created and enacted in its relationship to 'community'. During my fieldwork, I was unable to spend more than rare moments with the families of my informants; the following observations are therefore primarily based on the one family I came to know well—that of Angelina, Rommell, and Darnell.

The creation of 'family' within Angelina's home proved to be remarkably fluid, continually altering its boundaries and cross-cutting other expressions of 'community'. The nuclear family itself was marked by a closeness and level of support which was a source of strength to both its members and those who came into contact with them; it also formed the core of a wider, more inclusive and more loosely defined notion of 'family'. At its widest extent, Angelina's family formed a network with members in Jamaica, Grenada, Canada, the United States, and Britain—a truly 'diasporic' complex of relationships which transgressed and modified any absolute experience of 'nationhood'. Members of the extended family in Britain lived mainly in London, although one uncle lived in Huntingdon and his daughter was a regular presence in the family home every weekend. Other relatives, particularly her mother's brothers, lived locally and visited the house most days, providing a number of focal points for establishing relationships with and outside the local 'community'. These contacts were consolidated and extended by family- and community-based celebrations and activities, such as birthday parties, christenings, weddings, which moved outside the local area and mediated the boundaries of territorial networks, bringing new acquaintances inside the family structures and taking the family beyond the bonds of kinship. It should be noted also that some members of the family had white partners, so that there could be no simple correlation between 'race' and 'family'.

As mentioned earlier, Angelina's parents were in a 'mixed' marriage, her father being from Grenada and her mother from Jamaica. At a level beyond the bonds of biological kinship, this relationship formed the basis for the establishment of island connections and identifications within the area, throughout London and often at a country-wide level. Within the family, the island rivalries formed the subject of good-humoured wrangling between her mother and father; amongst their children, these 'differences' were not a cause of much concern or comment. Angelina was, however, a member of a local Grenadan organization and regularly attended island-based celebrations. Last year I accompanied her, her father, and two of her cousins to the Grenadan Independence Day dance in Wembley, where several hundred people of all ages, and from all over the country, were gathered to celebrate their shared island heritage. 'Family' in this context thus drew on a particular expression of 'community', which is based in the Caribbean, although it would be misleading to see this identification as in any way exclusive or conflictual with other constructions of either 'family' or 'community' in different situations.

Most strikingly, the notion of 'family' included within its structures many 'fictive' kin. Angelina's home was constantly open to a stream of friends from the local area and its surrounds, who were considered an integral part of the family group. Friends of Angelina, Rommell, and Darnell thus referred to their parents as 'mom' and 'dad', an arrangement which seemed to be largely reciprocal. The family home was, on the times I stayed there, full of young people, sitting and talking with their mother, working on cars with their father, eating dinner, seeking advice from Angelina, waiting for Darnell, running errands for one of the family group. At times of celebration and crisis, this 'fictive' kin group were always present for support and constituted an extensive, mainly local network, which cut across biological kinship, island or national origins—Angelina, for example, is godmother to a 'niece' of Ghanaian origin—'race' and generation.

It should be noted that, amongst others of my informants, the notion of family was less expansive and more nucleated, with comparatively rigid boundaries. The boys, for example, never referred to each other in kinship terms, nor were they uniformly received as 'fictive' kin within each other's family homes, although they would sometimes use kinship idiom to refer to a wider imagined 'community'. However, all knew each other's families and were careful to show their respect for the parental home and family commitments. Moreover, it should not be assumed from the above discussion that each creation of family carried an equal weighting and could be easily substituted for another. Within each, the primacy and uniqueness of the 'nuclear' family was undisputed and remained the central source of other imaginings. It is not thus the 'disorganized' (Duneier 1992: 10) and dysfunctional sprawl of undefined relationships often associated with black family life.

The relationship between 'family' and 'community' can thus be seen to be imagined and enacted as a fluid and contingent phenomenon; with the former both re-creating and traversing the bounds of the latter. 'The black family' should not, therefore, be seen as a simple component of 'the black community', its origin or its dominant symbol, but as a dynamic entity whose content, structures, and significance are constantly negotiated and reinvented. It should be noted, finally, that 'family' was always viewed by my informants as a *positive* expression of personal community, however diverse and elusive an experience it encapsulated.

CONCLUSION

Thus, even for one apparently coherent strata of black society—youth—'community' functions as a multi-faceted and ambiguous concept. At its most abstract, as an 'imagined community', it provides a source of solidarity in opposition to wider white society, which can be mobilized to act collectively and politically. The idea of 'community' can thus be seen, as Gilroy writes, to retain 'a special moral valency' (1993: 34), which is enacted differentially and contextually by its members. This can be clearly seen in relation to 'the community centre', which acts as a marker to the existence of the black community and which can be seen to embody attitudes towards, and of, this community. It can also be seen, however, to incorporate a number of divisions and varying standpoints which become visible and significant in different situations. This is not to invalidate the notion of community, but merely to suggest that what 'community' represents, and the way it is used, is more fluid than has been previously allowed.

The question of community also raises the question of nationhood. Since the arrival of large numbers of immigrants from the Caribbean in the 1950s, black people have been portrayed as an alien group within, but not of, the national culture. For the subjects of this study, however, the bounds of nationhood are neither discrete nor tied in any essentialist way to their sense of identity. The position of black youth in Britain can be seen to transcend the idea of national boundaries and absolute national identity, to allow a fluid and negotiable definition of identity, which is tied primarily to the assumption of shared experience rather than to place. Bhabha (1994) similarly writes of the 'counternarratives' of 'cultural hybrids', who challenge the 'totalising boundaries' of nationhood; while Gilroy has recently raised the notion of diasporic identity based on flow rather than fixity— 'routes' rather than 'roots' (1993: 193).

The notion of 'the community' thus exists at a number of levels and embodies shifting and often contradictory stances, incorporating roles and codes that centre around definitions of what it means to 'be black'. At a level lower than that of its relationship to wider social structures, therefore, any discussion of 'community' must take into account internal and contextual definitions centred around cultural origins, territory, perceived class and gender distinctions, and generational factors.

The definition of 'black', as of 'community', becomes a product of the situation, always changing, ever imagined and reimagined, open to inconsistency and ambiguity in its application. This does not invalidate the value of the notion of 'the black community', but recognizes both its strengths and limitations in the discussion of black identity. Particularly in response to the increasing pressures towards 'cultural insiderism' (Gilroy 1993: 124) and ethnically absolute notions of 'community', the imagination of 'the black community' recognizes the potential strength and unity of diversity.

3

Work

In the fifties, my people were told
That the
Streets of England were paved with gold,
They say,
'Come to England if you want money,
There's a whole heap of jobs for everybody'.
When they reach, what did they see?
Streets full of rubbish and doggie d . . . ,
Them made a joke,
'Them want *we* to clean it'.

(John MacLean, *Going Home*)

IN an article for *Guardian* Woman (June 1991), 'Flying Colours', Juliet Alexander writes of 'the widening gap between aspiring black women and black men' in the employment sphere. The article is significant not only for its assertion of black female success in the labour market, and the divisions this has caused within the black community, but also for its contrasting represen-tation of the position of black men. She writes: 'As the real suc-cess story of the Thatcher drive to create a black middle class, she [the black woman] has blossomed, while her brother is a sadder statistic of miseducation, disaffection and recession' (ibid.).

This portrayal of the employment sphere for black people is general and stereotypical; black women are seen as strong, inde-pendent, and hardworking; black men as lacking in the work ethic, underqualified, and alienated. The root of the 'problem' lies, inevitably, with the black family:

Many of the women . . . were products of single-parent households, where they learnt by example that women can and do get on. Their brothers weren't always so lucky: their role models were contemporaries and largely absent fathers (ibid.).

The position of black people, men and women, in the employ-ment market in Britain is undeniably discouraging. Alexander notes that black men are more than twice as likely as their white contemporaries to be unemployed; while the 1985 Labour Force Survey showed that over 30 per cent of African-Caribbean males and females between the ages of 16 and 24 were unemployed (Bhat, Carr-Hill and Ohri 1988; Brown 1992). Most of the men in work remain concentrated in skilled manual or semi-skilled jobs (48 per cent and 26 per cent, respectively) while women are mainly found in non-manual and semi-skilled employment (52 per cent and 36 per cent, respectively) (ibid.). The present study, however, is concerned less with 'the facts' of black employment or unemployment than with the way these have created an image, or series of images, surrounding black youth. As Alexander's article illustrates, there exists a clearly defined and largely uncontested picture of black employment, especially in relation to young black men, which both draws upon and reinforces popular stereotypes about the position of black people in the labour market and which are translated into a 'working' reality.

Colin Brown has recently argued (1992) that the present position of black youth in the labour market must be placed within the context of first-generation economic migration. What is revealed is a process of continuity and change, in which the sphere of black employment is outwardly transformed without significantly altering the overall structural position of black people: what Brown refers to as 'same difference' (ibid. 46). Thus he writes that 'the position of the black citizens of Britain largely remains . . . that allocated to them as immigrant workers in the 1950s and 1960s' (1984: 318). Brown argues further that the original marginality of first-generation migrant workers has been reinforced in the second generation by wider structural changes in the labour market throughout the 1970s and 1980s, which have seen the move away from traditional manufacturing industries and public-service employment towards high-tech and private service industries (1992). Such changes, compounded by continuing racial discrimination and exclusion in a labour market increasingly dominated by free-market principles (Solomos 1988; Brown 1992), have pushed black youth to the margins of the employment sphere (Jenkins 1992) or, indeed, beyond it.

Implicit to Brown's observations is the societal characterization of the types of employment considered suitable for minority communities. He notes that the overwhelming recruitment of black workers to manual work in the 1950s carried with it 'the assumption that non-whites were naturally less desirable people' (1992: 47), an assumption which was translated in the labour market of the 1960s and 1970s. Brown writes:

In the 1960s and 1970s an employment pattern developed which, while taking black and Asian people into a broader range of occupations than they were originally recruited to do, was *clearly centred on jobs that were deemed fit for ethnic minority workers rather than for white workers* (ibid. 52; emphasis added).

Solomos (1988) has argued that these assumptions form part of a complex of images which have served to construct black youth employment as a 'problem', particularly since the 1970s. Drawing together themes of crime, urban unrest, and unemployment, the image of unemployable and alienated young black men has been placed at the forefront of policy decisions, designed to control and contain frustration (Hall 1978; Solomos 1988). Policies formulated to tackle black youth unemployment have thus become inseparable from the issue of social control. Moreover, the equation of unemployment with criminality, urban decay, and disorder has led to an overwhelmingly culturalist definition of black disadvantage, manifested particularly through the language of 'special needs' (Solomos 1988; Wrench 1992). The emphasis has been placed firmly on cultural 'handicap' rather than structural or institutional exclusion, with the resultant emphasis on training and education.[1]

Without wishing to contest the statistics and lived realities of black youth employment, this study does, however, seek to confront and challenge the images that have been created and the position of black youth in relation to these images. In talking of black male disadvantage and black female advantage, studies of the work sphere have abstracted black experience, and have treated black youth—male and female—as distinct, autonomous, and internally homogeneous entities. This has served not only to obscure the type and quality of work with which the greater number of black women are engaged—usually the low-paid 'caring'

---

[1] This culturalist approach to black youth employment is clearly rehearsed, for example, in the Scarman Report (1986). For a challenge to culturalist definitions, cf. Brown 1984; Egglestone *et al.* 1986; Bhat, Carr-Hill, and Ohri 1988.

professions—but also isolates and denies the increasing numbers of young men entering higher education or attaining relatively high-status work. Moreover, at the level of ideology, and in its reproduction at the level of experience, the portrait of the successful black woman is central to, and inseparable from, the construction of black male employment. As Heidi Mirza notes: 'It is unfortunate that in one of the few instances where black women are highlighted as a central force, their success should be manipulated to undermine the position of the black male' (1992: 16). As Alexander's article shows, emphasis is placed rather on cultural determinants of achievement than on structural and economic constraints operating within the labour market. The way in which constructions of 'race' and 'gender' operate at an ideological level to restrict black success—both male and female— becomes secondary to the myth of the black matriarchy (Mirza 1992; Wallace 1990) and male underachievement.

In her study of young black women entering the labour market, Mirza notes that employment opportunities for men and women differed significantly, with 53 per cent of black women found in service industries, compared with only 20 per cent of men. The latter were concentrated in manufacturing industries, communication, and transport, mainly as skilled and semi-skilled manual workers. Women, by contrast, were employed by local authorities and the National Health Service (1992: 112). More significantly, Mirza claims that these employment positions were reproduced and reinforced by the employment choices of black school leavers, both male and female. Black youth entering the labour market would, therefore, turn to areas of employment known to be traditionally accessible to black people. Such choices reflected, however, more expectations than aspirations, particularly with young black men. Twenty-seven per cent of Mirza's sample aspired to professional employment, while 55 per cent expected to find work as skilled manual workers (ibid. 117). These two categories were not exclusive in membership, with aspirations outstripping the expectations of the individual. Black women were more likely to seek work in higher social categories and had greater expectations of the work arena than the men; nevertheless, they mainly sought to remain in service industries. Mirza writes: 'In spite of their determination to succeed, the career destinations of the young black women and young black men

. . . were characterised by a distinct lack of variety and scope' (ibid. 145).

Implicit to Mirza's findings is the existence of an image of what constitutes 'black employment', which defines and circumscribes the opportunities perceived as open to black youth. This image differs according to gender, but can be seen to have effect both upon the youth themselves and upon potential employers. Wrench notes, for example, that negative stereotypes about African-Caribbean young men, in particular, have denied them access to desirable employer-based training schemes, and that career services are often engaged in 'protective channelling', which directs ethnic minority youth away from perceived hostile work environments (1992). Young black people are thus pushed towards areas of employment perceived both by themselves and others as 'traditionally black'. Simultaneously, images of exclusion from other areas of work are reinforced and perpetuated. These factors help to perpetuate patterns of disadvantage, which can then become largely self-sustaining (Brown 1984, 1992).

Nevertheless, Mirza's study also shows an unwillingness amongst her sample to accept the limitations of ascribed 'black employment'. According to Mirza's findings, if 55 per cent of young men expected to find employment in the 'traditionally black' labour market, 45 per cent were expecting to move outside this arena. It is within such 'non-traditional' environments that the restrictive effects of societal representations of employment are most salient, and in which identity is most contested and negotiated.

This chapter seeks to explore some of the images of work which surround and circumscribe employment experience for young black people. It places the emphasis not solely on discrimination and disadvantage, but also on the ways in which image is negotiated in the workplace to facilitate mobility and empower the individual. Amongst my informants in London, there existed a range of employment experience, ranging from Ricky, who had been unemployed for nearly two years, to Clive, who worked as a computer operator in the City. This chapter will examine both areas of high black employment and those which have been considered traditionally closed to black people; it will also consider the role of representations of 'class' in the employment sphere. While acknowledging the significance of contributions by black women to the employment sphere, the focus of this study remains primarily on black male experience: the position of black women is seen here largely in comparison with, and contrast to, the role of black men.

It should be noted that the access I was able to obtain to my informants' work environments was relatively limited: it was, therefore, not possible to achieve the amount of direct observation available in other spheres of interaction. The material in this chapter thus relies more heavily on reported information than direct analysis. Nevertheless, the views articulated here are felt to be central to an understanding of the position of my informants in relation both to the black community and wider society: it was this position which both constrained them to enact specific roles and yielded the self-confidence to move beyond such roles. It was in the employment sphere that societal roles and expectations proved most intractable; the boys' behaviour was accordingly more restricted, more routinized, and less flamboyantly creative than in other areas of life. However, it was also this marginality which was the origin of, and impetus for, the fluidity and creativity of their constructed identities.

INSIDE THE IMAGE: 'BLACK EMPLOYMENT' AND IDENTITY

In *Britain's Black Population*, Bhat, Carr-Hill, and Ohri write that: 'Disappointment and disillusionment of many kinds was the everyday experience of the 1950s settlers. This is still the reality today for many black workers and their children' (1988: 62).[2] While it is true that the material position of black youth in employment has improved little from that of their parents, it is also true that the role of young black people in the labour market has altered considerably in kind, if not in degree (Brown 1992). Where their parents were recruited to specific jobs in transport, industry, and the Health Service, the perception of an employment niche for their British-born children has altered and diversified. What are considered 'traditional' areas for high levels of black employment are, therefore, not wholly replicated by later generations of workers. Indeed, the notion itself has undergone transformation

---

[2] Cf. also Cross and Entzinger 1988.

and created a new series of images and stereotypes about what 'black employment' actually is.

The change in perceptions of 'black employment' between the generations was clear with regard to my informants in London, whose parents were mainly involved in 'traditional' occupations. Angelina's father was employed as a signalman for British Rail and her mother worked for United Biscuits, as did both Fenella's and Eleanor's parents; Frank's mother was a nurse, as was Dion's mother; Clive's mother was a seamstress, who also ran a child-minding business from home, while his father exported second-hand typewriters to Nigeria; Ricky's and Shane's fathers were both loosely connected to the 'entertainment' business; Edgar's father, though a qualified lawyer in Ghana, worked for British Telecom, and his mother was also a nurse. None of the children had followed their parents into these areas of employment; instead, most had gone on to further education and entered new segments of the job market.

The actual employment choices of my informants will be considered later; what is of significance here is the career advice they were offered at school and college. This advice reflects the newly perceived areas of 'black employment'. Most of the boys were pushed towards semi-skilled manual work, loosely described as 'engineering'; but as Shane told me: 'I didn't want to do engineering. . . . I didn't want to do the motor mechanics or anything like they expect black people to do—drive a bus' (Interview, 5 Apr. 1991). Although not all the career advice was negative—Rommell and Darnell in particular found a great deal of support for their aspirations—most of their contemporaries eventually chose jobs in these areas. Darnell told me: 'Half of them, they goes "oh, try and do painting and decorating". I think a couple of my friends got "do painting and decorating" ' (Interview, 22 Mar. 1991).

Clive also noted that when he began his course in Business Studies at the local College of Higher Education, most of his friends did 'silly things; postmen, traindrivers, busdrivers or you just see them loafing around the street' (Interview, 5 May 1991), while his black contemporaries at college, when not 'playing pool in the canteen' (ibid.), were mainly found in electrical and mechanical subjects. Ricky expressed some scepticism at the advice that he and other young black men were offered at school:

In school you were well into this black militant thing and you ain't got no clear ideas of how you can manipulate the people so that you can get yourself into some of these positions. You just think it's totally impossible, and it doesn't really help some white person sitting down there and saying, 'you should go for this job because that's all you're qualified for and that's all you can do' (Interview, 9 June 1991).

During the course of my fieldwork, I met a number of black youths who were engaged in these 'typically black' jobs: at the community centre, the majority of men I knew were employed in fields such as decorating, vehicle maintenance, shopfitting, with a small number engaged in jobs geared specifically towards a black market—barbers, cooks, MCs. Several were unemployed or engaged in the 'alternative economy'. While not denying the experienced reality of these images of 'black employment', it can nevertheless be argued that these have denied the wider, more complex range of activities with which many black youth are engaged. For example, one man I met at the community centre, Tony, worked as a bouncer and a youth worker; he was also involved in the management of a private transport company and in the 'alternative economy'. Moreover, a large proportion of the men I knew were self-employed, a fact which reflected the increasing move of black youth towards the establishment of small businesses. Cross and Entzinger (1988) see this move as avoiding racial exclusion and achieving a measure of autonomy scarcely available in mainstream, white establishments; what Brian Jacobs terms 'the ideology of self-reliant capitalism' (1988: 183).

Although most of my informants were keen to define themselves away from images of 'typical' black employment, all had friends or family involved in these areas; all had also worked in jobs which employ relatively large numbers of black people—catering, retail, factory production. They were thus both acutely aware of the societal images surrounding black people in such employment and distanced from these images because of the temporary nature of their involvement. Angelina and Fenella, for example, had both worked as part-time shop assistants in British Home Stores while at school. Angelina started working four hours on a Saturday and earned £6. Although she, like all my informants, never experienced overt racism at work, she became aware of the image of black people within the work environment. She told me:

They had certain departments for certain people ... and in some of the departments they would have no more than two black people in any one department because [they think] otherwise they stand gossiping all day; they'd make their friends come in and nick all the items (Interview, 11 Mar. 1991).

In interaction with the customers, too, both Angelina and Fenella were aware of the expectations of black shop assistants. Fenella recalled:

I remember somebody once asked me to polish the bases of the stands, and I was going around cleaning these bases and I thought, I bet you most of the customers think black people are just good for cleaning, and I really hated that, and I thought to myself, would she have asked me if I was white? (Interview, 27 Mar. 1991).

Angelina also reacted against the assumptions that were connected with the image of this form of employment for black people. She told me: 'They all assume that that's all you can do; that you've got this job and you should be lucky you've got this job, girl, because you probably couldn't get anything better' (Interview, 11 Mar. 1991).

It should be noted that neither Angelina nor Fenella objected to the work itself, as much as to the image that was created for them, as black people, within that situation. Angelina pointed out that most of the black women she worked with were, like herself, filling in time between studying rather than full-time shop assistants. It was the temporary nature of the work which was the main defence against this external stereotyping. Fenella thus distanced herself from the mainly white, full-time workers, 'It didn't bother me because I knew that I wasn't going to stay there; this was not what I wanted to do for a career' (Interview, 27 Mar. 1991). Angelina, meanwhile, delighted in confronting these images:

All the customers used to assume that you can't do anything better, that it's your destiny in life, until some customers actually come in and they speak to you ... and then they've got to like swallow everything they thought previously and then they treat you as a decent human being .... Most of the time I didn't say anything; I just thought, Ha, Ha, if only you knew ... I thought, well, you think what you want, dear, but I know where I'm going (Interview, 11 Mar. 1991).

The position of men within the workplace differed slightly from that faced by the women, in that they were subjected to more rigorous stereotyping, which was accordingly more difficult to negotiate. For my male informants, the emphasis was thus placed more firmly on the establishment of control within the work situation. Ricky, who started working evening shifts in a Kentucky Fried Chicken outlet when he was 15, and was paid 70 pence per hour, balanced the vulnerability of his position by stealing money from the till, 'I knew it was slave labour, but there was food there all the time and if I wanted an extra fiver, it was in the till' (Interview, 9 June 1991). When he was eventually caught and dismissed, Ricky's account to me focused very much on his personal control of the situation. He told me:

After they caught me with the money from the till, he [the manager] says, 'oh yeah, I'm going to contact the police'. So I says, 'Go ahead, I'm under age and I'm not supposed to be working here and I want to see how you are going to explain this.' So we just said 'bye, and went (ibid.).

Ricky went on to work in factories, shops, and a Pizza Hut, last working two years ago. In each case, he laid stress on the temporary nature of the work, and on his refusal to be committed to, and defined by, his employment:

I know they're dead-end jobs . . . and I know I'd never settle down to anything like that. I know what I want, and I'll just be patient . . . if I'm a bit short and I need to pay for this, pay for that, I do a few weeks work, then I drop it (ibid.).

It is this perception of personal freedom, the ability to choose whether or not to accept employment and its incumbent definitions, which empowered Ricky, if within strict limitations. Ironically, it was the low status of the jobs that he, as a black man, could obtain that freed him from the negative effects of stereotyping, because such work exacted no commitment and carried no sense of personal success or failure. He explained:

I know that I'm walking into a job where they can replace me within five minutes, so why the hell am I going to take any mouth from them or any racist comments. . . . I'm just going to walk out of the job, because I know I can walk out of a dead-end job and straight into another dead-end job (ibid.).

Ricky's attitude to work was perhaps the most extreme, but was partially reflected in the attitudes of others of my male informants. Most viewed 'typical' employment as a means rather than an end, something that could be endured until something else, more suitable, came along—what Frank termed, 'just passing through' (Interview, 10 Mar. 1991). For several, this meant returning to education: Clive worked in a supermarket while at college, Darnell worked as a shop assistant in John Lewis while at school, and Edgar was employed in an Argos storeroom while submitting applications to polytechnic. Like the women, all felt the constraints of the image surrounding the employment; it seems, however, that the stereotypes surrounding black men were stronger and more clearly defined. Where the women were more easily accepted as departing from the perceived role, this was less true for the men. Darnell told me of John Lewis: 'the people in there thought because you're black, you don't know much, and only like the managers who are white—oh yes, he knows what he's talking about' (Interview, 22 Mar. 1991).

Like Ricky, Darnell's response was to attempt to take control of the situation on a personal level, while accepting that the overall definition would remain unchanged. In direct interaction, therefore, Darnell would attempt to obtain a sense of personal agency, while not directly challenging the suppositions of the customer: 'I don't pretend that I'm stupid; I'd pretend that *they* were stupid. Like if they go "what plug does it need", this is me—[speaking very slowly] "It says here it needs a 3 amp plug", like so' (ibid.). Darnell's usual response was to compensate for any implicit stereotyping by selling the customer the most expensive item in the range:

If they go, 'what does he know, we do this, we do that', then you just tell them a load of rubbish—like, 'this is good'—the shittiest one there, with just a high price. There's me, 'Take a look at the price for instance' (ibid.).

During the time of my fieldwork, only Frank and Shane were engaged full-time in areas of perceived 'black employment'. Both worked in men's clothes shops, as did Satish for a short time. For Frank, the work was 'just passing through', an attempt to make money to pursue his flying. Although Shane changed his job twice during my fieldwork, he took his work far more seriously than the others, and his personal success was a source of great pride. Perhaps because of this, Shane expressed more hostility than the others to the limitations of his chosen career:

It's cheap labour, do you know what I mean: they try to pay you the lowest wages—it's just like you see black dustmen; you walk in the train station, you see black people doing the sweeping: it's that they get low wages, but they'll take it because they need the money (Interview, 5 Apr. 1991).

Although Shane claimed to be taking home £250 per week from his present job, he was pessimistic about the prospects for career advancement, which were tied closely, in his mind, to his colour, and to a generalized image of black men. He told me:

My colour does interfere quite a lot with the positions I can get. . . . I think they think of me as another coon, a black person who thinks he's got a bit of brains, and *has* got a bit of brains, and you'd better watch him . . . people in general might look at me as aggressive, because I've been stereotyped—they think all black people are aggressive (ibid.).

The image of black men in the clothing retail business tends to be double-edged. On the one hand, the increased interest in men's designer wear and the equation of style with popular culture has created an image of the black shop assistant as fashion guide; on the other, negative stereotypes of black men have denied them access to legitimate power within the work environment. This was illustrated when Frank's manager, Kassim, tried to dismiss him, claiming that Frank had threatened him with violence and promised to return and 'do' the shop with his friends if he lost his job; a claim that clearly had more to do with Kassim's personal conceptions about black youth than with fact.

The nature of the employment situation amongst my informants makes it difficult for this study to comment in great detail on the position of youth in these occupations. As mentioned earlier, only Shane was fully engaged with this type of work in any committed sense, while most of the others had moved on to different areas, or were involved only on a temporary basis. Nevertheless, each was aware of the expectations and images surrounding such employment and had worked within these. The ability to negotiate identity can, however, be seen to be severely limited by social stereotypes; the actions of the individual being subsumed into the required role. Although it was possible to achieve limited personal control, this failed to redefine the image of the work itself, which in turn precluded the achievement of legitimate power.

For most of my informants, however, who were engaged in this type of employment on a temporary basis, or who perceived their future outside these environments, such constraints were something to be noted and dismissed; they were considered to be of more relevance to others, the 'typical' blacks, than to themselves. The boys, especially, tended to distance themselves from images of 'black employment', which they regarded as something that bore no relation to their personal aspirations—or their limitations. With the exception of Shane, the boys considered that for themselves, as individuals, everything was possible; skin colour was either irrelevant, or merely a factor which had to be negotiated. As Edgar told me:

I don't make an issue of my colour unless someone else does, that's it. I suppose it's being positive. I think people tend to make more of an issue out of my colour than I would. . . . I don't find it a problem; if you do, that's *your* problem (Interview, 17 May 1991).

OUTSIDE THE IMAGE: UPWARD MOBILITY AND IDENTITY

On a night out with Clive and Nathan, walking across Leicester Square to get to a winebar, Nathan told me about his brother, Robert, who had started up an import business with his Ghanaian girlfriend. The business was very successful, and the couple had moved out of South London to a house in Maida Vale, which both Nathan and Clive agreed was, indeed, the ultimate symbol of success. Nathan continued that his brother had not only changed his house, but also his circle of friends who, as 'typical niggers', were still blaming their lack of success on racial discrimination. Both he and Clive agreed that this 'excuse' no longer had any validity—that all things were possible for those who wanted it enough. Of all the boys, Clive and Nathan were the most successful: Clive worked in the City for a firm of stockbrokers and Nathan worked as a reprographic artist for an advertising company in Covent Garden. Their sentiments were, however, not uncommon amongst the boys. As Ricky echoed:

Anybody can become what they want; even if you're black, you can become what you want. Maybe you will have to take a few dodgy channels, but you can become what you want. I'll never use the excuse, it's because I'm black, or that's where I am; if you put your mind to it, you can achieve it, simple as that (Interview, 9 Sept. 1991).

The belief in individual success can be seen to reflect a new self-confidence amongst some black youth, who define themselves away from the view of traditional black employment and as part of a newly emergent black middle class. This aspirant class was nurtured in the wake of the uprisings of the early 1980s, largely as an institutional gesture of solidarity with anti-racist objectives (Gilroy 1987). Jobs were created, mainly in the public sector, to encourage a degree of upward mobility amongst black youth and to assuage the feelings of frustration and exclusion by enabling individual achievement (Cross and Entzinger 1988; Jacobs 1988).

This success is, however, riddled with contradictions. Cross and Johnson, for example, note that there was a 5 per cent decrease in the number of black men employed in manual labour by the mid-1980s, but continue: 'It is not possible to conclude that this small degree of mobility is occasioned by the lowering of barriers to advancement through opportunity' (1988: 79). Similarly, Brown argues that apparent improvements in employment statistics can be accounted for by increasing unemployment at lower occupational levels and the move towards self-employment (1992). Moreover, since most jobs for young black people were established in the public sector for a specific political purpose, the position of those thus employed was far from stable. Black upward mobility has therefore been largely channelled into specific and narrowly defined positions, which are economically unstable and politically vulnerable. A clear example would be the staff at the Community Centre, who were employed by the local council; when the Centre's funding was cut, over half the employees were made redundant. Moreover, within such positions, the emphasis is very much on 'colour'; 'blackness' thus becomes essentialized and reified as a basis for employment opportunities for the individual—'race' becomes a 'job issue'.

Amongst my informants, the advantage of being black in particular employment situations was recognized, and often manipulated. Darnell, who spent a year working for his local council before starting his accountancy course, told me:

They call it the United Nations building; there's everybody working there. . . . I reckon from [the council] it can be an advantage, because they're equal opportunities employers. So they keep up their numbers . . . . I'm all for it (Interview, 22 Mar. 1991).

His sister, Angelina, also found it to her advantage to stress 'race' both during her sociology course and in applying for teacher training places when she finished. In her sociology option on race and ethnic policy, she confronted her white tutor, who insisted upon the inevitable disadvantage of being black:

I said to him, you can theorize, you can quote literature, but you'll never know the real experience of a black person, because you're not black. . . . He thought basically that I was a traitor to my own race, because I did question that everybody had to experience racism: it's opportunities for people to meet, it's how you relate to people, all that together and that makes up your interpretation of it. It's not black and white; it's not as easy as that (Interview, 11 Mar. 1991).

For Angelina and Darnell, as for my other informants, phenotype was not an inevitable determining force within employment; it was not something which dominated their experience and excused their personal failings. 'Race' became one of a number of factors which came into play on specific occasions, and which had to be negotiated: as Angelina continued, 'I don't see myself as only black' (ibid.). However, although in particular situations being black was perceived to be an advantage, in most, it was recognized as more of an obstacle than a weapon. This was especially true with those who were employed in jobs which were outside 'traditional' black spheres, and were not within the public sector, which sanctioned and encouraged a degree of black upward mobility.

Within these new employment situations, my informants attempted to lay emphasis upon attributes other than 'race'; the stress was on themselves as individuals rather than as representatives of a minority group. Perhaps because all were aware of the image of black people in employment, and the closure of possibilities this signified, all attempted to impose alternative definitions, based on a common experience with their work colleagues. With most of my informants, this met with only limited success; most were forced back by those they worked with onto an image of 'typical' black employment, founded in the ideology of Empire (Cross and Johnson 1988), and were thereby constrained. The difficulty of creating alternative images within these new, middle-class arenas can be seen in a number of cases, each of which differed slightly in the way it was negotiated—or not— by each of my informants.

The most materially successful of the boys was undoubtedly Clive, who had been working as computer support for a firm of stockbrokers in the City for about two and a half years. Clive, like Ricky, had completed a National Diploma in Business Studies at college, and had worked in a number of junior office positions, in banks and for the DHSS, before starting his present job. The firm employed 700 people, of which only three black men were employed in the office, each in dealer support; there were no black managers or dealers. The only other black people employed were, inevitably, either security guards or cleaners. Although Clive claimed to be content in his working environment, it was well known amongst the boys that he had to endure a large amount of racial intolerance from his colleagues. This mainly took the form of racial jokes; on the several times I met Clive at work, many comments were made about the number of wives he had and his supposed sexual prowess. On one occasion, around the time of the Gulf War, Clive told me that the current office joke was 'I hear the Government are recruiting alphabetically for the Gulf War—Africans, Blacks, Coons . . .'. Clive's response was not to confront these stereotypes, but to laugh or, indeed, to play up to them. He told me, 'All the time, I get called "black bastard", black this and that. I just give it back' (Interview, 5 Mar. 1991).

When the others challenged him on this approach, he assured us that this was the only way he could avoid open antagonism and safeguard his job. Clive was of the opinion that the rewards of the work far outweighed any of the abuse he had to endure; thus he claimed:

If I have to beg, I'll beg; if I have to crawl, I'll crawl. . . . I'm not one of those chip-on-the-shoulder type of people—'just because I'm black you're not going to do this, or because I'm black you're doing this'. Just go out and get what you can get (ibid.).

Clive chose, therefore, to ignore any latent hostility and insist instead upon the communal spirit of the work environment; his favourite word was 'conformity'. He utilized all the external images to portray a façade of conformity; he wore designer suits to work, owned a new Alfa Romeo, carried a message pager, and cultivated an appropriate accent. He made sure that he always ordered the correct drink during lunchtimes and forbade his girlfriend from visiting him at work because he considered her 'too common' and therefore detrimental to his image. Significantly, however, this image was confined strictly to the work environment; Clive never socialized with his work colleagues, with the exception of Hercules, who was the only other black man in his department. Work and home environments were thus kept strictly separated. This enabled Clive to maintain his image at work, and also to continue to move in a black environment, without the risk of mutual disruption.

Although there is undoubtedly a 'class' element to Clive's situation, the primary identity which was negotiated was signalled by phenotype. It is nevertheless true that black identity has become equated with a particular social position (Ramdin 1987; Cross and Johnson 1988), and that skin colour is thus a symbol of both perceived 'racial' and socio-economic status (Rex 1986). Clive's primary concern was to obviate the imposed racial identity by manipulating the symbols of 'class', to create an image of upward mobility in which 'race' became irrelevant. To his colleagues, however, Clive's identity remained one defined on racial criteria. When Clive was 'made redundant' just after I left London, the reason given was that the company felt that Clive would be unable to adapt to future developments in technology. Although no overt reference was made to 'race', it is interesting that the company used lack of intellectual capacity as a reason for dismissal, especially when no such incapacity had been proved, or even tested. Clive claimed that his dismissal was due to personal antagonism between himself and his new manager; that the company should refer back to an image of what black people 'do', and are capable of, as a validation of a decision made for other reasons entirely, is a clear indication of how vulnerable Clive's position was. In the absence of alternative definitions of black mobility, the company was able to draw on societal perceptions of the 'typical' black male, and his incumbent limitations, to legitimate their actions. As a corollary to this, the man responsible for Clive's dismissal was reported to be afraid that Clive would wreak a violent retribution—drawing upon yet another well-worn construction of black male behaviour.

An interesting reflection on Clive's position and attitude can be found in Malcolm. Malcolm worked for his father, who owns a grocery shop in a market in East London, selling West Indian and tropical foodstuffs. Although self-employment is on the increase amongst black youth, Malcolm's position was unusual because his work was outside those spheres usually chosen by black businesses. Food retailing, especially in East London, remains a sphere more common to Asian and English businessmen. Like Clive, therefore, Malcolm can be seen to be working in an environment dominated by non-black people in a form of employment usually considered closed to black males. Also like Clive, Malcolm accepted racial abuse and intolerance as an inevitable part of his employment situation. Although he was of the same social and geographical background as the other shopkeepers, and was employed in the same type of work, Malcolm considered the ability to ignore this abuse as an essential tool in survival in a predominantly white arena. He told me:

Racism doesn't affect me; especially like in the market—there's a lot of whites there and they all have a joke. And if you can't take the joke you're finished there, really. . . . You have to be with them, otherwise they just cast you out (Interview, 12 May 1991).

Malcolm's position differed from Clive's in that, as a self-employed businessman, his job was more secure. It was, however, dependent on the goodwill of those around him, and it was this consideration which motivated his responses. Like Clive, Malcolm placed great emphasis upon his external image within the work environment; the desire to mark himself out from other 'typical' blacks. He drove a new Audi car with the latest sound equipment, wore handmade suits and a large quantity of gold jewellery, and owned two mobile phones and a message pager. He was also planning to buy his own house within the next two years. He told me: 'A lot of people think I'm flash and this and that, but I don't really worry about it. I'm a nice, down-to-earth boy who dresses smart. Because your appearance really counts a lot, doesn't it?' (ibid.).

This external image, based upon the expression of material wealth, can perhaps be seen as an attempt to carve out a model for black achievement. The acquisition of the material symbols of middle-class success can then be used to obscure the vulnerability of the employment position of black men, and attest to the infinite possibilities confronting them. On one occasion, Ricky's cousin, Kevin, who was an insurance salesman, came to the flat, and spent over an hour assuring myself and Anne of his ultimate power over women and over other men because of his new car, his designer clothes, his mobile phone. He could, he told us more than once, have anything he wanted. The reality was often, however, somewhat different: for example, when Ricky's brother, Mike, gave up his job in insurance in Birmingham to return to London, he was unable to get similar employment, and is currently working in McDonald's.

The manipulation of a 'class' image is best understood as an attempt to exercise some control within the work environment; to achieve an element of personal power. Too often, however, the lack of black role models in positions of real influence leads to a definition of the situation over which the individual has no control and no recourse. After completing a B.Tec. Course in Distribution Studies at a college in Watford, Rommell undertook an eighteen-month management training course with John Lewis. He was the only black person on his course, and when it was completed, he was one of only two people who did not get promoted to management status. He told me:

The management report said, first of all, you weren't assertive enough, so I did that; then they said, you don't have good organizational skills, so I worked on that; but there was always something on the management side, so by the time I'd got to this stage they still say, you've got to get the best out of others (Interview, 14 Apr. 1991).

To be promoted, the trainees needed positive reports from the managers of each of the three departments they worked in. Rommell told me that of his three departments, only one gave him training which was adequate to ensure success. In the first, Rommell claims that the manager was concerned only to teach him to be a salesman, not a manager; while in the third, he was told, 'Well, you're a very good salesman, you get on well with the team, but at the moment I don't see you as a manager' (ibid.).

This was despite reports from the second department which confirmed Rommell's managerial capabilities. Rommell was convinced that the other managers considered him unsuitable management material because black people generally were perceived merely as salespeople. Of 120 managerial positions in the store, there was only one black department manager and five section managers, while over 10 per cent of the sales staff were black. Rommell claimed:

If I was white, then I basically know I would have been promoted a long time ago. Like when I was talking to this Section Manager—he's Asian—and he goes to me 'Well, to tell you the truth [Rommell], if you were white they'd be pinning medals on you by now' (ibid.).

Rommell finally decided to leave John Lewis and return to college to pursue a degree in accountancy. He remained bitter about his treatment and, like Shane, expressed serious doubts about the future for black youth in retailing. Rommell's main source of bitterness, however, was his lack of control over the definition of his position. Nothing overtly racist was said; nothing could be proved and there was no recourse within the structure of John Lewis to defend his position. All depended ultimately upon the word of the Department Managers, and there was little consideration of the perception that these individuals may have of the position of black trainees. Rommell was determined that such a situation would never happen again:

As long as I've got a degree I know that any job I actually go for . . . if I don't get it, I'll know, well, it's not because I didn't have the qualifications; OK, it's the black thing. So I'll say, well, I've got my degree, so why can't *I* do that job. . . . I will fight a lot more (ibid.).

An interesting contrast to the experiences, and attempted resolutions, of Clive and Rommell can be found in Frank, who worked as a land surveyor for several years, before moving to the clothes shop during the year of my fieldwork. At its best, he told me, he was being paid £12 per hour, but received on average £7 per hour for contract work. Like Clive and Rommell, Frank was acutely aware of the expectations of himself as a black man within a mainly white environment, especially one where black males were concentrated in the lower echelons of the trade. He told me:

I always thought being black, I always had to make a point very clear that I was capable of doing it. . . . I was always working twice as hard as the white partner to try and prove I was capable of doing it. I've been on sites where the white boys are engineers and they are useless, but no one is going to say anything to them. But if you're black—ah, you can feel it in the air, you can smell it (Interview, 10 Mar. 1991).

Frank's approach differed from either Clive's or Rommell's, however, in that he negotiated his 'racial' identity by subsuming it into an assumed 'working-class' identity. Although, of all the boys, Frank's background was the only one which could be described loosely as 'middle-class', Frank was able to utilize a black working-class identity to establish a bond with the builders on the site. This inevitably distanced him from the management, but because Frank saw himself as 'passing through' on his way to a career in flying, this was of little importance. He explained:

I spent most of the time on the building site playing the diplomatic part of it. . . . Because I get away with that easily; I know when to smile, know when to lose my temper. . . . Respect them for what they are, because they know their trade. . . . That's what I used to do, I respected them for what they did and how they did it, and that's why they liked me . . . at the end of the day I go out and have a drink with the tradesmen. I never saw myself being an engineer as someone special or different (ibid.).

Frank acknowledged, however, that this negotiation would have been more difficult if he had been concerned to establish a career in this area. He told me of one Asian graduate who antagonized the workmen by his attitude:

Some of the workers hated him because he had been to university and he thought 'yeah'; and he used to tell the lads 'do this, do that'. I thought, I had the power to do that, but what would I gain from doing it? But you see everyone looks at it in a different way; he's probably striving coming onto this stage and this is what he wants to do and like his next stage is to be like the site director or something like that, yeah? So he's probably got that tendency, but I had no time for that. The only time I had was to make my money (ibid.).

Had Frank been interested in establishing a permanent career in this field it is possible that, like Clive and Rommell, he too would have faced problems of definition. It is ironic, but significant, that Frank should choose instead to draw upon a traditional notion of black identity—as essentially working class—because the work itself was unimportant to him. Had it been more important, he would have been forced to construct an alternative definition of black identity, which incorporated the possibility of personal mobility. Until such an alternative can be established, however, it seems that the possibility for a secure and successful black middle class remains in doubt. As an illustration of this, it should be noted that four of the boys—Clive, Nathan, Frank, and Satish—lost their jobs in the six months following my fieldwork, with Rommell resigning his position with John Lewis and returning to college. To date, only Nathan has been able to find comparable alternative employment, at a reduced salary.

BLACK AND SUCCESSFUL: A CONTRADICTION OF CLASS?

The relationship between 'race' and class is perhaps one of the most contentious theoretical issues in contemporary debates around the black presence in Britain. A range of Weberian, Marxist, and neo-Marxist writers have argued a plurality of positions (Solomos 1986; Gilroy 1987), from Robert Miles's deterministic assertion of the primacy of economic structure and capitalist production over the ideological mirage of 'race' (Miles 1982; Solomos 1986), through John Rex's portrayal of the 'black underclass' (Rex 1986), to Ben-Tovim and Gabriel's demand for the absolute separation of the two categories and the recognition of the supremacy of agency and anti-racist struggle (Solomos 1986; Ben-Tovim *et al.* 1986; Gilroy 1987). Whether 'race' is seen as an ideological falsification of the mode of production, determined by and instrumental to economic relations, or an autonomous dichotomy, discussions around 'race' and class have tended to abstract and homogenize historically specific and disparate experiences in the search for general and unified theories (Gilroy 1987).

As the work of Hall (1980), Gilroy (1987), and the CCCS collective (1982) has consistently argued, however, the analysis of both 'race' and class—and their interaction—needs to be placed within a historical framework which recognizes the dynamic and transformative nature of their encounters and the heterogeneity of the experiences that these social and ideological categories encompass. In particular, Gilroy has asserted the 'crisis of representation' posed by the black presence to any continuous, unified, and ahistorical conception of 'the working class' (1982*b*; 1987). Following Hall, he writes:

Racism plays an active role, articulating political, cultural and economic elements into a complex and contradictory unity. It ensures . . . that for contemporary Britain 'race is the modality in which class is lived', the medium in which it is appropriated and 'fought through' (1987: 30).

He thus argues for the 'relative autonomy' of 'race' and class (CCCS 1982; Solomos 1986; Gilroy 1987), in which 'Class politics . . . do not precede the encounter between black and white, they are created and destroyed in it' (ibid. 34). Formations of 'race' and class are seen as a continuous and contingent process in which meanings are fought over, translated, and negotiated.

'Race' and class are thus to be understood as part of a process of 'articulation' (Hall 1980), in which both structure and agent are engaged in an ongoing and incomplete dialectic, located within a historically specific framework. What is of most significance to this study, however, is not the theoretical articulation of 'race' and class, but the way in which *representations* of these constructions are used to negotiate control in the mediatory space between structure and actor, constraint and agency. While not denying the determining nature of structural, economic and political constraints in this sphere, it can be argued that such structures are confronted, contested, and mediated by the actions of the individual actor or group, particularly through the use of symbolic markers. The relationship between 'race' and class becomes contingent and malleable, rather than absolute and deterministic, with the markers of one both confirming and displacing the other. Thus, as was mentioned earlier, while 'race' itself has become a marker of class status, it also transcends narrowly defined class interests in the assertion of 'community' (Gilroy 1982*b*), while the external symbols of class can be wielded either to obviate the categorizations surrounding 'race' or to consolidate them. All these processes can be seen in the above material, however ambiguous and contradictory the results.

The experiences of my male informants are significant as an illustration of some of the problems and contradictions facing black youth who seek to redefine the bounds of black employment; to re-create structure through individual action. All were the first generation of their family to move outside the roles defined for black people since the beginning of mass migration; each was moving into an area in which they were often the only black employee. Nevertheless, it is only with reference to the image of the group that the position of the individual actor can be fully understood. It is from this image, constructed through 'race', that the role of the individual is defined externally and his performance judged.

For my informants, the emphasis in the employment sphere remained very much upon their position as individuals; most were concerned to define themselves away from the view of 'typical' blacks, defined and constrained by the structural markers of 'race'. This was reflected in Ricky's dismissal of the members of the Community Centre as 'layabouts' and 'no hopers', even though many were working, and he himself had been unemployed for two years. For the boys, the difference lay in the construction of their personal image: this was touched on earlier in connection with Clive. Clothes, style of speech, leisure activities, choice of women, all reflected the concern with creating an image of upward mobility. Most stressed the status of their job as of primary importance; although money was regarded as the main indicator of status. Clive, for example, told me that he was attracted to office work because it more easily afforded the material symbols of success: this was epitomized for Clive by designer suits.

This image of upward mobility—the mediation of 'race' through class—was undermined, however, by the economic insecurity confronting most black men, which rendered the encounter profoundly ambiguous. As often the first generation of black people to enter new employment markets, and with family and friends still employed in 'traditional' spheres, most expressed a degree of ambivalence about their position, and a reluctance to separate themselves from the 'community' image. For the boys, the resultant duality—the desire to be both successful and yet remain part of their perceived community—led to the manipulation of symbols of both 'race' and class identities and the separation of their work and home environments. This manipulation can be seen most clearly with regard to their social life, which will be considered in the next chapter. It also led to an ambiguous attitude towards the symbols of upward mobility, which was usually expressed as 'going white'. There are a number of well-known terms for the individual who is seen to be deserting his or her 'roots'—coconut, Bounty Bar, black blonde; black on the outside, white on the inside. The focus is placed on the acquisition of material symbols usually associated with the white middle class. Such symbols are also equated with personal success. This ambivalence was expressed by Rommell:

Like I say, you've got to be three times better than the white people to get anywhere and it may mean you lose some of your morals. You become like them, sort of change your whole attitude, your whole lifestyle, that sort of thing. . . . I admit when I first started I was sort of going over the other side, then soon as I realized I was getting all those bad reports, it sort of knocked me back, so I'm even more into my culture now . . . so I think like, well, I'm black and that's it; it's the way of life (Interview, 14 Apr. 1991).

Rommell's argument is that, in order to be successful, the individual must give up all symbols of his 'culture' and become more like his white counterparts; the intimation being that it is, therefore, impossible to be both 'black' and successful. While some of my other informants were less pessimistic, all acknowledged that a degree of compromise was necessary in order to succeed within a work environment. This meant conforming to standards normally perceived to be 'white'. Shane termed this 'hypocrisy', though acknowledged its necessity, while Ricky confirmed, 'Well, of course you have to compromise' (Interview, 9 June 1991). On other occasions, he asserted more vigorously that, to succeed in business, black men must behave like white men; this did not, however, carry over into more 'private' spheres of life, in which 'black' identity was reasserted and maintained.

Within the work sphere, then, most agreed that the individual must adopt the 'white' symbols of success, or remain a 'typical' black male, with all its associated negative imagery, yet with a solid 'community' foundation. For my informants, black identity was often equated with an unproblematic working-class status, the maintenance of which became a central marker of 'racial' authenticity. Ironically, therefore, to succeed in these environments as a black man, the individual will be judged by his contemporaries to be no longer 'black', which in turn precludes any redefinition of black success. This situation seems unlikely to alter until the economic position of black employment becomes more stable and those thus employed are less dependent upon the whims of the white establishment.

It is also true, however—and as a further complication—that large numbers of black youth have become mobilized around these same symbols of material success. This has created an image of lifestyle and wealth which belies the insecurity of black youth in employment, but has also helped to focus and mobilize black youth aspirations. These symbols have been adopted as markers of the 'alternative economy' as well as of more traditional forms of black employment. They have thus become an integral part of black youth style, which has served to integrate disparate groups of youth, rather than distinguish them as they might wish. It has also served to blur the symbolic boundaries of perceived class identities, and further obfuscate the race/class dichotomy. As one of my informants commented, if one sees a black man with a BMW, a mobile phone, a designer suit and gold jewellery, he could either be an insurance salesman or a drug dealer—or both. Or, he might have added, he could be a plasterer or a car mechanic.

The meaning attached to such symbols, therefore, shifts according to context. If, for example, the individual works in a white middle-class environment, he may be seen as 'going white'; if, however, he is employed in a predominantly black context, then he becomes the icon of black style. Within this latter context, the symbols constitute the symbols of black success; ironically, however, these cannot be utilized in the mainstream environment without changing their significance. Moreover, to an external, dominant gaze, these symbols may reflect 'typical' black values and will carry a negative value assessment.

This study does not intend to consider the workings of the so-called 'alternative economy' other than to note its use of the same symbols. Although some of my informants had limited contact with those employed in this sphere, its activities were not of direct significance to them. What is interesting, however, is the way that the symbols of black mobility were manipulated in the somewhat grey area of activity between legitimate and alternative employment.

Of my informants, only Ricky was engaged in this area, but his activities are significant because they draw upon the image of the black male and manipulate it to create an appearance of black success which, unlike those working in white professional employment, is unchallenged. The stereotypical equation of black men with illegality, and also with street credibility and machismo, enabled Ricky to create an image which was within the traditional view of 'black employment', yet which did not preclude individual success. This made use of the same symbols of lifestyle as those used by Clive, but they were considered to have more validity because they were in accordance with an external perception of what black men were and did. Ricky was never involved with overtly illegal activity; he was, as he described himself, a 'hustler'. His work was mainly opportunistic and small-scale:

Little things, like for an example I meet some guy that I know and he's selling these lighters or something small like lighters; I say 'Well, you've got a box full' and he says yeah, they're selling them, just trying to flog them off, you can offer him a price that's below the market value and just sell it after (Interview, 9 June 1991).

Within such work, Ricky acknowledged the advantages of being black: 'Black is becoming the in-thing; like if you're black and you're into something slightly dodgy, everybody loves you. They know they can deal with you, you know' (ibid.). More than this, the advantage lay in not being 'typically black' in any narrowly defined stylistic sense, while retaining the credibility of black street style:

If you're going to be a Rasta and you're going to be like dealing drugs, you're only going to be hitting one side of the market: if you're going to be black and you can bounce on either side . . . you can be an Eastender if you want, and you can hit both markets—the white guys and the black guys—that's the advantage (ibid.).

Ricky's main area of activity was, however, with women: Shane once told me, when I first arrived in London, that Ricky 'used to be a gigolo'. Ricky admitted that, before settling down with Anne, he used to spend time in the West End with a group of young black men who would meet young women and hustle money from them. Within this 'work', black street style was the crucial factor; exploiting the mythology surrounding black male sexuality. Ricky told me:

It's easy, it's so easy. As long as you've got the right assets—you're not ugly, you dress nice, and you can dance; you can go into any place and without creating too much attention you can make people look over to you and after you pick out the one that looks very vulnerable and just go over—just like that (ibid.).

Ricky always chose white European women, preferably those on holiday, because they carried large amounts of cash and would be leaving. They were also believed to be more susceptible to the 'exotic' charms of black men. Before I moved into the flat, Ricky had been sharing with three women, two Danish and one Swedish, all of whom he had affairs with and all of whom would give him money—for the rent, for clothes, to go out. He finally moved them out on Anne's demand, but they often returned to the flat to see Ricky and attempt to reinstate their relationship. Normally, however, the approach was more short-term:

The easiest way to do it is, you see the girl often, you be with her every day and after she says she's just over here for two weeks; and then after you say, 'next week I can't see you because this guy is supposed to be giving me £200 and I've got to chase him'—she wants to see you next week of course, doesn't she, so she's going to give you the £200 so you can spend the week with her instead—and you just keep playing it that way (ibid.).

Within this arena, Ricky was able to manipulate black stereotypes to create an image of success and of personal power. He remained aware, however, of the limitations upon this image, because of its failure to penetrate beyond the bounds of a narrowly defined sphere in which black masculinity was both positively defined and circumscribed. Within this arena, his primary, if not sole, identity was defined by phenotype; to move beyond this would be to redefine this identity and render it powerless. Ricky's situation became self-defining and self-perpetuating; he told me:

And after, you keep on and keep on and keep on, but you see a lot of cash keeps going through your hands all the time, and I mean at the end of the day what do you have to show for it? . . . I'm trying to hustle the money so I can buy more clothes and spend more time in the city. So basically I was more or less burning the money, you know (Interview, 9 June 1991).

When I first moved to Ricky's flat to live, he informed me that he was intending to start a business importing and selling Italian designer clothes. The project was to be funded by one of the women Ricky had met while 'working' in the City; she had apparently offered him £20,000 recently inherited upon her father's death. During the year I lived with him, the money was a source of much discussion, but never materialized. It soon became clear to everyone but Ricky that the woman had no intentions of giving Ricky the money to start a business, but was using it merely as a means of control. It is significant that she was determined to keep Ricky within his former role rather than enable him to redefine his position as a businessman with a source of independent power. As with the others, therefore, the role of black male was defined and circumscribed to limit any expression of personal success and power within a work environment.

WOMEN AND EMPLOYMENT

As the *Guardian* article mentioned at the start of this chapter illustrates, the role of the 'successful' black woman has been defined rather differently from that of her black male counterparts. Where for the black male, 'success' seems an impossibility, for women, it has become almost an inevitability. This image has tended to marginalize a large number of black women who are either not working, or who are employed in low-paid, unskilled manual work. It has also, as mentioned earlier, created an image of female employment which ignores the type of work with which black women are mainly engaged, which is often within local government or the caring professions (Mirza 1992). Such work, though of higher status than black male employment, tends to be badly paid and offers as little chance of personal advancement. The successful black career woman is, in part at least, as much a creation of sociological categorization as of employment realities.

The images surrounding black female employment have, however, created more opportunities for black women and this is reflected in employment realities. Although a number of the women I either knew or heard about were engaged in low-paid manual work—Dion, for example, used to work as a chambermaid to supplement her state benefits—many had gone on to higher education or had returned to education after having children. One, Yvette, who worked in the Community Centre, started a degree course in social administration during the time of my fieldwork; she was in her early thirties and had one son. Similarly, Angelina and her friends, Eleanor and Fenella, were all undertaking degrees at university and polytechnic.

The situation of black women in employment is beyond the scope of this study and deserves separate consideration. What is of interest, however, is the differing image of black women in employment and the way this affects their employment status in comparison with their male counterparts. As mentioned earlier, all the women I knew had been involved in 'typical' black employment at various stages and were aware of the negative stereotypes that confronted them. However, when removed from this arena, women were more easily accepted into mainstream white working environments than men. It is perhaps the lack of pervasive negative social stereotypes surrounding black women that facilitates upward mobility. Moreover, the presence of an alternative image that embraces black female success provides the possibility of redefinition of 'traditional' black roles within an employment situation.

The image of the independent, well-educated, successful black woman has therefore become something of a self-fulfilling prophecy. This is not to deny, of course, that racism affects their working life, nor to underestimate the significance of gender discrimination. To what extent these factors will prove significant will become more apparent once my female informants leave college and look for work. As Fenella assured me, however:

Let's put it this way, I'm not a person that gets easily discouraged. If I don't find it straight away, then I'll have to go round the back door somewhere. If there's something I really, really want to do then I'll find a way (Interview, 27 Mar. 1991).

CONCLUSION

This study does not deny that for the majority of black youth in Britain employment prospects remain bleak (Solomos 1988; Brown 1992; Jenkins 1992). Most are concentrated at the lower end of the labour market, in poorly paid manual or semi-skilled work, where employment is at its most vulnerable. While not denying the 'reality' of black employment, then, this chapter maintains two things. First, the nature, if not the quality, of 'traditional' black employment is changing from that encountered by their parents; secondly, that the notion of 'black employment' has created an image of the black male which precludes any expression of personal success. Black men have thus become stereotyped within the employment sphere, in a way which denies access to any legitimate power by either individuals or groups. For those men who attempt to move outside this sphere, the absence of alternative definitions of black employment renders their position vulnerable, both economically and ideologically. This can be contrasted, in part, with the position of black women, for whom an alternative definition has been created, and which both incorporates and facilitates a degree of upward mobility. For men within the new employment markets, there remains a need to create—and sustain—an image which incorporates personal success; this may be based upon the manipulation of symbols of 'class' rather than 'race'. This in turn requires a recognition of the dynamic articulation between 'race' and class categorizations, which embraces heterogeneity and personal agency. Such an approach requires, moreover, a widening of the definition of black employment away from the 'traditional' arenas of work, and 'typical' avenues for black success, such as sports and entertainment (cf. Small 1994), to encompass the increasingly disparate activities with which black youth are engaged.

4

Social Life

No more need to fuss or fight—
I'll just enjoy my life.
Whatever gives you the greatest pleasure
And joy.

(Soul II Soul, *Joy*)

ONE Friday night in November, I accompanied some of the boys on another of their regular 'boys' nights out' in the West End. Having been refused entry to two of their regular winebars, we were walking to a third when we stopped outside an off-licence waiting for Frank, who was looking at video games in a shop, to catch up. We had been standing for less than a minute when the shop-owner ran to the shop door, locked it, and pulled down the metal grille. The incident passed without comment and seemed not to be regarded as an unusual—or, indeed, bizarre—occurrence by any of the boys. Such reactions, reflected also in the common refusal of entry to venues, appeared to be an accepted part of the night's events. This was despite the fact that all the boys were smartly dressed, neither drunk nor particularly rowdy, and were frequent patrons of the West End bars and clubs. The boys themselves shrugged and claimed that the reactions were not so much racially directed as against the size of the group: although why a group of five black men should constitute such a problem remained unclear and unconsidered.

The perceived threat of young black men remains a powerful image, especially in relation to the leisure sphere. On 6 November 1990, *The Voice* quoted John Carlisle, MP, on the 'terrible nuisance' of black youth:

The main problem is with the young aggressive blacks who run these parties. They are a scourge, many of which go on for three days. But, understandably, the police are wary about stopping them. . . . You can't deny that there is a lot of alcohol at these parties and a great suspicion of drugs. These youth also get up to some pretty disgusting things in the backs of people's gardens.

Carlisle's objections are familiar and overworked; black youth are seen as an aggressive, anti-authoritarian and anti-social collectivity, whose life revolves around endless parties, alcohol, drugs, and unspecified general debauchery. By extension, black leisure events are seen as a focus for criminal activity, violence, and social irresponsibility. As Gilroy notes, the long-standing equation of black leisure with unemployment, drugs, and violence has led to the criminalization of black culture (1987: 72–3), in which any gathering of black youth is seen as counterposed to the social order and a threat to it. In a recent article on so-called Yardies in *The Independent Magazine*, for example, Peter Popham rehearses the commonplace connection between black social life, criminalized subculture, and violence: 'Shootings in crowded dance halls have become commonplace, and the motive is often trivial—a guy has knocked over your beer, made eye contact with your girlfriend' (30 Oct. 1993). As Gilroy writes of the Deptford fire of 1981: 'the "black party" had become such an entrenched sign of disorder and criminality... that it had become fundamentally incompatible with the representation of black life and experience in any other form' (1987: 102).

RITUALIZED RESISTANCE?: LEISURE AND POLITICS

Analogous to the representation of black social events as criminal is the image popular in most academic studies of black youth culture—that of black leisure as political struggle. Although apparently opposed to the criminalization of culture, both represent the black social sphere as one distinct from mainstream culture and inherently opposed to it (Cashmore 1979; Cashmore and Troyna 1982). Such studies have focused mainly on the culture of Rastafari and reggae music, and have created an image of a discrete and enclosed social sphere, which is monolithic both in its form and intent. Hebdige, for example, describes reggae as essentially oppositional from its very roots in slave culture:

It was never dirigible, protected as it was by language, by colour and by a culture which had been forced, in its very inception, to cultivate secrecy and to elaborate defences against the intrusions of the master class (1976: 147).

The form, he continues, is thus inherently subversive and politicized, and remains impenetrable to white outsiders. This viewpoint is echoed by Troyna and Cashmore, who see Rastafari as a negative centripetal force which 'assumes a critical role in both structuring and reinforcing negative attitudes towards Britain . . . and encourages their retreat into an alternative sub-cultural milieu' (Troyna 1979).

For Troyna, echoing Pryce, the reactions of black youth to life in Britain fall into three categories: mainstreamer, compromiser, and rejector, which can be read off from the forms of social life enjoyed by the individual. The mainstreamer listens to pop music; the compromiser to soul music and 'sweet' reggae; while the rejector, inevitably, turns to Rastafari and its associated culture of hard reggae, shebeens, and sound systems (ibid.). Black culture is thus seen as a refuge for personal failure and feelings of inadequacy, which expresses a negative stance towards the wider society from which it is excluded. The equation of expressive cultures with deviance and hence with criminality is easily, and consistently, drawn. For example, Abner Cohen's recent study of the Notting Hill Carnival conflates black culture and political action with violence and drug dealing—the markers for Cohen of a 'distinct and homogeneous West Indian Culture' (1993: 6). Thus he writes of 'the customary ritual of youths rioting and behaving with violence' (ibid. 42), of 'a tense event with violence ever lurking just below the surface' (ibid. 45), of 'steaming gangs' (ibid. 71), 'no-go areas' (ibid. 58), and of the streets of Notting Hill itself as 'notorious for drug dealing and mugging' (ibid. 2). While acknowledging the historical development and transformations of the Carnival, Cohen's account nevertheless fixes black expression within an enduring legacy of pathology and cultural anomie; black culture becomes dehistoricized and essentialized.

The perception of black youth culture as existing within a vacuum, impervious to outside influence and changes over time, undiluted and inviolate, ignores the dynamism that marks out black expression both historically and within a contemporary context. Forms of cultural expression, which are constantly changing and transforming themselves, are envisioned as direct reflections of the political concerns of black youth; as if they can be read as markers for the social orientation of black youth at any given moment. Black youth expression and, indeed, black youths themselves, are portrayed as a homogeneous entity, bound by time and by present concerns. This perspective is reflected in recent debates over the misogynistic, homophobic, gun-culture lyrics of ragga artists such as Buju Banton, in which, as Gilroy notes, musical expression becomes 'a cipher for authenticity' (1993: 6).

As Hewitt notes, however, 'it would be a travesty to reduce *all* black culture to expressions, reflexive or otherwise, of the conditions of political and economic struggle' (1986: 214). Seeking to define and limit black youth expression through an insistence upon an 'authentic' black sphere denies the dynamism of black culture as it is lived and precludes any possibility of meaningful interaction. As Hewitt argues, such an approach represents closure rather than engagement, and black youth become ' "ghettoised" within their own fictive realm' (ibid. 215). Black youth culture should be seen rather as 'a constant process of manipulation through socially structured interactions mediated by the ideological terms within which they operate' (ibid. 214).

Such an approach allows for a range of social options and cultural affiliations, amongst which the individual can select and alternate. This enables the recognition of processes of both change and continuity within black culture; and for the mediation of black culture upon and by mainstream culture (Jones 1988). This is not to deny, or underestimate, the existence of—or desire for— a 'black' cultural space; it does, however, argue for a more complex and multi-faceted understanding of Black British culture, and resist the reduction of its expression to the mere rehearsal of immediate desires. As Gilroy notes, black expressive culture in Britain has been created from a complex of diaspora images and influences which constitute a syncretic and multiplex field of interaction and transformation (1987, 1993). Thus, he writes, 'Black culture is actively made and remade' (1987: 153). It is by recognizing the plurality of black cultural expression and the diversity of experience to which it relates, that black culture escapes reduction and achieves significance.

This chapter aims, therefore, to explore the plurality of black cultural expression as it is lived and experienced through social interaction. It focuses less on the forms and content of Black

British youth cultural expression than on the social arenas in
which these are played out. It will consider first the range of
options open to black youth in London, together with their incumbent images and ideologies. It will then discuss the role of
the individual in relation to these options. The chapter contends
that individual youths select from amongst these options to construct a self-image and identity which positions them in relation
to both 'the community' and mainstream society, and in which
meanings are manipulated and negotiated. The black leisure
sphere can thus be seen as a site for the creative contestation
between the individual and the collective; what has been described as the tension between black pleasure and black joy (Dent
1992).

SOCIAL SCENES: OPTIONS AND IMAGES

The leisure arena for black youth in London is comprised of a
number of options, ranging from events which are almost exclusively black to predominantly white venues. These are distinguished not so much by clientele, who could attend any of these
events and move between them, but by the image associated
with them. These images articulated certain standpoints towards
'the community' and towards mainstream society, which proved
remarkably consistent amongst the boys and others I spoke to;
the differences lay not in the way the events themselves were
perceived, but in the way the individual positioned himself towards them. This distinction will become clearer in the second
section of this chapter; it suffices now to say that there were
generally held images of the leisure options open to black youth,
which are the subject of the following section.

Houseparties

Perhaps the most clearly localized and informal leisure option is
that of houseparties. These are held usually, though not exclusively, to mark specific occasions—birthdays, christenings, weddings, and so on. They are thus the leisure option most clearly
associated with family and 'community'; 'community' in this
respect referring to a personal network of people who are known

to the host, rather than a wider, more idealized perception of 'the black community'. Indeed, those houseparties I attended were often strictly by invitation only and were watched over at the entrances by male friends or family to guard against unwanted intrusion. These social events are often held within the home itself, but a more recent trend is towards hiring external venues, where more people can be accommodated. At a party for Clive's brother's twenty-first birthday, a converted church-hall was hired in South London, with two large rooms and a kitchen. About three hundred people, friends and family, attended the party, which began around midnight and ended at eight o'clock the following morning. In one room was a band and sound system playing African music; in the other, a sound system playing more conventional forms of youth expression—reggae, soul, hip-hop. Other parties I went to were less lavish, but shared similar features: there was always a large sound system, with black MCs; a quantity of usually 'traditional' food, such as fried chicken, curried goat and rice, fish and corn; a surprisingly small amount of alcohol; and very little room. Most of the food and drink was supplied by the host or family and close friends. The venues were always very dark—a feature I came to associate with 'black' social events—and very cramped: one complaint I heard often from the boys about such occasions was their inability to dance. Indeed, at one houseparty I attended in Walthamstow with two women from the Community Centre, Sonya and Margaret, we were unable to get beyond the hallway.

The defining ethos of houseparties can be perhaps best encapsulated by the notion of 'respect'. Because these events were closely associated with the idea of home, family, and 'community', they tended to be marked by little trouble and a high degree of self-control. This was a function partly of the internal norms of behaviour at such events and partly of the external constraints wielded by those on the door, which stopped 'roughnecks' (Darnell, Interview, 24 Mar. 1991) from entering. Those within the party were known to each other and acted as mutual constraints; it was considered to be very damaging to a person's reputation if any trouble was started by someone he knew or had brought to the party. Similarly, the community nature of houseparties ensured an atmosphere unmarked by overt personal competition; there were no attempts to compete in dancing—

even if there were room—and little attempt to pick up women, which characterized other social options. They were seen rather as purely social events; a chance to meet friends and exchange gossip; as Darnell described to me:

we'd just like meet up at the party and chat to that person and probably see our next friends and you go over and have a chat to that person; so you just circulate round the party. Then, when it's time to go home, somebody else would say they're going home at the same time as you in the same direction, so you just walk off with them (Interview, 24 Mar. 1991).

The mix of people attending houseparties, because of their informal nature, depends very much on the person hosting it. Those I attended were predominantly black events, although a few white people were occasionally present. These were usually either friends or work colleagues of the host or, more rarely, the partner of one of the guests. The hostility to white people at such gatherings was not marked as at other 'black' leisure events. Houseparties were also one of the few places where the men I knew would take their girlfriends; partly because of the associations with the private, family sphere, which was considered to be safer and more 'respectable', and partly because they were not intending to meet other women at these events. They were thus not perceived as the public, male domain of other leisure spaces.

Blues Dances and Sound Clashes

With their roots in the rent parties and shebeens of the early migrants, blues parties were unanimously agreed by my inform-ants, and others I met, to be the 'blackest' social events, as well as the least formal. Like houseparties, they are held usually within a private house; they are, however, held for commercial pur-poses, charging an entrance fee and open to all. Although tradi-tionally held in deserted houses, with electricity for the sound system wired from outside street lights or from neighbours, they are more often held in private homes by people wishing to raise money. A more recent trend is towards hiring premises from local estate agents for the night. Entrance is charged, usually between £3 and £5, although more can be asked if a well-known 'sound' is playing. Like houseparties, blues start in the early hours of the morning and continue throughout the night, and perhaps the next morning. Drinks and food are on sale for those attending. The music played is almost exclusively reggae, in all its forms—revival, ragga, lover's rock.

Blues parties are perhaps the most 'community'-based form of public black social event and the most closely related to the idea of a distinct 'black' subculture. They are informal gatherings whose existence is publicized through word of mouth or, until recently, through local pirate radio stations. These stations were often run by sound systems, who would publicize their activities through the radio and use them to build up a following. These have to some extent crossed into the more formal black leisure scene and play at commercially run black clubs. Sounds such as Mystery, G. T., and Latest Edition now tour the black clubs and have a large following from all over London. More frequently, however, a sound system builds up a locally-based reputation, and tends to attract local youths when they 'play out'. This is mainly a function of the somewhat eclectic publicity strategies; blues parties are often advertised without addresses, and almost always without house numbers. Attendance is thus dependent on a knowledge of the area and of the people associated with the event. Angelina told me that she and Darnell once spent two hours driving up and down the streets of Ladbroke Grove looking for a blues party which had been advertised on a local pirate radio station, but to no avail. On other occasions, however, the strategies were more successful; Darnell told me:

two years ago, New Year's Eve, there was a pirate radio, Fresh FM, having their New Year's Eve party and it was in this hall, Anson Hall, which is just a massive hall about as big as a football pitch and this place was just jammed packed with people—there must have been over 4,000 people in this place. . . . I reckon the whole of Harlesden was there, because I saw everybody I knew; I reckon half of London was there as well (ibid.).

Blues parties are generally regarded as the most 'community'-oriented events within the public leisure sphere. They are almost exclusively black events, popular both with older men, who had grown up in the Caribbean, and with younger British-born youth. The informality of blues dances, marked by the lack of a dress code and no restrictions upon weapons and drugs has, however, given them something of a reputation for violence. None of the boys attended blues dances, which most regarded with a mixture of terror and scorn. Clive told me: 'Some of them are a bit nasty . . . . You smoke, you drink, you don't think twice about pulling out a knife on someone, do you, for something really silly' (Interview, 16 Apr. 1991).

Although Darnell and Rommell did attend blues dances on occasion, they too were careful in making this choice. Darnell explained:

Like I wouldn't go to a blues dance in Stonebridge, because you don't know who you find in them places. I've been to a couple in Harlesden, but it's like you sort of know who's holding the blues anyway . . . so you feel safe, because if anything, they're holding your back. . . . But if it was like someone goes 'there's a blues dance in Brixton, I've just heard about it' then *I* ain't going to it! (Interview, 24 Mar. 1991).

Blues dances were more popular with the men I knew at the Centre, although these were mainly held within the locale. Also popular were the larger, more commercialized 'sound clashes', in which two well-known sound systems set up in a hall and compete for the audience's approval by alternately playing records— preferably new, imported, and hard to obtain. My direct experience of such events was, however, very limited. This was mainly because, as I was frequently told, 'nice girls' did not attend these events. The men I knew that did go to blues dances were, therefore, reluctant to take me with them. When I asked Maurice the barber to take me to his next blues dance, which he regularly attended, he demurred, claiming that if I went with him people would assume I was his girlfriend, and that this would make me a target for the black women there. When I did finally attend a blues dance, held by a Rastafarian friend from the Community Centre, I was made to stand in the kitchen and was escorted whenever I left the room. I suspect, however, that this action represented more a symbol of 'ownership' on his part than any real threat to my well-being.

Blues dances tend, therefore, to be a predominantly male arena; men do not generally take their partners with them, and the girls who do attend are considered to be 'rough'. Blues dances are thus partly associated with a negative image of 'community', discussed in the earlier chapters. They are also seen as exclusively black events: to take a white person, male or female, to these would be considered a provocation and an insult. At the blues I attended, I was the only non-black person there, and was accepted largely because I knew a number of the men from the Centre. The atmosphere at the party was relaxed and friendly; most of the people knew or recognized each other, and there was no trouble. As with houseparties, there was no overt competition, in either dress or action. This was a general feature of these events remarked upon by both Ricky and Darnell; when I asked about dress codes, the latter told me:

if it's a blues, don't dress up too tough, because half the people in there are going to be of the older era and they're just going to be in their dirty jeans and trainers, and you just look out of place.... You've got to look better than them, but you don't want to look too good (ibid.).

Ricky similarly claimed:

From you don't bother nobody, nobody bothers you.... You just go in there and just mellow out: don't make too much big stuff of yourself, just stroll through, buy your drinks and just mellow out in the corner. That's how most black guys are (Interview, 9 June 1991).

Black Clubs and Winebars

During my fieldwork, I attended a number of black clubs and winebars with various of my informants. Although these were not the most popular leisure option with some of the boys, for reasons which will be discussed later, they are perhaps the most widely patronized by the majority of young black people. A large number of black clubs have opened in London in recent years, mainly in areas of high black population, although there are several within the West End area. Like 'white' clubs, the format and style of black clubs varies widely, from those which are closely associated with blues-style events, to those portraying a more 'upmarket' image. There is also a recognizable difference between those black clubs within the West End and those outside the City.

The term 'black club' is thus somewhat open to question, since these can range from wholly black institutions to those with a large white clientele, often playing different music and portraying different images. The term was one, however, used by my informants with some authority: there was no doubt which clubs were 'black' and which were not. For those clubs outside the West End, the definition is less contentious; at those I attended, there were very few white people present, and the music was predominantly reggae or rare groove. Indeed, it was the lack of variety in the music which was the boys' main excuse for not frequenting these places, while for others this was the biggest attraction. The black venues in the City tend to have a larger white clientele and play a variety of music, including some reggae (though usually not much ragga),[1] rare groove, and a high input of commercial American hip-hop and dance music. Within such places, the description 'black' is more questionable and seems founded upon a general notion of 'atmosphere' and style by those who attend them. It should be noted that the white clientele of these places are almost always women, which is not true of the 'white' clubs. It is perhaps the predominance of black men, both in numbers and stylistic influence, which is the defining characteristic of these places. These clubs differ in some features from those outside the West End and encapsulate a different image; for the purposes of this study, therefore, they will be considered separately. The former will be referred to as 'City Clubs', and the latter as 'Inner City Clubs', to reflect both geographical location and a wider associated ambience.

Inner City Clubs

As mentioned earlier, black clubs are the most popular leisure option for young black people, both male and female. Those I attended during my fieldwork were often large, inevitably dark, and usually very full. In 1990/1, most charged between £5 and £10, although prices increased if a well-known sound was 'playing out' in the club. Unlike the City clubs, those in the 'Inner City' tend to open their doors at around midnight and close around 4 or 5 a.m., or later. These clubs are, then, not far removed from the blues parties and houseparties which are their origin. As such, they encapsulate the ambiguity of image associated with 'community' leisure activities, which is further complicated by the commercialization of this community subculture.

---

[1] These and following comments are based on fieldwork observations in 1990–1, and recognize the continued transformations in popular music, notably the crossover of ragga music into mainstream popular culture.

Thus, although the majority of the Inner City clubs are located in areas with a large black population—Hackney, Brixton, Stoke Newington—the patrons of these venues are by no means as locally-based as with other social events. The ideal of 'community' associated with these places exists, therefore, as an imagined, abstract notion rather than being linked with a geographical area, although some overlap does occur. Most of the young black people I knew were prepared to travel widely and frequently to different venues, and although they often met people they recognized, the community base was very diluted. The popularity of clubs waxed and waned with alarming speed, and the knowledge of which clubs to attend, on which nights, was generally seen as a token of the individual's street credibility. Such knowledge became less easy to obtain with the clampdown on pirate radio stations in the middle of my fieldwork, and returned very much to word of mouth street advertisement. When I began, one of the most popular venues—as well as one of the largest—was All Nations in Hackney, which has three dancefloors, a kitchen, and large bar and seating areas. When I went with some of the boys several months later, the club was nearly empty, although this could have been attributed to a bad choice of night rather than representative of a wider decline in popularity.

The 'community' ideal was manifest in a number of ways in these clubs. At an institutional level, as with the Community Centre in Chapter 2, the clubs were perceived as open to all black people, in a way that other options were not. Ricky assured me, for example, that although most black venues had strict dress codes, none would turn away Rastafarians, whom 'the community' regards, theoretically at least, with a high degree of respect. When a new black winebar, Splash, opened in Hackney and invited Michael Prophet, the reggae artist, to perform, there were a large number of Rastafarians present, with little seeming regard for the venue's usual demands. Generally, however, these clubs tend not to attract Rastafarians, so Ricky's assertion is difficult to validate; it does, however, reflect his own perception of the defining ethos of such places.

At a personal level, also, the ideal of 'community' was significant. As with houseparties and blues dances, there was no overt competition, although greater emphasis was laid on appearance and dress. Ricky explained, 'Black people have a good time just

standing up and drinking their drink and listening to the music'
(Interview, 9 June 1991). Dancing tended therefore to be largely
uniform; more an expression of a shared experience rather than
individual achievement. As Darnell told me:

you've got to know how to dance or you'd look childish. But like most
people, when it's soul, just nod their heads anyway; when it's reggae,
they just nod their head same way, right? . . . You can't really tell who's
a better dancer because there is only like one thing you can do—so
someone might move their arms a bit better than you, but boy, that's it
(Interview, 24 Mar. 1991).

It was, however, crucial to know the latest dance forms, the execution of which can be seen as the constant re-creation and
reassertion of a communal identity.

Similarly, there was no obvious competition for women. This
was because, the boys told me frequently, black women are 'feisty'
and 'ignorant', and are therefore impossible to approach. Within
the mythology of the group, some of the favourite stories were
of the others receiving notable rebuffs at the hands of black
women in clubs: the version current at the beginning of my
fieldwork concerned Nathan, who had asked five women at a
black club to dance, each time in vain, and had been reduced in
his exasperation from a polite 'Excuse me but would you like to
dance?' to a desperately screeched 'Wanna dance?' Even Darnell,
who frequented the Inner City clubs almost exclusively, told me
that although he always found women to dance with, these
meetings were rarely followed up: 'We just like go out there,
right, and we don't expect to chat to no girls because we don't
want that; just like one or two dances and then go "yeah, safe"
and so move on to the next one' (Interview, 24 Mar. 1991). Incorporated within this perspective was the notion of 'respect'; of
maintaining community solidarity, of which women are seen to
be the primary mainstay. This will be considered in more detail
in the following chapters.

The association with community, and the links with 'typical'
black expressive culture, also led, however, to the creation of
negative images surrounding these clubs. Most of the boys saw
the clubs as potentially violent and often dangerous, although
none had direct evidence of this. This image was reflected by the
clubs themselves in the surprisingly strict door policies. At all

the clubs I attended, those entering were searched for weapons and drugs, all displayed prominent 'No Drugs' policies, and all applied stringent dress codes. This can be seen perhaps as an attempt to exclude undesirable elements from their establishments, but also forms part of an ideological struggle to distance themselves from the stereotypes surrounding black social establishments. The boys themselves expressed some ambiguity about their success: it was a standing joke that some of the clubs were *so* violent that if the door staff searched you and you were found not to have a weapon, they gave you one before you went in. Interestingly, the only club I attended which evidenced any sign of weapons was a black club in the West End, which is generally perceived as an area of the City hostile to the majority of black people. In this club, those entering left their weapons in a stack by the door, which could perhaps be seen as symbolic of a perceived boundary between 'safe' and 'unsafe' public spaces.

City Clubs

The black clubs in the West End can be seen to occupy the interstices between perceptions of 'the community' and wider white society, both blurring and exploiting the perceived divide between black and white social spheres. They are generally much smaller than the Inner City clubs, with smaller dancefloors and more lights. They are thus, at least in decor, closer to the West End 'white' clubs than their 'black' counterparts. They are also more expensive to enter, starting at around £8 for a weekend night. There are, of course, differences between the City clubs, with places such as Moonlighting—one of the most popular black clubs in the West End, frequented on occasion by black celebrities such as Prince and Eddie Murphy—resembling one of the more upmarket white venues; while others such as Gossips, a reggae club in a rather dingy basement, remain closer to the blues parties atmosphere. Hardly surprisingly, the former attract more white customers than the latter.

The notion of 'community', which defines the ideological framework of the Inner City clubs, is noticeably diluted in the black City establishments. Although, by contrast, the door policies are apparently more relaxed, in reality, entrance is strictly controlled and more difficult to negotiate. The door policies are unstated and seem to centre more closely upon the image of the patron, and the 'type' of black person the clubs wish to attract. These unstated policies of exclusion can be wielded at any time and are not open to negotiation; unless, of course, you know the door staff. On one evening, when the boys went to meet Nathan and Arif in Gossips, Frank was refused admittance because he was wearing trainers; this was despite the fact that the trainers were new, that the club allowed jeans, and that women were allowed to wear whatever they liked, including trainers. Ricky explained that this effectively excluded from the club those youth who favoured hip-hop style and dress, who may have been considered detrimental to the club's image. Significantly, this is a male image; women generally are more easily accepted in any of the clubs, both within and outside the City.

If the notion of 'community' can be seen to be limited as it is encapsulated within the structures of the City clubs, this is equally true of its clientele. Unlike the Inner City clubs and other 'community' leisure options, the atmosphere within these places is marked by a high level of competition, both in dress and dance. Emphasis is thus more strongly placed upon individual status rather than communal solidarity. When the boys were in these clubs they were noticeably more vociferous and active than at other times, and on several occasions I witnessed a 'dance-off' between one member of the group and another black man—or woman—who was seen as threatening to their status. The most memorable was between Nathan and another unknown man, who were alternately 'busting splits', jumping on tables, and generally demonstrating their physical prowess, while others in the club watched and judged. On this occasion, the other man was judged by all to be the better dancer, although I found it impossible to understand the criteria: Nathan's defeat was held to be a reflection on the standing of the whole group, who agreed unanimously that, if Ricky had been present, the situation would have been very different.

The image associated with these clubs was very much one of upward mobility; this was contrasted sharply with the Inner City clubs, which were constructed as being for those with few social prospects and little ambition. This was, of course, not an image held by the Inner City clubs themselves, their patrons, or, indeed, grounded in reality; it constituted more a created image against which the City clubs defined themselves. Ricky explained,

'In the City, you get a different set of black people. It means they come from all over, they most likely work in the City, they're most likely in better jobs . . . the ones in Hackney are a bit more rough' (Interview, 9 June 1991).

In reality, however, these distinctions proved to be more a matter of self-perception than actual difference. Of the boys, only Nathan, Arif, and Clive worked in the City; Ricky had been unemployed for two years, yet the City was his constant haunt, and the others, Shane, Malcolm, Frank, and Satish, worked in jobs which, by Ricky's definition, would have led them towards the Inner City clubs. Moreover, as Ricky was aware, there was a degree of ambiguity surrounding these clubs: those in the City were, he told me, 'less black' than those in Hackney. This implied both a positive and negative value judgement; that they represented at once both higher status and betrayal of one's 'roots'. This was echoed by Darnell, who had only once attended a City club, Moonlighting: 'People that go to those clubs look like they were working people, who are getting ahead in life and are successful. They just seemed like they were white people with black faces' (Interview, 24 Mar. 1991). Darnell claimed that this was not how he saw himself, although he was starting college to become an accountant and planned to be successful:

When I'm successful, I might go to it, but it doesn't seem right. It seems like false, like, you know (in a high-pitched English accent), 'see you, darling'—that's what it seemed like in that club. But like in the clubs down the east, they go (in black English accent), 'yeah, what you saying', not 'oh, darling' (ibid.).

White Clubs and Winebars

As with 'black clubs', the description 'white club' serves more as a general term of analysis than a generic specification. It thus covers a range of venues, from more upmarket and exclusive clubs, such as Stringfellows, through popular City clubs, such as the Hippodrome, to 'acid' raves. For the majority of young black people, including the boys, the extremes of this range were considered 'white only' events; this is not to claim that black people are never present at these places, but that the numbers involved are comparatively small, if not stylistically insignificant. At an 'acid' club in Southall I once visited with Angelina, where a friend worked as a bouncer, there were less than ten black people present out of several hundred; that this was not considered a 'black' venue was made clear by the door staff, who asked us several times if we were sure we wanted to go in. The middle range of clubs also varies widely in image, from acceptably 'trendy' and 'credible' clubs, such as the Hippodrome, to those regarded by the boys as catering to a more downmarket, 'East End' clientele, such as Hombres. The boys rarely attended any 'white' clubs outside the City and never went to pubs; they were, however, frequent visitors to the City clubs and winebars. At these places, the numbers of black people were small, almost exclusively male and generally composed of individuals or small groups. On our 'boys' nights out', the boys usually formed the largest group of black men in any venue, as well as the most boisterous. In the absence of any larger numbers, my observations about white establishments are restricted primarily to the boys.

The white clubs can perhaps be more accurately defined as 'mixed', in that they cater for black and Asian youth as well as white English people. The term 'white' was, however, that used by the boys, except when they were seeking to avoid accusations of 'selling-out' or 'being white'; it is the term, therefore, which this study will continue to use. It is certainly true that the label 'white' defines these clubs and winebars in opposition to the perception of 'black' venues, and hence against the value systems and expectations of the latter. It is also true that these places carry none of the restrictions of the 'community' ethos. It was these places in which the boys were at their most competitive and most active, seeking constantly to outdo the other patrons in dancing, dress, and general 'attitude'. As Clive, who was the strongest advocate of these clubs, explained:

A white club, something like Hombres, is a bit more faster music; people jumping up and down . . . and basically, the atmosphere is a bit more enjoyable, and much faster. . . . When I'm in a white club, I like to jump about and be noticed and be seen (Interview, 16 Apr. 1991).

It is significant that this competition was directed first and foremost at other black men present: white men were generally considered unworthy opponents, and women were primarily objects of conquest. This was especially true of white women, who were the primary purpose for the attendance at these clubs:

I was frequently told that if the boys wanted to dance and be together they would go to a black club, if they wanted to pick up women they would go to a white club. This adage existed more at the level of public myth than private reality: it did, however, seem to have a noticeable effect on the behaviour of the boys when in these places.

The clubs, as with the black City clubs, cost from about £8 entrance at weekends, although the Hippodrome can cost up to £20 per night. They start at around 11 p.m. and finish around 2 or 3 a.m. The clubs themselves are usually large and well lit, but with comparatively small dancefloors. Music varies, but tends to be a mixture of rap, American dance music, and some popular old-style reggae: those white clubs I attended rarely played ragga (although this has since 'crossed over' into mainstream popular culture). More popular with the boys, however, were the winebars, which often played dance music and which were usually free to enter. They were also held to attract a 'better' class of women. The favourite haunt of the boys, almost every weekend during my fieldwork, was Corks in Bond Street. The boys would usually spend the evening there, dancing, drinking, and chatting up women, before either going home or proceeding to a club, when the winebar closed at 11 p.m.

The boys generally considered those white clubs and winebars they frequented to attract a more successful, upwardly mobile clientele than the other leisure options. This image had, however, rather ambiguous implications for the black men that were attracted to them. On the one hand, it was felt that allying themselves to this image gave them status within a wider white domain; on the other, a general antipathy towards black youth by these institutions made their choice of this leisure option one that was severely constrained by external forces. Restrictive door policies, and the knowledge that certain places were simply not open to large numbers of black youth, must be taken into account when considering this leisure choice.

SOCIAL CONTROL: LEISURE AND POWER

It can be seen from the broad typology of leisure options described above that black youth culture forms not a homogeneous, bounded sphere, but rather a range of choices, each with its associated image and prescribed modes of action. Those I have described are those which were of most significance to my informants, and other young black men of my acquaintance. It may be that there are other options not included within this discussion that are of relevance to other groups. The boys themselves were not limited to the options discussed above: however, other forms of leisure entertainment—sport, cinema, restaurants— tend to be participated in on an individual basis and were largely neutral in terms of the image associated with them. What is of greatest significance to this study is, however, not the form and content of these options, but the way these are manipulated by individuals to articulate a self-image which in turn expresses a stance on wider concerns. This is not to claim a primary politicized intent for black youth culture; leisure choices do, however, provide a useful insight into the creation of individual identities and their dynamic relation to 'the community' and mainstream society.

It should be noted that the leisure sphere for black youth does not allow for complete freedom of expression; that there are limitations upon movement and choice amongst the available options. This was mentioned briefly in relation to black City clubs, but is more true of white establishments. Within the leisure arena a number of exclusions operate which must be taken into account in any discussion of black youth culture. This can be seen in turn as a reflection of the relative lack of power wielded by black people in the wider society and of the negative images of black youth which have proliferated. It was these exclusions which were mentioned briefly in the opening story.

Amongst my informants, there was a clear recognition of these limitations, which could be seen to impinge on their leisure activities. Darnell and Rommell, for example, rarely ventured into the City and never went to white clubs there: this was partly the expression of an individual preference for other options, but was also due in part to a perception of these places as hostile to their presence. Amongst the boys also, there existed some variation in attitudes; Malcolm told me:

In a white place, I'm thinking, say they decided to tear down a bit of nigger, for a laugh—because they do those type of things—what'll happen to me? Because I've seen them do it. They say, let's have a laugh, let's cut the niggers or cut the Pakis, or kick the shit out of them, because they do when they're drunk (Interview, 12 May 1991).

Significantly, when Ricky got into a fight with a group of white youths at Hombres, a white club, after they had spent the evening pushing him and touching his girlfriend, it was we who were thrown out and barred, while his white opponents remained inside the club.

A number of the West End clubs and winebars were generally known to be antipathetic to black clientele, particularly black men. The boys often went to great lengths to circumvent any restrictions, and the attitude to be adopted when approaching certain venues was invariably a matter of deep discussion and advance planning. The boys would often enter the place individually or in couples, rather than together; they would ask women who were going into the venue to accompany them. One of the benefits of my presence was that I, as a woman, lessened the perceived threat of the group. They also went to such places early, knowing that admittance became more difficult as the evening wore on, and would attempt to cultivate the friendship of the door staff. If the group were ever turned away, there would always ensue a large amount of analysis and the attribution of blame—it was Clive's fault because his shirt was too loud; we should have gone in individually; Frank looked too aggressive; Nathan should not have argued with the bouncer, and so on. It is interesting that these difficulties seemed not to lessen with familiarity; the boys would often get turned away from places they knew well and frequented often. All were, however, loath to attribute these refusals to racism; most accepted the exclusions as part and parcel of this leisure option and found other reasons —which were both more palatable and more easily circumvented —for their implementation. Indeed, the ability to control these refusals was considered something of an attribute of character— the assertion and validation of individual worth.

The recognition of group powerlessness was thus offset by assertions of individual control. For the boys, this meant persuading a reluctant bouncer to admit them to a club, or, once inside, establishing and maintaining control over the other patrons. This was achieved mainly through dancing and through the attraction of women. As mentioned earlier, the element of competition was not directed at other members of the group but, first, at other black men and, then, white men. The boundaries of the group were thus always fairly open, and outside elements were constantly drawn into the group at different times.

In this context, Ricky and the others would often recount to me stories of their younger days in the City, at the age of 20 to 22 years, when large groups of up to fifteen or twenty black men would congregate in Cork's wine bar in Leicester Square, where they were renowned for their exuberance, dancing, and general stylistic presence. Even at the time of my fieldwork, several years later, the boys tended to judge places on the degree of impact they felt they could make; on whether or not they could 'run things'. Although in these social environments black youths were in a minority, the group laid claim to the predominant stylistic influence of black men. Frank told me: 'I don't think you'd call clubs in the City white clubs, because in most . . . it's black men make them look what they are. They give the clubs that image' (Interview, 10 Mar. 1991).

Amongst the boys, far greater emphasis was laid upon the popular stereotypical image of black men in these clubs than in other places. Styles of dress, the ability to dance, the capacity to attract women, all became of much greater importance in establishing and maintaining control. For example, all the boys were competent dancers—although this was a matter of some dispute within the group itself—and all set great store by their ability. That this was an essential part of their 'image' was expressed by Frank:

The style of your dance means what kind of person you are, what kind of styles you are attracted to and why this particular style. I mean, you can know a certain dancer by the way he dresses; you know what kind of dance to expect from him from the way he dresses. And girls do appreciate a bloke that can dance good (ibid.).

It is interesting, and significant, to contrast this with Darnell's comments on dancing in black clubs mentioned earlier. Ricky, turning away from the City to the black Inner City clubs, also noted the shifting interpretation of dancing within these contexts:

Dancing is something I feel, not something I try to learn. When we used to hit the City, *then* it was important to us. . . . *Now* if I hear something and my body feels like picking it up, it will pick it up; if it doesn't, it doesn't (Interview, 9 June 1991).

The boys now, however, tended to go out in smaller groups of four or five—rarely more—and chose their options according to the mix of the group, and the image they wished to ally themselves with. This image had changed over time and was always open to negotiation; it is significant, however, that during my fieldwork the groups tended to fragment further and more conflict arose over the choice of social option. This was articulated by most as reflecting a divergence in life choices and aspirations. Within the City, however, the emphasis remained always upon 'control', at an individual and group level, and was opposed to the institutional control wielded by the City itself. By contrast, the notion of 'control' was significant by its absence in the 'community' leisure options.

SOCIAL CHOICES: LEISURE AND THE INDIVIDUAL

Within the limitations mentioned above, the individual is able to select leisure options in accordance with the lifestyle and image he wishes to reflect at any given time. Amongst the boys, those who most clearly favoured the City environment were those who either worked in the City, such as Clive, Nathan, and Arif, or those with whose self-image it most clearly correlated, such as Frank. Others of the group, particularly Shane and Malcolm, tended to favour the black social venues, while, during the course of my fieldwork, Ricky underwent a major change in attitude, turning from the City to the black Inner City clubs. As mentioned earlier, Darnell and Rommell preferred to stay within black clubs in East and North London, and rarely considered the City as a social possibility. Edgar, who considered himself something of a non-conformist, mainly frequented the jazz clubs and winebars of Camden.

The correlation of social images with lifestyle was most clearly reflected by Frank, who favoured the more upmarket winebars in the West End and tended to avoid both black venues and the less salubrious white clubs. He claimed to have explored most

social options—with the notable exception of blues parties—
when he was younger and went out almost every night, but told
me that as he had matured he had become more selective. He
explained:

The kind of places, the *right* places, I like is where I'll be up to date with
anything that's happening. I'll be moving with the people, moving with
the times, moving with people who've got things going for them. . . . It's
the image the club has; as I said, it's all to do with image again (Interview, 10 Mar. 1991).

For Frank, black clubs had the wrong 'image', which was defined against the upward mobility and image of success reflected
by the winebars he frequented:

It's what the people who go there make it to be; so, as I say, I like
meeting people, exciting people, but most of the black clubs aren't that
exciting for my liking. Those clubs are always like a set routine; you
know what's going to happen next (ibid.).

The same can also be said of the white clubs, like Hombres, the
image of which Frank was keen to distance himself from:

They've all got a set type of people that go there; like Hombres is East
End kind of people; they go there and kind of fit into times. You can tell
by the way they dress. See, my kind of person likes—not a wild look,
but a kind of freestyle look. . . . A place you can show off a bit: what you
wear, how you look, how you dance. Show other people what they
probably want to do or want to be (ibid.).

Frank was quick to assert that his leisure choices did not reflect any personal fears or ambivalence, especially in his relationship to the more 'community' leisure options: 'Like most of the
black clubs I've been to, I don't feel comfortable in them. It's not
my kind of scene. I like reggae, but not too much. . . . The people
I don't mind at all' (ibid.). When pushed further, however, Frank
expressed a more negative reaction, based upon the image of
black social events as violent, and the people who attend as being
socially marginalized:

In a club like that you don't really want to express yourself too much,
because you've got people that envy you so much. And like in most of
the clubs they show it to you straight away; they'll come up and stab
you or do anything stupid to you. . . . It's not that I'm scared of showing

it, but then again, if you show my kind of image, I'll rather show it to people who will probably appreciate it (ibid.).

This attitude was echoed by Clive, who was slightly less discerning in his choice of social venues but, like Frank, tended to avoid black Inner City clubs. He told me:

When I'm in a white club I like to jump about and be noticed and be seen; if I was in a black club I'd curb my jumping about . . . because black people, some of them are ignorant, and if you're seen to be really enjoying yourself, you know, you get stares, you get looks (Interview, 5 Mar. 1991).

On one occasion, when a group of us went to Splash, a black winebar in Hackney, Clive got drunk and began dancing wildly and pulling girls up to dance—much as he would in a white club: the others moved away and denied any association with him. Such behaviour, which transgressed the norms of these events, was rare in a black venue and reflected, for Ricky, Clive's inability to maintain a credible 'black' persona:

In a black place—apart from C[live] right, everybody, if a black guy get drunk, he will keep himself quiet; he's not going to walk around like Rambo inside the place, or make a fool of himself or anything. . . . Now if that's C[live] and he gets drunk, he's on the floor. That's why you can easily tell C[live] has been brought up here, like in a white environment, because it's only white people make fools of themselves when they get drunk, black people don't (Interview, 9 June 1991).

Although this was an undoubted generalization—yet one that seemed on the whole true of my visits to both black and white clubs—Ricky's comments reflect the existence of accepted norms of what constitutes 'black' behaviour in a particular situation. Any deviance from these norms is defined in opposition to them: to fail to behave appropriately is a slur on one's 'blackness'. The attitudes of Clive and Frank to black clubs incorporated this notion of 'black' norms, yet neither would accept that deviance from these denied or undermined their identity as 'black'. Both rather articulated the difference in 'class' terms; that black social events were associated with marginality, with negative images of 'community'. Clive thus told me he never attended blues dances, because those who go are 'roughnecks':

CL. Someone who hasn't got a job—which is wrong, because they might have a job: basically, my definition of a roughneck is someone as you would say hangs around street corners.
C. The stereotypical black youth, in other words?
CL. Yes, standing on a street corner with a tape recorder (Interview, 5 Mar. 1991).

It is interesting that Clive himself was aware that his perceptions of black social events were coloured strongly by stereotypes; what is more significant, however, is the way in which he used this stereotype as an identity marker against which to define himself. By setting up an image and then claiming his distinction from it—in this case in spatial, as well as ideological, terms—Clive was able to establish an alternative identity for himself, which was based on material and social success. It would be misleading, however, to regard this distinction as absolute; both Clive and Frank, as well as others in the group, were careful to stress their identification with the wider black 'community' when the occasion arose. For example, all the boys went often to houseparties, which were almost exclusively black, and although they usually socialized in a mainly white environment, the group itself was always entirely black.

The contextual and permeable nature of these distinctions can be seen clearly with Ricky. When I first began my fieldwork, Ricky's favourite social options were always closely associated with the City environment, which he had frequented since he was about 18. Edgar, for example, informed me that it was Ricky who had first introduced him to the West End bars and clubs, and it was in this environment that Ricky, Clive, and Frank had met Nathan and Arif. During the first few months of my fieldwork, I accompanied Ricky and Anne, his girlfriend, on many occasions to Corks, the Hippodrome, and Moonlighting. He told me then that he preferred the City to black clubs which were, he claimed, small, sweaty, and full of very aggressive black people, especially women. After Christmas, however, he began spending more time in the Inner City clubs and less time with the boys. He now told me that he was tired of running around looking for women and attempting to be the centre of attention; a view that was echoed at various times by others of the group, although few changes were made. Ricky explained:

I like this idea that there's not too much put on you; too much emphasis on you that you must be jumping around and showing that you're having a good time. Black people have a good time just standing up and drinking their drink and listening to the music. And that's how *I* feel. I enjoy that. Maybe it's a sign of getting old, but I enjoy that. And so do a lot of other black people (Interview, 9 June 1991).

It should be noted that when Ricky was frequenting the white winebars, he constructed an image of 'black' venues against which to define himself, and that this role was reversed when he returned to the black clubs. It is also significant that Ricky should choose to appeal to the image of 'community', of a collective black identity, in justifying his choice. Ricky's action caused some friction amongst members of the group, which prided itself on the unanimity of its interests and aspirations. This seeming unanimity had, however, begun to fragment during the time of my fieldwork, mainly because various members of the group were either settling down with their partners or were spending more time on their careers. These tensions were partially reflected in the social habits of the boys. For most of the others, Ricky's change could be attributed to his unwillingness to work and his frustrations with the lack of opportunities within white mainstream society; the return to black social environments was thus seen as symptomatic of personal failure. For Ricky, however, the change reflected a positive choice which was based upon a clear perception of his position in society; it was thus a reclamation of 'blackness' as a source of communal strength rather than weakness. This strength, ironically, made use of the same images as those used by Frank and Clive as a means of distinction; 'control' in this context arising from the knowledge of how to handle the situation as a 'black man'. Thus, Ricky explained:

There's ways to deal with things, right, and black guys know about this. F[rank] says 'I don't want to step on some guy's toe and him cut me up' and all that. I mean, the only one reason why one guy steps on another guy's toe and he cuts him up is because of the attitudes. . . . It's knowing the right attitudes, that's all it is. . . . Because if I walk around in Splash and there's this guy and I step on his toe, and I say 'Sorry, Boss', he'll say 'yeah, safe' (Interview, 9 June 1991).

For Ricky, social identity in this instance pivoted on the distinction between black and white social venues; 'black' thus became a collective and oppositional identity in which the individual was judged on his ability to operate within certain value systems. This can be contrasted with the attitudes of Frank and Clive, which were founded on distinctions which can be loosely described as 'class' issues. The primary site for opposition in this case was over internal definitions of 'blackness' as an individual, rather than collective, stance.

The lines for these divisions proved, however, to be highly flexible and were manipulated by all concerned. Thus, in a black club, the boys tended to adopt the standards of this environment and assumed a posture based upon a black collective identity; in a white club, this would fragment and provide the material for competition. Moreover, it was apparent that within a black social environment, such as the Inner City clubs, other lines of distinction also operated. Darnell, for example, distinguished between blues dances and clubs he would attend and those he would avoid as being 'too rough'; even within the former, he would define himself against the image of other black youth present. As was usual with Darnell—but also with my other informants, if less explicitly—a primary source of image definition was women. He told me of blues dances he had attended where the women were 'rough'; when I asked him to explain, he turned to an image of the 'raga girl':

It's the way she looks, right? If she's wearing little yardie boots, the silver ones with gold and red stars on it and . . . when they smile you can see the brilliance of gold and, not all the time, but they've usually got big earrings; some of the nice girls got big earrings, but you know, the big chunk of gold and they've got their head waxed, like when they oil it down and they've got little waves there; finger waves (Interview, 24 Mar. 1991).

This image was associated for Darnell with a particular lifestyle: 'She'd probably be sitting at home, smoking her weed all day and not working and just talk bad . . . and going to every man "yeah come here and boy, I've got two kids behind me already but I don't mind"' (ibid.). His attitude to these women, as differing from his own self-perception, was clear, 'I can't associate myself with them sort of people' (ibid.). It is interesting, however, that this distinction did not extend, at least in theory, to male acquaintances. This can probably be related to a general perception of black men as constituting a peer group, the core of collective identity, and of women as providing a measure of individual status.

A NOTE ON WOMEN

This chapter has been devoted almost entirely to men. This is not to deny the role of black women in the leisure sphere; it is true, however, that the public leisure arena remains one dominated by men and largely defined by them. There are some signs that this situation is changing; during the time of my fieldwork, I noticed increasing numbers of black women participating in the City leisure environments, while women are more generally assuming a far more active role in cultural and leisure expression. *The Voice* recently proclaimed the arrival of the 'raga girl' ('Raga girls are in town', 21 Apr. 1992) as a definable presence on the black social scene.

Amongst the women that I knew, however, the leisure practices seemed very distinct from those of the boys. They generally went out less than the men, and usually frequented only house-parties or some of the Inner City black clubs. These were considered safe and respectable leisure options. The women also did not form a definable and bounded social group on these excursions; they tended to go out either with family members or in small groups. They rarely attended black clubs with their partners, although they would go with them to more family-oriented events. Perhaps because women were considered less of a threat, the same forms of restrictions and exclusions that were exercised on the boys did not appear to apply. The emphasis seemed less on control as a social group and more on the maintenance of 'respect' for their position as black women. As an interesting corollary to the male view of black women as 'feisty', I was told by Sonya and Margaret on a visit to La Belles nightclub in East London, 'If someone asks you to dance, just say No!'

CONCLUSION

This chapter does not pretend to offer an exhaustive account of the leisure options and choices available to young black men. It can be seen, however, that rather than constituting a discrete and bounded sphere, marked by the preservation of an 'authentic' and homogeneous black expressive culture, the leisure sphere for many black youth comprises a fluid range of social options and individual choices. It represents neither the criminalized debauchery of popular myth, nor the inevitable political stance of opposition and hostility of most academic studies. The black leisure arena provides rather a gamut of environments and images amongst which the individual can move, allying himself to, distancing himself from, or re-creating these as he chooses. Although the images themselves appeared largely consistent amongst my informants, the position of each individual towards these images, and the meanings they attached to them, was neither consistent nor predictable, changing over time and according to context. The identities of black youth expressed in the public leisure sphere are dynamic, multi-faceted, and contested; it is in this dynamism that the strength of its relationship to black life and experience lies. Black leisure explores and expresses the tensions and continuities between the individual, the 'community', and society: more than this, it is an expression of both individual pleasure and collective joy.

5

Black Masculinity I
The Peer Group

In fact, what most people see when they look at the black
man is the myth.

(Michele Wallace 1990)

ABOUT six months into my fieldwork, Dion and Satish split up.
This event was not unusual nor unexpected; indeed, the couple
had already separated twice since my arrival in July 1990. In each
case the reason was the same: Satish's continual infidelity with
the numerous women he met while out with his friends. Satish
had moved in temporarily with Clive and his parents, waiting
for Dion to calm down and allow him to return to their house
and two children. One Saturday morning, Dion asked me to drive
her to Clive's house, so she could give Satish 'a present'. When
we arrived, she handed Satish the 'gift'—which turned out to be
a pair of his dirty socks and a used condom—telling him that,
since he preferred being with his friends, he could stay with
them permanently. Moreover, if he could have other lovers, so
could she—indeed, she already had. Satish's reaction was dramatic: he pulled Dion from my car and started ripping her clothes,
shouting that if she behaved like a whore, she should look like
one. Dion, in turn, was punching and kicking Satish, while Clive
and I looked on bemused. After about fifteen minutes, Dion and
I made our escape while Clive pinned down Satish in the back
of his car.

This episode, it transpired, was by no means unique in the
seven-year history of Dion and Satish's stormy relationship. Indeed, the past several years had been marked by Dion's occasional discovery of Satish's recurrent indiscretions, followed by
a major row, retribution, and final reconciliation. In the past,
Dion's revenge had always been dramatic: she had, she informed
me, cut up all Satish's clothes on several occasions, thrown all his

possessions on to the front lawn of their house, and once heaved his hi-fi system through the windscreen of his car. The present confrontation was, however, significant in focusing a number of attitudes surrounding questions of masculinity and gender roles which were a primary feature of the construction of the boys' identities, both as individuals and as a group.

Dion's stance threw into relief two seemingly opposed relationships: that of the individual to his male peers and that towards women. Satish's main 'problem' in Dion's eyes was the influence of the male peer group and his conformity to internal expectations regarding women in the public sphere. These were seen as opposed to, and incompatible with, the demands and responsibilities of long-term domestic relationships and family duty; an opinion often echoed by women involved with members of the group. Dion's demand was that Satish should make a choice, and that if he opted for his friends, they should assume a permanent responsibility in all spheres of life—including his dirty washing. Failing that, Dion demanded equal rights to act in the public arena. Satish's response was equally revealing. Dion, as 'his woman', was seen as an integral part of his individual status as a man, both within and outside the group; for her to be unfaithful to him thus became a source of personal shame and disrespect. More than this, it undermined his assumed control of her sexuality. This attitude reflects both the perceived difference in gender roles and expectations on the part of men, and a distinction between public and private spheres of action. In reality, of course, the two are closely connected, with actions in each affecting the other; moreover, gender roles alter within each arena. Dion's action on this occasion, unlike earlier and subsequent confrontations, challenged the perceived divisions between both gender roles and spheres of action, through the medium of sex. Her supposed infidelity transgressed the boundaries of private action and thus confronted Satish, as well as the other boys, with an inverted image of their own much-vaunted masculinity.

Dion's gesture, therefore, represented far more than an act of simple retribution; it questioned the whole issue of control and power, which was central to the group's existence, and its public stance towards women. The following chapters will consider these dual aspects of masculinity, focusing first on the male peer group, and secondly, on attitudes towards women. It is argued that these seemingly opposed foci are inextricably linked through issues of power which cannot be fully understood in isolation. Moreover, they are both concerned with wider constructions of gender and of social inequality. However, for the purposes of analysis, they will be considered separately: this chapter will examine the role of the male peer group, while attitudes to women will form the subject of the following chapter.

BLACK MACHO: MASCULINITY AND THE PEER GROUP

Very little has been written on issues of black masculinity in the British context. Although both Pryce (1967) and Cashmore (1979) remark on the significance of the male peer group in black youth culture, this remains very much an institution whose existence is assumed and significance unquestioned. Both place the peer group within the context of personal failure and frustration; a retreat to a collective identity—in each case, Rastafari—as a coping strategy in the face of racial rejection. For Pryce, the peer group is associated closely with the 'hustler' lifestyle, where older men act as role models for teenagers who are 'unemployed, homeless and in conflict with their parents' (1967: 35). Drawing upon the ascribed pathology of the black family, Cashmore similarly claims that the peer group constitutes the primary source of socialization for black youth; an alternative to their parents who 'provided only models of degradation and deprivation' (1979: 85). The black peer group thus constitutes a recoil from the forces of racism into a negative and hostile structure, which is oppositional in both form and intent. It also becomes inevitably associated with deviance and criminality (Lawrence 1982b).

The attitude of both Cashmore and Pryce towards black male peer groups can be seen to have its roots in traditional approaches to youth deviance. This places the peer group, black or white, within the context of social and psychological maladjustment (A. K. Cohen 1955), in which the individual turns to a male subculture in order to compensate for social rejection. This forms an autonomous entity which is defined by 'negative polarity' (ibid. 28) to the norms of wider society, and creates an alternative value system through which marginalized youth can create the illusion of status and power. Although later studies recognize that such groups are neither inevitably delinquent (Matza 1964; Downes 1966), nor necessarily opposed to social norms, it is this power inequality which remains the central feature of youth subcultural groups. Peter Wilmott notes in his study *Adolescent Boys of East London* that within the peer group, 'the adolescent boy can enjoy a freedom and equality he cannot find at school, at work or inside his family' (1966: 40). That the peer group constitutes a bid for power by marginalized groups lies at the centre of many studies of youth subculture; that this reach for control reinforces such marginality and re-creates the conditions for its existence has become something of a truism (Willis 1977, 1978; Hebdige 1979). Within this arena, black youth are seen as doubly disadvantaged—by race and by class position—and are perceived as inevitably 'contracultural' in their stance (Downes 1966: 229). The black peer group is thus seen more as a cathartic expression of frustrated power and social maladjustment than of positive action and control.

Although youth culture is seen as an exclusively male arena, few studies focus directly on the construction of masculinity. Paul Willis's studies of working-class youth culture are the main exceptions in this area, although even these do not fully consider the position of women in subcultural discourse. The general dearth of material on gender relations can perhaps be explained partly by the absence of work on and by women in this area, but also by the highly structured perception of social realities which marks out subcultural theory. Subcultural groups are usually regarded as internally homogeneous and positioned in direct opposition to an overarching hegemonic order which constitutes 'Society'. Hall and Jefferson note (1976) that subcultures are not placed in simple opposition and have relation to both 'Society' and the parent culture; in practice, however, these subcultures are viewed as autonomous entities locked in conflict with an omnipresent and static social structure, by which they are ultimately subordinated. The focus has thus been placed on 'class' struggle at the expense of the multiple layers of social structure, which enable subordinated groups—both male and female—to enter into conflict with each other as part of an ongoing search for control. It is at these levels, lower than that of the ubiquitous and undefined 'Society', that black masculinity is lived out and achieves significance.

The 'living out' of black male experience has been considered more fully in relation to African-American men. In *Tally's Corner* (1967), Elliot Liebow studies an all-male, 'street corner' society, which considers the role of the man as father, lover, husband, and breadwinner, rather than as 'social problem'. His study reveals the complexity and variation within these roles in relation to the individual, and in their relation to both women and other men. However, Liebow's emphasis throughout is on problem-solving; on the expression of powerlessness rather than control. He writes, 'Here, where the measure of man is considerably smaller, and where weaknesses are somehow turned upside down and almost magically transformed into strengths, he can be, once again, a man among men' (1967: 136). Exploitation, or power, becomes for Liebow a 'public fiction' within the street-corner context, an illusion distorted by the inevitability of personal failure. Liebow's study is of a world largely separated from wider society, denied its concerns, and set apart from its values and structures; a vision shared by Hannerz in his study of a black 'ghetto': 'The fact about the power of the ghetto . . . is that most ghetto dwellers neither have any nor are actively working to acquire any at present' (1969: 15). With a lifestyle characterized by sex, drinking, and women, the 'Street Corner Men' (ibid. 57) are seen as symptomatic of personal limitation and lack of control, the product and enactment of absolute powerlessness. Ronald Taylor thus argues:

A combination of contemporary social and economic factors conspire to limit the black male's access to status and economic resources. . . . The inability to function successfully in the male role . . . may be experienced as a loss in masculinity and social identity, which he may attempt to recoup by active involvement in the life of the streets (1977: 2).[1]

This pathologized approach to black masculinity has recently been challenged by Mitchell Duneier in *Slim's Table* (1992). Focusing on a small, loose collectivity of older black men in a Chicago diner, Duneier writes of the group affirmation of respectability,

---

[1] Similarly, David Schulz writes of the 'problem' of black masculinity as a direct extension of the 'problem' of the black family: 'The problem of the Negro lower-class family is . . . the absence of an *adequate* masculine role model *enabling adaptation* to the *values* of the larger culture' (1977: 10–11; emphasis in original). This leads to the retreat into street life, where masculine roles are exaggerated and played out in what Schulz terms a 'ritualised exorcism' (ibid. 15).

self-esteem, and communal identity which lies at the heart of working-class black masculinity:

They are consistently inner-directed and firm and they act with resolve; their images of self worth are not derived from material possessions or the approval of others; they are disciplined ascetics with respect for wisdom and experience; usually humble, they can be quiet, sincere and discreet, and they look for those qualities in their friends (1992: 163).

Duneier contrasts this with the public expressions of 'ghetto-specific masculinity' (ibid. 148) which characterize the younger black 'underclass'. He thus distinguishes between working-class 'maintainers' and the subcultural 'creators' of alternative status systems, such as drug dealers and gang leaders, who dominate the public arena (ibid. 131). While affirming the heterogeneity of black masculinity at an individual, private level, therefore, Duneier simultaneously rehearses and reinscribes the homogeneity of 'black macho' at a public, 'street level'. Like Liebow, Hannerz, and Anderson (1978) before him, he finally adheres to a view of expressive young black male identity as a form of status-inversion; the catharsis of ultimate male powerlessness.

There is little doubt that the concept of power is central to any discussion of black masculinity. Most studies have, however, regarded black masculinity as an *alternative* to social status, rather than as an *extension* of it. 'Black macho' has been portrayed, therefore, as differing in kind rather than degree from the wider gendered power relations within Society at large. Machismo becomes a symbol of, and substitute for, the lack of power, rather than constituting an aspect of that power. It has thus been seen as inauthentic and illusory; something apart from, and opposed to, the wider structures of Society. As bell hooks argues:

The portrait of black masculinity that emerges in this work perpetually constructs men as 'failures', who are psychologically 'fucked up', dangerous, violent sex maniacs whose insanity is informed by their inability to fulfill their phallocentric masculine destiny in a racist context (1992: 89).

It is, however, only within the context of wider power relations —and as an extension of them—that black masculinity can be fully understood. In *Black Macho and the Myth of the Superwoman*, Michelle Wallace argues that it is in the search for 'manliness', as defined by dominant white society, that the origins of 'black macho' are to be found. It thus constitutes, for Wallace, a 'façade of power' (1990: 199), which is concerned with the negotiation of personal control through interaction. This control is, however, taken as a prerequisite for the attainment of social and economic power: the assertion of masculinity constituting an expression of individual worth. Lynn Segal notes, 'The issue of "manliness" was thus crucial to the confrontation between white men and black' (1990: 188). Black masculinity can be seen, therefore, to reify white Western notions of masculinity in the search for wider social control and to incorporate these within its creation. Kobena Mercer writes:

There is a further contradiction, another turn of the screw of oppression, which occurs when Black men subjectively internalise and incorporate aspects of the dominant definitions of masculinity in order to contest the definitions of dependency and powerlessness which racism and racial oppression enforce (1988: 112).

However, rather than a static, autonomous, and essentialized ideology, with a direct relationship to action, constructions of masculinity should be viewed as both historically and synchronically contingent, inescapably intertwined with the expression and contestation of power. Michel Foucault writes in *The History of Sexuality*:

Sexuality ... appears rather as an especially dense transfer point for relations of power. ... Sexuality is not the most intractable element in power relations, but rather one of those endowed with the greatest instrumentality: useful for the greatest number of maneuvres and capable of serving as a point of support, as a lynchpin, for the most varied strategies (cited in Jones 1992: 95).

Black masculinity is then perhaps best understood as an articulated response to structural inequality, enacting and subverting dominant definitions of power and control, rather than substituting for them. Rather than a hostile and withdrawn entity, the black peer group can be seen as a base for interaction and negotiation with wider society. It forms a loose collectivity, which is internally neither homogeneous nor unified, and externally disparate in its intent and attitudes. The enactment of dominant norms and the restrictions of macro-structural constraints, however, render the lived expressions of black masculinity complex and often contradictory. Such tensions question the bounds of social constructions concerning 'race' and 'masculinity' and underline the fluidity of black male identity. As Segal notes: 'Black culture is also questioning the very notion of the "Black" subject .... In looking at the oppositional meanings inherent in Black masculinity today, the stress is on diversity' (1990: 203).

'ONE OF THE BOYS': CONTROL AND THE PEER GROUP

During my fieldwork, the constitution of my core group of informants proved remarkably diffuse. At times, it expanded to include men who were comparatively unknown to me; at others, it contracted to around four or five men that I knew well. My knowledge of the peer group was thus rather uneven, but reflected the dynamism and fluidity of the group as it was experienced by those it encompassed. Some general observations can be made, however.

First, the group was exclusively male; although women were sometimes present—as I myself was—at their meetings, they were never regarded as an integral part of the group. Far from being the 'honorary male', women tended to be 'carried with' the group more as an external adornment than an active participant. Secondly, the group was almost exclusively black; the notable exception being Satish, who is of Indian origin. Although he was generally accepted as part of the group, his ethnic origin was used frequently as a form of ridicule whenever tensions within the group arose. Thirdly, the peer group structure existed primarily in the public sphere. The boys were rarely together for any length of time within their home environments—although each knew the others' families—and usually gathered together only as a prelude to going out. Moreover, private knowledge between some members of the group was surprisingly slight; for example, when questioned, Ricky was unable to tell me Nathan's age or employment circumstances. Lack of knowledge of other spheres of life was relatively common, although this is not to deny the existence of close friendships between individual members of the group.

The core group, defined by Ricky and confirmed by others I asked, consisted of Ricky, Frank, Clive, Satish, Nathan, and Arif; it had formerly included Ricky's brother, Mike, and Shane, who was intermittently part of the group but had moved away the year before to pursue other interests. Its boundaries often expanded to include others such as Malcolm or Edgar, and more rarely to include occasional members, such as Ricky's cousin, Kevin, or Nathan's brother, Philip. The core group remained, however, relatively constant, although it did begin to fragment towards the end of my fieldwork for reasons which will be considered later.

The boys were, Ricky assured me, 'a unique group' (Interview, 9 Dec. 1990). In reality, however, this proved more a matter of self-perception than fact. Each of the core members moved outside the boundaries to form parts of other groups, perhaps with a degree of overlap in membership; these interacted with the other groups only sporadically. Clive, for example, formed part of a sound system, of which Malcolm was a member: although the other boys knew this group, they met only rarely at dances and parties, and were never included en masse within the structures of the boys' group. Clive also spent an increasing amount of time with some of the men from work, whom he introduced rather selectively to his other friends. Frank had a number of friends from the period of his return to England, with whom he spent time; Satish had a circle of rather dubious acquaintances from his days as car thief and amateur fence; while Shane, as mentioned earlier, had moved away from the boys towards a group of musicians, whom he considered more in keeping with his future plans. Although these other groups were not considered threatening to the structure of the original group, in the way that relationships with women often were, they were often a site for role tensions. Each group was seen to appeal to a different facet of the individual's identity, of which the other groups had only limited knowledge. Ricky explained of his other friendships:

They weren't part of the group really; basically they were my friends, but they just find it hard to like deal with C[live] and N[athan] and all that. Because them sort of guys, they feel rejected by guys like C[live] and N[athan]. They feel like someone's taking the piss out of them ... there's a lot of frictions basically (ibid.).

It is interesting to compare the boys' 'unique' group with Darnell's peer group. He told me: 'Like, a lot of people from round my area, about six or seven of them, we go round, and then you get like fractions; like this friend knows that friend. Then it's a lot of people' (Interview, 24 Mar. 1991). Darnell, it should be noted, is younger than the boys; his circle of acquaintances stemmed mainly from school and the locale, whereas the boys' friendships—with the exception of Clive and Ricky—were established after this period and tended to be more diffuse. Even so, Darnell's friends had decreased in number since leaving school and had become more tightly focused around shared ambitions and interests. He explained:

When you are at school, you mix with all of them, but now they've gone their ways; some of them moved out of the area and like there's only a few of them left still. So you mix with less and less people . . . when you were at school, there was about forty people walking around same way (ibid.).

His closest friends were those he 'raved' with, and, like Ricky, he admitted to some tensions between this group and those with which it overlapped. Darnell thus told me of one friend, Owen:

I see less and less of him everyday; he's strange. He raves, but he doesn't rave with *us*. He raves with his *other* friends. He might not like the people we go with: because if you like smoke weed 'Oh my God, you're bad', but with us, we don't mind what the people are really, as long as it's a good party. But if he doesn't like the look of the people, he doesn't want to go there (ibid.).

The 'uniqueness' of the boys lay, therefore, not so much in the closed structure of the group, nor its particularity within black youth culture, as its self-perceived cohesion. That is, it was not the group itself which was unique or unusual, but the singularity of its defining ethos—at least in its own terms.

It is this ethos, an internal perception of what the group stood for to its members, which was the main source for membership. As mentioned above, the group was not particularly distinguished by its history: although Clive and Ricky had known each other for about eight years, other relationships were more newly formed. Frank met Mike, Ricky's brother, about four years previously while they were both working in Pizza Hut; Arif and Nathan were introduced in a City winebar only about two years before. Other, older acquaintances, such as Edgar, had more recently moved away from the group and defined themselves against it.

The boundaries of the group were thus perceived as relatively open to new members—male, of course, and generally excluding Asians and whites. These exclusions were articulated not on 'racial' grounds—indeed, most of the boys were keen to assert the existence of white friends—but on the grounds of 'cultural difference'. White men, I was told, do not share the same interests and expectations as black men. Malcolm told me:

I've got some [white friends], but not that many. I don't rave with them. . . . They're not so close; not close at all. I'm not racist, but the white ones, they've got their ways; they go to the pub a lot, and I'm not into it. I'm not someone [who] says 'let's go and have a pint', do you understand me? That's the reason why (Interview, 12 May 1991).

On closer questioning, it transpired that the boys had very few non-black friends, and that these were regarded more as distant acquaintances. The boys were concerned, however, not to be seen as 'racist', and, more importantly, not to be seen as having an inability to deal with white people. Clive, who socialized occasionally with people from work, told me:

Basically, what I gather is that they don't have any black friends, so I'm a bit of a novelty. . . . It can be to your advantage, it can also be to your detriment as well. Sometimes you get all the old jokes 'you shouldn't be doing that, you should be cleaning', or 'you should be nicking videos or car stereos'. As I say, I'm thick-skinned, it's no problem. . . . I can go somewhere where I'm the only black guy in there and that's alright (Interview, 16 Apr. 1991).

During my fieldwork, on only one occasion did the boys take a white man out with them—Danny, a friend of Satish's. The boys explained that because Danny had grown up with mainly black people he was able to relate to them and understand them in a way most white people could not. That power was a consideration in his inclusion was also obvious. Danny was accepted because in any confrontation he could be relied upon to take the part of the black group against any white men. In the fight in Hombres, he did so; he was thus dissociated from the power dynamic of most interactions with white men. Moreover, because Danny was short, round, and considered by most to be both quite stupid and slightly unstable, he was regarded as no threat to the image of the group or to its control.

Most of the boys defined the internal cohesion of the group in terms of shared expectations and ambitions. In theory at least, anyone who was male and black and shared these ambitions could become part of the group. Ricky explained:

To keep up with the pack is exactly what it takes to go out with that lot. . . . It's almost like a pack of wolves running, and if you can't keep up, you're not part of the group. You know, keep up with the wildness, chasing girls, everything (Interview, 9 Dec. 1990).

Ricky's metaphor is apt in a number of ways: first, it captures the overtly masculine nature of the group; secondly, it reveals the dynamic way in which the group functioned. The group itself only functioned *as* a group in relation to others; it thus incorporated movement and interaction within its very boundaries. When this external stimulation was not present, the group became much looser and more internally divided and competitive. The metaphor also encapsulates the notion of control, of power, which dominated the group in its external encounters; how this was inscribed by the group is hinted at in his last sentence, 'the wildness, chasing girls, everything'. This element was echoed by Frank, who defined the qualities of the group as:

Personality. To do something that—to stick out among a crowd, not to blend in with the crowd; to be different. Just to show themselves as being themselves, not to be affected by what society says, or basically doesn't give a fuck. . . . Most of them are loud people; they're party people, they're the kind of people who make the atmosphere totally different; people walking up to their house would go 'wow, what have I been missing?' Those kind of people (Interview, 5 Apr. 1991).

To a large extent, therefore, the internal cohesion of the group relied on the ability to elicit external responses; the relationships amongst the boys were primarily based upon external stimuli rather than internal, personal knowledge. When I asked Frank what had formed the core group from the much larger crowd in which they had previously moved, he told me:

There were more then, but out of that more there was always that same group that would always be together. . . . I would say we were the liked. They all wanted to be with us, because they liked the way we moved; they copied what we did. If we wanted to do this, do that, they always wanted to know what we were doing, how we were doing it (ibid.).

For Frank, the ability to elicit these responses, this control, was a reflection of personal attributes, notably in relation to wider society: 'At the end of the day, I always knew what I was looking for; always knew what I wanted; always knew how to have a good time; always knew the kind of environment I liked to be in and didn't like to be in' (ibid.).

These personal ambitions were, in turn, translated into and reflected by the ability to 'perform' within a given social setting. To be able to control external responses in a social environment became a measure of one's ability to assert control in other spheres. In this, the values expressed by the peer group were a translation and transformation of wider societal values rather than the creation of an alternative; they were not 'contracultural' but rather an extension of wider social concerns and status judgements. For the boys, the ability to 'perform' was focused very much in the attraction of women: this was seen as asserting control as much over the other men present—black or white—as over the women themselves. Closely associated with this attraction was the presentation of external image, including the ability to dance, styles of dress, and the ability to communicate verbally. This latter ability, which Ricky termed 'the gift of the gab' (Interview, 9 Dec. 1990), was perhaps most central to this image, and the most closely connected to the wider issues of power, both within and outside the group.[2] Also of crucial importance in the reach for control was the ability to assert physical control, should the need arise.

Membership of the peer group was thus grounded in an ability to conform to certain internal expectations and perform to an external audience. Such abilities were not, however, unproblematic in their execution. Ricky explained:

It depends; if you're no good with women, but you can fight, you're part of the group; if you're good with women, but you can't fight, you're still part of the group. It works that way, but it's better if you can do both (Interview, 9 Dec. 1990).

In practice, the group proved rather uneven in its application of these standards. Arif, it was generally acknowledged by the others, was neither good with women, nor reliable in the event of any confrontation. He was included in the group primarily because of his association with Nathan. Nevertheless, Arif was accorded full status within the group, despite many personal

---

[2] Cf. Edith Folb, 'Words . . . are tools for power and gain' (1980: 90).

animosities and misgivings by the others. Of primary importance in these decisions was the maintenance of at least the appearance of external unity. Clive told me: 'As long as they show the same values whilst in the company. . . . Whether they've got it or not—as long as they can show it' (Interview, 16 Apr. 1991).

THE INTERNAL DYNAMIC

Within this often impressive display of external unity, the reality of the boys' peer group was far from harmonious and uniform. Although there was no status hierarchy within the group, and no developed sense of personal competition—at least where the internal group norms were concerned—there existed a number of latent divisions and private hostilities which were manifest within the private arena. This 'backstage' could occur either within the domestic sphere or during an evening out, if no external audience was present. I never witnessed any conflict within the group when it was performing to an audience. The internal dynamic of the group was, however, revealing of the personal attitudes towards status and control, and towards the peer group itself.

On the whole, the enactment of personal hostilities remained very much at a verbal level; it was rarely translated into action. On only one occasion did a fight occur: this was between Frank and Satish over the use of the telephone in Ricky's flat, which I shared. Frank, who had long thought of Satish as ill-mannered and manipulative, accused Satish of exploiting our goodwill; while Satish, who thought of Frank as arrogant and bossy, accused him of interfering in his private business. In the row that ensued, the long history of this antagonism was replayed, with Frank finally threatening to hit Satish. The fight was prevented through Ricky's intervention, and Frank left. The others present, Ricky, Malcolm, and Clive, merely shrugged and told me that Satish was renowned for provoking Frank's infamous temper, and that it would all be forgotten within days—which it was. More generally, the boys were loath to admit openly to any private dislikes or conflict with their friends. They would, however, point out tensions between other members of the group. Moreover, as I lived with the boys for twelve months, it became possible to observe these tensions as they were enacted, both privately and within the group setting.

Personal tensions were both played out and assuaged through the constant verbal interplay which marked out any interaction within the group. This was focused primarily on the physical defects of the individual, which became the constant markers for ritualized insult. In her study of African-American teenagers, Folb has argued that 'These verbal games expose the points of genuine tension, anger, hostility and self-deprecation . . . experienced by young people in this society' (1980: 32).

Amongst the boys, however, these interactions were directed primarily at the individual rather than pointing to wider concerns and tended not to focus upon matters of personal social status. The main exception to this was the ridicule of the individual's girlfriend or partner, in which the man usually joined with some enthusiasm: the overall effect was thus more cathartic than injurious. Meetings of the group were characterized by references to Frank's receding hairline, Clive's mouth and weak chin, the gap in Nathan's front teeth, Arif's lack of height, Ricky's skinny legs, and so on. The focus moved from one individual to another, with the rest of the group uniting against the man under attack. Ricky commented:

That's how they normally do it, they switch from one to the other; it's either they might start on C[live] and they go on to S[atish] and they go on to A[rif], you know, then they might take the piss out of F[rank]'s forehead. They look for something they can say, 'yes, that's a fault in that person' and then they won't leave it alone (Interview, 9 Dec. 1990).

These insults also served to denote the core group at specific moments, although the content of this core remained quite fluid. More occasional members of the group, such as Malcolm and Satish, thus came under more intense, if not more hostile, fire. Malcolm was targeted mainly because the others considered him effeminate and Satish because of his ethnic origin and his lack of control over Dion. Ricky told me:

It's like M[alcolm], even though he's part of the group, it's like one person takes the piss out of him, then everyone does. . . . He finds the guys a joke, but then again, as soon as he hears N[athan]'s name, he knows that he's in for a *hard* day (ibid.).

Both Satish and Malcolm were especially valued within the group for their role as stooge. Resistance to this role by any of the boys was almost impossible to achieve; indeed, negative reactions tended merely to make the insults even more intense. Ricky told me that the ability to take the jokes was part of being in the group. Individual control could be asserted only by shifting the focus onto someone else.

The in-group joking thus functioned as a boundary marker, serving to include members and exclude outsiders, although these categories tended to shift according to context and the constitution of the core group at any given moment. Nathan, for example, was hostile to Malcolm and to Frank; Frank and Satish were often antagonistic; almost all the boys, except Ricky, despised Shane. These members were thus open to more intensive group ridicule at particular moments and personal antagonisms were more openly displayed when these parties were together. Such personal tensions did not preclude, however, the smooth functioning of the group. As Shane constantly made clear, although he disliked most of the boys intensely on a personal level, considering them 'hypocrites' (Interview, 5 Apr. 1991), this did not prevent him being part of the group. He told me, 'They amuse me when I want to be amused; they're there for me to have a laugh if I want to have a laugh: that's it' (ibid.). Shane's view of the group was thus primarily functional and expressed its externally-directed purpose: 'We like going out, dancing, talking to girls sometimes: but you know that's not really the thing I have in common with them, it's the thing I do when I'm with them. . . . I'm with the crowd' (ibid.).

The perceived functionality of the collective marked out most responses to the peer group. All the boys denied that they would go to their friends if they had personal problems; all articulated their relationship primarily in terms of external forces. Frank assured me that this was very much a gender difference:

Men are not like women. Women come home and go to their friends— 'I missed my period': men don't talk like that. Obviously they don't have their period, but a man won't come and go 'F[rank], there's something wrong downstairs'. A man won't say that—we just talk about normal things (Interview, 5 Apr. 1991).

As mentioned earlier, private, personal knowledge of other members of the group was often very slight. Liebow notes in *Tally's Corner* that 'Friendship thus appears as a relationship between two people who, in an important sense, stand unrevealed to one another' (1967: 206). Amongst the boys, however, this private knowledge was considered largely irrelevant; what was of significance was the social function of the group. This is not to deny that within the group some close friendships did exist at the personal level; however, these were not the foundation of the group's existence.

Darnell, for example, explained of his friends: 'We are all after the same things when we go out together. Check women and all that . . . we all like the same sort of music, we all like rare groove and a bit of reggae' (Interview, 24 Mar. 1991). Although Darnell was very close to one friend, Richard—'My mum says, "if D[arnell] tells you a lie in Harlesden, and you go round towards Willesden and ask R[ichard] the same thing, he'll tell you the same lie"' (ibid.)—this friendship was expressed in terms of mutual interest rather than personal, private support. Darnell told me: 'You don't talk to the guys about your problems. Because they just go "forget them, man, come on, let's check a next one [girl]"' (ibid.).

Unlike Liebow's assumption that without private knowledge such relationships 'do not stand up well to the stress of crisis and conflict of interest' (ibid. 180), the group's relationships were primarily turned outwards and oppositional in their formation. They functioned, therefore, largely autonomously from personal relationships and in response to external forces. This partly accounts for the fluidity of group boundaries, which worked to include and exclude as occasion demanded. Thus, when Ricky got into a fight at Hombres, the other boys present were immediately there to assist him: on this occasion the boundaries of the group expanded to include Danny. Depending on the nature of the oppositional force, the boundaries would also expand to incorporate other groups or be incorporated. On one occasion, the boys were called upon to help exact retribution on a group of white youths who had attacked a black acquaintance of theirs. Ricky immediately assembled as many of the boys as he could find, who left to seek out the offenders; this time as part of a much larger body of people. Of course, the oppositional nature of the group did not necessitate conflict; the boys would unite as strongly to assist the others in attracting women as in fighting. It should be noted that 'oppositional' in this context refers to a relational position rather than a hostile and absolute distinction.

The group functioned, therefore, mainly in the public arena, and internal interaction remained largely between generally perceived public persona. This can be compared to the 'drop-in' area at the Community Centre, where public interaction was clearly distinguished from private knowledge and was symbolized by the use of public names, such as Ticker, Yardie, or Tyson. These were rarely applied to women, who were seen as part of the domestic, private sphere. Amongst the boys, each had an internally ascribed role, which was enacted whenever an audience was present. Clive, for example, was seen as the loud, extrovert member of the group, who could always be relied upon to break the ice in any encounter. As Ricky told me:

C[live] has no conscience; he will go with any group of girls, or anything like that, and if I wanted C[live] to go and chat with a group of girls, I'd say 'C[live] let's go over there' and C[live] would go over there and he breaks the ice and then I move in, and N[athan] and A[rif]—the rest of the vultures move in (Interview, 9 Dec. 1990).

Nathan was seen as the aggressive member of the group; Frank as the intellectual and pacifier, the 'father figure'; Satish as being good with women. Ricky was generally accepted by the others as most personifying the desired qualities of the public role—attractive, a good dancer, a strong fighter, and, until he met Anne, something of a womanizer. It is significant that this role had little to do with what the other members of the group thought of Ricky's abilities in the private arena, where most considered him unemployable, lazy, and exploitative. Moreover, the public persona had little to do with what the boys were like in one-to-one private interaction, where most were quiet, serious, and reflective. The public roles were to some extent interchangeable: on the boys' nights out, each member of the group acted at different times both as a spur to, and a constraint upon, the group's excesses. Each reflected, however, a different aspect of the group's personality and enacted its norms.

The norms and internal mores of the group were inculcated and relived whenever the boys met. This mainly took the form of what may be described as an internal mythology, composed of stories surrounding the notable successes and failures of the group. After most evenings out, the events of the night were retold, discussed, and placed in an overall group context; notable happenings then became part of an 'imagined' history, which was often recounted at these sessions. Through stories of victorious fights, successful liaisons with women, triumphs over hostile police encounters, the boys celebrated and reasserted their control of their immediate environment. They also relived notorious failures, such as the time Nathan was turned down by women in a club five times in a row, or the time he split his jeans while busting splits in a dance-off; the time Shane was beaten up in a club for chatting up someone's girlfriend; the time Frank and Mike (Ricky's brother) picked up two especially unattractive Italian girls, and Mike leapt off the bus to avoid being seen with them. These latter stories served to remind the group of the situations which were to be avoided, and encapsulated by their denial the norms they sought to uphold.

The peer group is thus perhaps best understood as a collection of individuals joined internally by a set of assumed shared values and welded in opposition to external forces. Although within the group, divisions and personality clashes did occur, these were largely irrelevant in the enactment of a common aim; that is, control over the public sphere. This was achieved largely through the creation of a public image focused around dance, dress, and the attraction of women. Although this image has been traditionally understood as an alternative status system (Liebow 1967; Folb 1980), it can also be seen as the extension of mainstream concerns; a means of actively engaging in, rather than opposing, traditional criteria of power and success.

EXTERNAL INTERACTION

'The boys' can thus be seen primarily as an interactive force, achieving significance only in opposition to other groups. The means of interaction was not, however, uniform. It should be noted that, since it functioned only in the leisure arena, the main groups it faced were of similar age; it rarely confronted either older people or figures of authority, except occasionally the police. Amongst its contemporaries, group action differed according to both gender and 'racial' origin; it also altered according to the environment and, indeed, the constitution of the group and its dominant mood at any given time. The interaction with women, at both a group and individual level, will be considered later; it should be noted, however, that attitudes to women were an integral part of control in a wider sphere and were therefore partially reflected in the attitudes towards other men.

As mentioned in the previous chapter, black social events were usually marked by a lack of overt competition and the assertion of communal solidarity. The boys' actions within these contexts were normally characterized by almost a lack of interaction. The boundaries of the group became much less clearly defined and more fluid, and its members functioned more as a set of individuals than a bounded collectivity. They were less likely to roam the venue, or seek to dominate, as they did in other environments, generally preferring to stand, drink, and occasionally dance a little.

Reactions to other black groups within a predominantly white environment proved more ambiguous. On the one hand, the boys were reluctant to 'run' other black groups, and there was rarely any sense of conflict. In many places the boys frequented, they recognized and acknowledged other black men, and often entered into friendly exchanges with groups they encountered on the street. On one occasion, we met a group of young black men who were on their first excursion in the City. The boys approached and surrounded the youths, who looked only about 19 years old and seemed intimidated, but the banter remained amicable and almost protective, rather than confrontational. They discussed places to go, commented on the clothes the youths were wearing and generally behaved as city-wise mentors. A similar approach was adopted with the many black men they encountered walking through the West End, notably around the Leicester Square area. Talk was of parties, new venues, and encounters the other groups had had with the police or white groups. This exchange of information was, of course, only between men—women were generally excluded. As one black woman I met in such an encounter commented, when we were both ignored, 'Girl, that's what you get for hanging around with niggers.' Among the black men frequenting the West End, then, there existed some feeling of solidarity. Ricky told me:

You tend to see that you don't go and start trouble with your own blacks, basically because you're black yourself. . . . I mean, black people are in enough trouble as it is—so you don't start on your own black person (Interview, 9 Dec. 1990).

On the other hand, black men were seen as the first targets of competition. The boys would always measure themselves against other black men in terms of dress sense, dancing ability, and general presence; they would then seek either to ally themselves with the competition, or—more often—to annihilate it, usually through dancing. This can perhaps be best understood as a struggle for control of the stereotypical symbols of 'black' style, which were the main source of status within these environments. The major concern, therefore, centred around issues of control; on the boys' continued ability to 'run' a place and make their presence felt. If they were ever defeated or felt a loss of control, the group would not return to the site for many weeks or perhaps ever. It is revealing that the boys tended to avoid venues that attracted a large black presence. Such a presence was articulated as a sign of decay, yet should perhaps be placed within the context of increased pressure to compete and a corresponding loss of assured control.

The main source of confrontation within these environments was, inevitably, white men. Although, on the occasions I was with the group, there was rarely any trouble, the boys did generally behave provocatively towards white men, and in the past there had been a number of fights. Interaction was not, however, necessarily confrontational. On many occasions, the boys would engage white men in friendly, if challenging, banter and draw upon their shared experience as London youth, City employees, East Londoners to assuage any conflict. Such encounters were, however, almost always competitive. One of the favourite themes for 'discussion' was, inevitably, penis size and sexual competence. In these, the boys retreated to a racial characterization and focused upon women as the basis for their control. The white men they challenged were then forced to compete for this control, yet from a shared overtly masculine stance. In the absence of other groups, this sexual competition was continued within the group, though in a less provocative manner.

That such provocation was intentional and instrumental is undoubted. Ricky told me, 'You go out to have fun and cause trouble, that's basically it. . . . It's a way of releasing tension'

(Interview, 9 Dec. 1990). Rather than directly starting fights, the boys would act in such a way as to provoke a response and then act upon this response. They thus exerted dual control: first, in provoking action on the part of the white men and, secondly, through physical strength. The initial manipulation of response was a crucial part of this activity and did not necessarily need the physical element to prove satisfactory. Ricky explained:

You start trouble with the white guys. . . . C[live] would be over there like a shot, telling them that they're motherfuckers and everything else. It's that sort of thing. Or you can see a guy with a drink and say 'Oh, thanks mate' and you start drinking it. It depends how the white guys see it; we don't go and pick trouble with white guys because you say 'yes, pick some trouble with some white guys'; we have a laugh with them, and if they take it seriously, *then* you fight them; that's the way it works (ibid.).

It is significant that 'having a laugh' always meant provocation by the boys directed towards someone else. On the occasions I was with them, I never saw them allow this initiative to be taken by others and directed towards them. The need for external stimuli meant, however, that the group was always open to outsiders and to constant interaction. Both within and between social venues, therefore, the boys were constantly drawing others within their boundaries. This often occurred within the context of the street. As the boys moved between winebars and clubs, they would often stop other groups, male or female or mixed, and engage them in conversation, which usually remained friendly. On other occasions, however, the boys would rely on their size and perceived racial stereotypes to challenge people they met directly; this challenge was exclusively directed at other men, but would often use women to achieve this. As Ricky explained to me:

Say we're like walking down the street, there might be a girl and a guy walking; you touch the girl and you don't care that she's walking with her husband or boyfriend. You don't care, you just did it, just for a laugh (Interview, 9 Dec. 1990).

In these encounters, which took place exclusively in the predominantly white environment of 'the City', the boys often articulated 'race' as a primary marker of the group's self-definition. This was used to exclude other groups which were then set up in opposition, so that the limits of control could be tested. However, 'race' was not the sole factor shaping the group's existence; indeed, the peer group was often posited upon general perceptions of common background or aspirations, gender roles, or socio-economic factors. The significance of 'race' was most obviously elided in confrontation with other black groups in the City, where 'race' was a unifying factor and difference was created and maintained using alternative symbols. Ironically, however, competition between these groups focused upon ownership of symbols in which 'race' and 'masculinity' have become indistinguishable (Gilroy 1993: 7). 'Control' in these situations thus carried with it the implication of wider power relations in which 'race' was an integral factor.

It is interesting to compare the boys' behaviour in the West End with that of Darnell and his friends, who functioned almost exclusively in predominantly black environments. Like the boys, Darnell's group encompassed a fairly fluid membership, but, unlike the boys, it constituted at its largest a community-based grouping. The boys were, by contrast, a geographically dispersed entity which was formulated only within the public social arena, rather than related to any latent sense of 'community'. On the level of everyday interaction, Darnell's group tended to be inclusive rather than exclusive and was not inclined towards the confrontation and competition which marked out many of the boys' encounters. It thus became more like Liebow's 'personal community' (1967: 162), in which a network of acquaintances forms a locus for personal action rather than group interaction; an expression of community rather than control. This inclusive personal network, indeed, exempted the individual from the need to exert control within particular situations. Darnell told me of one night when, returning from a friend's house, he was confronted by a group of black youths. He continued:

I saw all of them and like, you know, they was all reaching for their knife and whatever, and I walked up close to them and goes 'yeah, so what you load going to do?' And I knew about five of them anyway. And they goes 'oh, we didn't realize it was you, you know'. And I go 'if you didn't recognize me, what would happen?'; 'Don't worry, man, we would have stopped' (Interview, 24 Mar. 1991).

Because Darnell knew members of the group, who formed part of his extended 'personal community', neither side felt the need to enact a display of power. The boundaries of the group dissolved and enabled Darnell to form part of it, if only temporarily.

Similarly, the extended peer group was crucial as a source of community identity and security; in this role, it functioned in opposition to other groups. Darnell told me of one occasion when his group, consisting of about forty youths from Harlesden, went to a park near Wormwood Scrubs, where one was attacked by some other youths for talking to a girl. He told me:

So next Sunday, there's about 100 people. . . . Can you imagine it, two guys and about 100 people running after them . . . and they were hitting them and they was getting kick up and bruck [sic] up some ways. . . . It was bad, bad (ibid.).

It seems likely that the extended base of Darnell's peer group was more a matter of context than essential difference. Were his friends to function outside a black environment, the group would almost certainly become more tightly bounded. This, indeed, was the case even in unfamiliar black environments, as Darnell explained:

If you was out in the sticks, right—in some club in the country, like Birmingham—then you'd all go round like bad men. And then when people look at you and they want to say something to you; when they know you're from Harlesden, then they won't say nothing to you (ibid.).

It is significant that Darnell should choose a geographically-based group identity amongst other black groups: this can be contrasted with the primary definition of the boys' group as 'black' within a white environment.

It would be misleading, however, to see Darnell's group as entirely free from the search for control. Although, unlike the boys, they did not compete overtly with other men, the group was formulated primarily as a force for social interaction. The focus for this interaction was not, however, other male groups—black or white—but women. The group's structures, in a predominantly black context at least, thus tended to include men and define themselves against women; 'Gender' not 'Race' became the primary basis for identification. Within a mainly white environment, the boundaries of definition and self-definition proved more complex, incorporating 'racial' as well as gender considerations.

CONCLUSION

The male peer group should thus be seen neither as a naturally formed and harmonious entity, nor as a defensive enclave in which the inadequacies of the group in wider society are turned inwards both to compensate for and consolidate these short-comings. For the boys, the peer group formed a basis for inter-action with wider society at street level and enacted issues of control and status within this arena. It was a loosely-based collectivity, whose boundaries were fluid, and internal relations complex. This enabled the boys to interact with different social groupings at street level in an attempt to empower themselves. Its operation was thus oppositional and relational, altering its definition according to context. Within a predominantly black environment, the peer group could expand to provide a 'community' stance, or contract to two or three men in interaction with women. Within a mainly white environment, these boundaries became more rigid in their opposition to other men, and more antagonistic.

Inter-group competition is then a primary force in the enactment and subversion of power relations; images of 'masculinity' in this arena constituting the yardstick by which success is measured. 'Race' in these encounters becomes a symbol denoting group boundaries. It is employed in relation to other groups, usually, but not exclusively, as a means of opposition. 'Race' is not, however, a sufficient or necessary basis for peer group formation: its meaning may alter according to the situation or be cross-cut by other considerations, such as those based on gender or class constructions.

6

Black Masculinity II
Attitudes to Women

> I love white women too. But as long as white men are talk-
> ing about niggers, I ain't walking out with any white girl.
>
> (Mike Tyson, *The Voice*, 4 Dec. 1990)

IN an article in *The Sunday Times* (24 May 1992), on the increasing
number of black women dating white men, a black female TV
producer is quoted as saying:

Black men are in the main still very chauvinistic and women of my
generation don't want that. . . . We have somehow outgrown the black
men of our age. Putting it crudely, for whatever reason, there just aren't
that many middle-class black men around. They just don't want to marry
bus drivers.

The author, Dona Kogbara, concurs: 'Black girls I know are
abandoning ship with a vengeance because they say their black
brethren are more chauvinistic, more unfaithful and less success-
oriented' (ibid.).

Although this chapter is concerned less with black women
directly than with attitudes expressed towards gender relations
by men, the article quoted above is significant in focusing a number of issues. First, black men are portrayed homogeneously and
unproblematically as more 'chauvinistic' and less faithful than
white men, as if this were a 'natural' or inherent cultural quality.
Secondly, it is assumed that black men are less successful than
black women and are therefore without the relevant status attributes required to maintain what is viewed as a hypogamous
relationship. Thirdly, dating white men is interpreted in two ways:
as a 'breaking free' from the control that black men have
wielded—mainly hypocritically—over black women for decades;
but also as the transgression of group loyalties, a betrayal of the
race. This latter attitude is expressed in the above article by Paul

King, a City accountant: 'For black women to turn around and willingly give white men what they used to forcibly grab [*sic*] without permission is like rubbing salt into a centuries-old wound' (ibid.).

Black women are here perceived as the core of black society: to date white men is seen to be a betrayal of the collectivity in the way that black male–white female dating is not. Central to this issue is the question of control. Black men are concerned with losing control of 'their' women; black women with assuming control of their own sexuality. That the issue of interracial dating is of intense concern to the black community is apparent from the long-running correspondence and series of articles in *The Voice* in recent years, while it recently formed the focus of a series of debates on Channel 4 in 1993 called 'Doing it with you . . . is Taboo'. It is significant that social status is seen as a primary legitimation for such unions or for a denial of this legitimacy. Kogbara writes:

If you go out with a nice white window cleaner, you are really slapping black men in the face for preferring 'white trash'. But if you opt for a white man who is Somebody, you are allying yourself with a descendant of supremacist forces that colonised, enslaved and raped us (ibid.).

What black female–white male dating confronts, therefore, is the issue of power. More than this, it throws into question the relationship of power at the level of social structure and at the private, domestic level. Put simply, the control of black women in the domestic sphere can be best understood within the context of power relations with wider social forces.

The use of women in the enactment of male power relations has long been recognized. Cynthia Enloe notes in her essay 'Nationalism and Masculinity' (1989) that women have been co-opted into nationalist struggle both as symbols of cultural continuity and solidarity, and of external colonial possession. The ability to control and exploit another group's women is seen as the ultimate expression of power. Thus, Enloe writes: 'for a man, to be conquered is to have his women turned into fodder for imperialist postcards. Becoming a nationalist requires a man to resist the foreigner's use and abuse of his women' (1989: 44).

Within the context of external power relations, women are objectified as possessions, culture-bearers, reproducers; they are thus both the most valuable and the most vulnerable of a group's assets (ibid. 54). To a large extent, these struggles have ignored or repressed women's voices in the interest of internal unity, or in the search for external possession and control (Wallace 1990). For black men, black female–white male relationships are seen as a weakening of their cause, a loss of their internal control and thus of their ability to negotiate external power. These threats were often articulated by the men I knew as a form of impurity; as a dilution of the blood of the 'race'.

The interaction between 'Race' and 'Gender' categories has proved perhaps one of the most hotly contested and controversial issues within the black communities, both in Britain and America. The Anita Hill–Clarence Thomas hearings, the Tyson rape trial, the censorship controversy over the cultural misogyny of the Two Live Crew, or, indeed, of the ragga lyrics of Shabba Ranks and Buju Banton, have clearly focused popular attention on a perceived gender crisis of black cultural life. In a recent article in *Ms* Magazine, Marcia Ann Gillespie argues:

we are equally aware of the fact that for the good of the race, we women have routinely been expected to put our men first, no matter what. But many of us are also painfully conscious of the way that the misogyny in our community is often both heightened and disguised under the banner of racial consciousness (Jan./Feb. 1993).

'Race' is thus privileged as the primary signifier of the black experience, whether male or female, into which gender is subsumed, reduced, or simply lost. As Gilroy notes, 'today's crisis of black social life is routinely represented as a crisis of masculinity alone' (1993: 7). More than this, constructions of black male sexuality have become reified and naturalized; transformed through the lens of new racism into an inherent and inescapable part of black cultural life and expression. Gilroy argues further that the increasing uncertainties and contradictions surrounding racialized identities are lived through and symbolized by an insistence on the 'naturalness' of gender categories (ibid.).

In a much quoted passage, Liebow writes:

Men and women talk of themselves and others as cynical, self-serving marauders, ceaselessly exploiting one another as use objects or objects of income. . . . The men prefer to see themselves as the exploiters, the women as the exploited (1967: 137).

Within such relationships, the element of power on either side is of crucial importance. Black men have been traditionally viewed as emasculated by society and turning upon black women to create an artificial sense of masculine power through exploitation. Thus, hooks writes of the construction of black men as 'tormented by their inability to fulfill the phallocentric masculine ideal' (1992: 89). Black women, by contrast, are seen as financially and emotionally autonomous and comparatively successful. This has led to a dual image of black male–female relationships, in which men are characterized as weak and frustrated, and black women as strong and independent. Taylor writes:

Women are said to view men as irresponsible, exploitative, aggressive—even depraved. Black men, on the other hand, may view women as domineering, untrustworthy and often indifferent to their plight (1977: 3).

As Liebow notes, such images exist primarily at the level of 'public fiction' (1967: 145), and of external social stereotype. His intimation is that the powerless are in no position to exert any meaningful control, through exploitation or otherwise. Such public fictions thus form part of a male fantasy which has little relation to social reality. The former he terms the 'ideal mode', the latter the 'real mode'. Liebow's division is useful in that it acknowledges a distinction between a collective masculine myth and individual attitudes towards women. It is misleading, however, to consider the distinction between the two modes of action as in any way absolute. As was mentioned in reference to the peer group, control can be enacted at a multiplicity of levels, and powerlessness in one sphere does not presage powerlessness in another. Hooks writes, therefore, of the failure of both white sociologists and of black male activists 'to acknowledge that the phallocentric power black men wield over black women is "real" power, the assumption being that only the power white men have that black men do not have is real' (1992: 108). Within different arenas, ideals can become reality, part of a limited and ambiguous enactment of masculine control.

At the level of 'public fiction', therefore, the ideology of black masculinity is perceived, even—or perhaps especially—by its practitioners, as inherent and inevitable. In practice, however, the enactment of its norms in interaction with women is far from absolute and unequivocal. Gilroy writes of black masculinity as 'an austere Spartan masculinity that constructs its patriarchal techniques from blending a blunt authoritarianism with the shape-shifting cunning of the black hustler' (1993: 8). This description encapsulates both the apparent rigidity of its ideological framework, and the fluidity and ambiguity which it incorporates and which is manipulated at the level of praxis to maintain and subvert notions of control. Amongst my male informants, there existed an oft-articulated understanding of gender relations, but this proved far from unambiguous both in its ideological structures and in its application, especially amongst groups differentiated by race, and by social and economic factors. 'Women' cannot be understood as a homogeneous and undivided category; the values and attitudes of black masculinity are similarly not uniform. Control is thus enacted differentially and with varying aims and effects. It constitutes rather an interactive process, which alters according to context and intent.

The following chapter will seek to unravel some of the complexities of the 'black macho' stance as it was conceptualized and practised by my male informants. It will consider the divisions between public and private spheres, between 'types' of women and between 'ideal' and 'real' modes of action (Liebow 1967). These divisions are, however, primarily a tool to facilitate analysis and cannot but render a complex reality somewhat artificial in its categorization. By placing power at the centre of the construction of black masculinity, it is hoped merely to contextualize and explore some of its manifestations and some of its inherent ambiguities. This study is unable to take into account the voices of either black women or homosexual black men,[1] although it acknowledges their significance in the continued struggle over racialized and gendered meanings.

'BITCHES AND WIVES': WOMEN AND CONTROL

During the period of my fieldwork, most of the boys were involved in long-standing 'committed' relationships with women.

---

[1] The denial of black homosexuality can be argued as one of the silences implicit in the construction of black masculinity. A forthcoming paper by Kendall Thomas, delivered to the 'Race Matters: Black Americans, US terrain' conference at Princeton University, Apr. 1994, makes this argument most forcefully.

Clive had been with Pat for seven years, Satish with Dion for about the same length of time, Malcolm with Valerie for about four years. Ricky had been settled with Anne for two years, and Shane had recently left a four-year-long relationship and had been seeing Nellie for over six months. Both Satish and Clive had children with their partners. Of the group, only Frank, Nathan, and Arif were completely unattached. Satish was the only member of the group to live permanently with his partner, although both Ricky and Shane spent the majority of time with their girlfriends, either at their flats or at the hospital in West London, where the women were student nurses.

Despite these attachments, however, the boys functioned as an exclusively male group. During my time in London, and in spite of my closeness to the group, I rarely met these women, except in passing, and found it impossible to negotiate access to them. This was with the exception of Anne, who was often at the flat I shared with Ricky, and Dion, whom I met through Clive. The latter relationship proved explosive in the wider context of my fieldwork, for reasons which will be explained later. On the whole, the boys were rarely seen in public with their partners, never took them out with the group, and were loath for them to have sustained contact, either with me, as another woman, or with each other. Again, the exception to this was Anne, who went every-where with Ricky, but whose presence was generally overlooked.

These women were generally referred to as 'wives'; a term which denoted the serious nature of the relationship between them and the individual man, and which was acknowledged by the group. The existence of 'wives' did not preclude, however, the frequent dalliances which were initiated on the boys' nights out, and which were the cause of the perennial conflict between Satish and Dion. These other women, who were seen as casual flings and considered apart from, and irrelevant to, their primary relationships, were often referred to—though mainly in jest—as 'bitches'. The term itself was often used in reference to all women the boys encountered in the leisure sphere, although its usage was by no means uniform and consistent. It was also, of course, a term normally used within the boundaries of the male peer group rather than with the women themselves.

The 'wives' were thus opposed to, and defined against, the 'bitches'. This can be compared with Liebow's distinction in *Tally's*

Corner, between 'nice' and 'not nice' women (1967: 151); the latter category being those designated for exploitation, whereas the former were those to whom one demonstrated emotional, financial, and social commitment. This also corresponded to a distinction the boys made between public and private spheres of action, between the leisure and the community domain. The wives were thus closely associated with 'home' and the community, the bitches with wider society.

Private Women, Private Power

For the boys, there existed, in theory at least, a clear distinction between the two arenas. I was told that men did not meet 'nice' women in the West End or in clubs and winebars. Shane told me, though with his usual affectations, that he only met his girl-friends in libraries, in the park, or at church. He continued, 'I don't go out to clubs to look for girls. They don't appeal to me much' (Interview, 5 Apr. 1991). This does not mean, it should be noted, that Shane had never met women in clubs, merely that these were considered primarily as casual, sexual liaisons. Darnell similarly told me that he never met his girlfriends in clubs:

I don't really go in for that, because in a club it seems like too many things are so obvious and it just looks so bad; that you go to a club just to pick up a girl. Boy, I can't handle that, because some of them girls might just be out to get picked up (Interview, 24 Mar. 1991).

It is significant, however, that Darnell's distinction functioned largely internally to his perception of 'community': the clubs he was referring to were black clubs; the women, black women. For the boys, the distinction was between two perceived commun-ities, and 'race' became a major signifier of these boundaries. This will be considered in more detail later: it suffices here to point out that the 'wives' in this instance were either black or Asian. Valerie and Dion are both of Jamaican origin; Pat is 'mixed-race'; Nellie is Trinidadian-Indian, and Anne, Malaysian-Indian. More-over, in no case was contact initially made in the leisure sphere. Satish and Clive met their 'wives' during holiday work in a supermarket; Ricky and Shane met Anne through friends at the hospital where she was studying; Malcolm was introduced to Valerie by family friends. It is interesting that Darnell met his last girlfriend, Jackie, at a houseparty: as was mentioned earlier, these events were seen as closely connected with notions of 'community'. They are thus a 'respectable' place to meet 'nice' girls.

In theory, the association of 'wives' with community and home accorded them a degree of respect not granted to other women. Even when the boys were unfaithful—as they frequently were— to their wives, they were careful to distinguish between this primary relationship and others. Shane told me that when he was with Marion, his last girlfriend, he was occasionally unfaithful to her, but that this did not affect his feelings for her. I was frequently told, 'You make love with your wife, you only have sex with other women.' Thus, Shane said: 'I treat the one that I'm serious about like a flower, like a butterfly; I treat the other one like a dog. . . . And that's it—either you like it or leave it' (Interview, 5 Apr. 1991).

Hardly surprisingly, this was not a freedom granted to their wives. Shane told me that if Marion had been unfaithful to him, he would 'Beat her brains out' (ibid.). It is revealing that other men I knew referred to their partners as their 'personal women'; a term which captures the notions of ownership and exclusivity associated with these relationships. Indeed, I was informed by Ricky, Shane, and Frank that they would never take seriously a woman who had had other lovers, because she would then have 'belonged' to someone else, and sexual ownership would have been in question. Others of the boys were less stringent in their demands, but all were concerned with the concept of sexual purity; at least in the private domain. The primary reason for Satish's fury at Dion's 'gift' was that it brought into question his 'ownership' of her sexuality and threatened the boundaries of the private sphere.

The notion of power and ownership expressed in these relationships rendered the apparently simple status of 'wife' very ambiguous in its application. Although the boys presented themselves as very much in control of 'their' women, the enactment of this power was by no means consistently adhered to by either side, nor were the women as powerless in the relationships as the overarching ideology would have rendered them. Indeed, an alternative label often used amongst the boys for their partners was 'tyrant'. This acknowledged the primacy of the women within the domestic sphere, both socially and often economically. On

several occasions, the boys were at the flat and one of their partners would call and demand their presence; each time, despite
many taunts by the others, the man in question would leave.
Once, when Clive had 'borrowed' Pat's car to visit Ricky, she
paged him and threatened to call the police and tell them the car
had been stolen if he did not return at once: Clive left.

As mentioned earlier, the lack of control wielded by individual
men was a subject for much in-group ridicule. This often made
the woman a focus for much disrespect, both as a way of lessen-
ing her perceived power and of reminding the man of his weakness. The wives were generally caricatured as large, domineering,
and potentially violent. Clive's girlfriend, for example, was known
as 'The Elephant', and the boys would sing the children's song
'Nellie the Elephant' and swing their arms as trunks whenever
Clive was around. They even did it when Pat was present, although she had no idea of the 'joke'. On these occasions, Clive
was enjoined to enter into the entertainment: to refuse to do so
would have served to underscore his weakness and enhance his
status as a 'pussy'—that is, a man who is controlled by women.
Moreover, any refusal would be interpreted as a denial of the
primacy of the peer group and an attack upon it.

Dion's attack on Satish illustrates the tension that was felt to
exist by both men and women between the peer group and the
domestic relationship. For Dion, this was articulated as a simple
choice: Satish should leave his friends or leave her. For the boys,
however, the choice was not so clear: to deny the peer group was
seen as an admission of weakness, but the relationships with
their partners were crucial both to their connection with ideas of
family and community, and to the future. This led to tension and
some role conflict, which was articulated against the power
wielded by the women. The situation was intensified especially
where children were involved, since they committed the man
financially and emotionally to the woman. Most saw this as being
'trapped', a diminution of their control. Ricky told me:

You can always see when it's starting to happen. There will be a girl that
they were serious with before—you know, it doesn't just happen out of
the blue when this girl says 'I'm pregnant' . . . it'll be a girl they were
serious with before, the relationship started to die and she always seems
to get pregnant at that moment. Then they're trapped, officially trapped
(Interview, 9 Dec. 1990).

This position, the boys claimed, was then exploited by the women to control the men. As Ricky explained of Pat and Clive, 'she threatens him with not seeing the baby, taking you to court and everything else and he just bends to it' (ibid.). Children were not, of course, the only foundation of female power. It seems likely, in fact, that these external reasons for control are themselves public fictions, by which the men explained and legitimated their relationships within the context of the peer group. In reality, most of the boys were keen to maintain their relationships with their partners, which were founded on strong and enduring emotional ties. This in itself was seen as a source of potential struggle. Shane thus told me of his last girlfriend, Marion: 'I was really in love and she abused it, so I dropped her. . . . I felt that she was in control and I wasn't, so I decided to drop her' (Interview, 5 Apr. 1991).

The boys generally concurred that Marion had controlled Shane and had driven him away. Indeed, in most of the long-standing relationships within the group, the women were generally held to be in control. This was symbolized by their ability to exact financial commitment from the men, as with Valerie and Malcolm, or Clive and Pat; but also, with Dion and Satish, through physical power. Ricky told me of the latter: 'when she wants to, she lifts up her hand and boxes [Satish]. She hits him; she doesn't spare the rod, she beats him like a child' (Interview, 9 Dec. 1990).

However, the extent of this female control was admitted to be ambiguous: 'they get what they want, but I mean they never truly have them, do they?' (ibid.). The appearance of female control was undermined by the men through their activities in the leisure sphere; indeed, it can perhaps be argued—as it was by Ricky—that feelings of powerlessness in their relationships with their 'wives' were translated into power through their exploitation of women in the leisure sphere. Moreover, the power that the women possessed was itself flawed because they were dependent on the men financially, especially if they had children. For example, it was generally noted that Satish had much more freedom to act with the peer group when he was in employment.

It is significant that relationships between the boys and their 'wives' were conducted between individuals, not between groups. Although the boys often commented on these relationships, they were careful never to interfere in them. They were considered largely separate from the actions of the group. The question of power was also a personal, individual interaction; a man was expected to be able to control 'his' woman, but this did not extend outside the confines of this relationship. For example, although Ricky felt entitled to call Anne from her sick bed to cook his dinner, the other boys always treated her with deference and respect; moreover, Ricky never made the same demands on other women. The women involved in these relationships were always regarded as individuals; they were never approached as representatives of other categories. The same cannot be said of the public sphere, in which women were important primarily as representatives of other groups and other interests.

Public Women, Public Power

It should perhaps be noted that the conception of 'public women' was not in complete correlation with the boundaries of the public leisure arena. Indeed, the notion of 'public women' can be seen to exist more as a categorization of mind and attitude than of space, although there was often a large degree of overlap. Thus, women who were considered 'bitches' were often admitted into private space; Ricky lived with three women in his flat the year before I moved in and conducted relationships with each, he told me, 'on a rota basis'. Similarly, Shane had been involved in a casual relationship with Nellie's cousin, who lived in the adjacent room in the nurses' home.

The distinction between these women was, however, a clear one in the minds of my informants, at least in theory. Most told me that the division was often made upon meeting the woman initially, and that there was little chance of movement between the categories. Some, Frank informed me, were women one was only interested in for sex; some for longer relationships: only the latter could ever become 'wives'. He told me:

There's some birds you meet, sex is not what's on your mind; if sex was on my mind, I'd probably be in her knickers now. But it's not on my mind; what's on my mind is getting to know her, seeing her more (Interview, 5 Apr. 1991).

Central to this distinction was the question of sexual control: if a woman was seen to be sexually experienced, she was considered a threat to the man's control and became a 'bitch'; someone who existed purely for sexual pleasure. Frank explained:

If I'm trying and I get into your knickers the first night—fuck me—I mean, tens of thousands of blokes can do the same thing as well. You've got no security whatsoever. Come on, where's all the security down there, do you know what I mean? (ibid.).

Ironically, the ideology of the public arena uniformly categorized women within this space as sexually available and thus potentially both exploitable and uncontrollable.

Overt expressions of female sexuality, the consideration of which dominated the public domain, were always viewed as threatening to the boys' sense of their masculinity. Their response was almost exclusively to attack it, either through exploitation or through group censure. Ricky thus told me of a friend of Clive's, Jane:

them lot is always trying to get—not trying to get a leg over—but a quick thrill basically, a quick touch here, mess around her, this and that. She's got a nice body, not very attractive but, you know, she's very easy. You know, they all mess around her and after they walk away 'bleeding hell, man, what a dork'. They're just having a laugh. It's a quick thrill .... If she said 'yeah, let's go in the bedroom', none of them would, they just wouldn't bother. She's too easy.... They do have *some* respect for themselves (Interview, 9 Dec. 1990).

The disrespect displayed towards women in this arena was manifest in often public, group situations, particularly through the use of public ritualized insults. Frank told me:

C[live] will go up to the girl's face and say 'hi; you're an ugly bastard, aren't you?' He would! I met this girl, right; she had a big nose . . . when she turned sideways you can't see, it casts a big shadow the other side of the room. And C[live] goes up to her 'cor, you've got a big nose, ain't you?' (Interview, 5 Apr. 1991).

It should be noted that this type of ridicule was only conducted in a group situation, for the benefit of the other men present. This served to objectify the woman and lessen her perceived threat by reasserting group—and hence male—control. When they met friends of mine, for example, who were university educated and employed in comparatively good jobs, group insults were frequently used to retain power. These were primarily addressed at external or physical features which defined their sexuality—styles of clothes, hair, size of breasts, and so on. Clive's favourite line was, 'My, your skin is so smooth; what shaving cream did you use this morning?' On other occasions, the boys would draw upon gendered power relations in wider society to assert their primacy; this usually took the form of 'It's a man's world' discussions, followed by a triumphal, if self-parodying, 'A woman's place is in the kitchen or the bedroom. Get in the kitchen and make me some food, woman.'

Women in the public domain were, then, usually considered as objects, whose sole purpose was for financial or sexual exploitation. Although some were considered 'nice', and were exempted from this categorization, the vast majority were, to all intents and purposes, simply 'bitches'. Their status as object in this arena was symbolized by the use of the pronoun 'it' rather than 'she' in much conversation. At the level of ideology, public women were used to express external power rather than internal control; although, of course, the former was largely dependent on the latter. Exploitation becomes the public expression of this power.

Relationships in this sphere were thus discussed in terms of personal gain; of what the man concerned could 'get', financially or sexually, from the woman. These were more public tokens of control, discussed and displayed within the group, than objects of necessity to the individual. Clive, for example, occasionally brought out one of a number of women, whom he had known for some time, on the boys' excursions. These were present, I was told, because they would cover all the night's expenses and then have sex with him. This was despite the fact that Clive was well-paid and did not need the money; and that he had a long-standing girlfriend. The women were used to increase his status within the group and as a public declaration of his control as a man. During these evenings, Clive would generally leave the woman standing in a corner, while he danced and flirted with other women. This functioned as a method of controlling both parties simultaneously, by announcing his attraction for, and independence from, each. It also worked as an assertion of masculine power directed at other men present. It was thus an expression at once of internal group status and external competition. Ricky similarly told me that a few years ago when he had 'worked' the City, he and his brother would enter familiar haunts and do a 'head count'; whoever had had sex with the least number of women there bought the drinks. This assertion of power was as much directed at other men present as at each other.

It is significant, but not surprising, that the boys considered these relationships as important only for what the man could exact from them: what the woman wanted was of no concern. When I asked Shane about the reciprocity of these public relationships, he told me, 'they want a piece of the action. . . . This big thing in me trousers' (Interview, 5 Apr. 1991). It would be misleading, however, to see this ideology of exploitation as overtly and actively hostile towards women; indeed, the women themselves were largely irrelevant, except as objects. Moreover, the ideology as public fiction did not preclude the establishment of several long-standing and close 'friendships' with 'public women'. The sexual element in these relationships was, however, an essential one. None of the boys had any female friends with whom they had no sexual contact, nor wished to have; indeed, they denied the possibility of platonic relationships with women. Frank explained:

I find it very hard to have just like a female friend. . . . If she's attractive, I mean someday you're going to be in that kind of circumstance where you're going to think 'oh dear, it's raining outside and I haven't got a car and it's two o'clock in the morning and you're really tired—Can I stay the night, please' (Interview, 5 Apr. 1991).

Frank insisted, moreover, that he did not have any female friends with which this would not be a temptation. Most of his women friends, as with the other boys, were ex-girlfriends, with whom he continued to have intermittent sexual contact.

The category of 'woman friend' is significant because it undermines the qualitative division between 'bitches' and 'wives'. Although these women were portrayed as targets for exploitation, this attitude often remained solely at the level of public fiction and intra-group humour. In reality, some of these relationships were long-standing and involved a large extent of non-exploitative interaction. Ricky, for example, helped one of his ex-flatmates move house many months after he had forced her to leave the flat and allowed her to stay for several days while the move took place. Moreover, on many occasions, the boys would assume the financial responsibility within the relationship—

especially in the early stages—although this was never admitted. These relationships often reflected a larger degree of respect and emotional attachment than the ideology would suggest.

The attitude towards women friends was partly a product of the categorization of women at the ideological level. Women were either family, your partner, or your friends' partners; or they were available for sexual conquest. The perception of a public sphere meant, moreover, that women met in this arena would be categorized automatically. Frank, who met many of his girlfriends in the West End winebars, would circumvent this categorization by introducing the woman to his friends in what he considered to be an appropriate context. He explained:

It depends on what kind of relationship you're looking for with this girl. If it's just a playtime relationship, any time of day you can make an introduction to your friends. Or if you believe that this girl has got something different—a special quality—. . . then you take your time. . . . It won't be at a club, it won't be at a winebar; it'll probably be, say, I'll bring her round his house—somewhere where he's slightly sober (Interview, 5 Apr. 1991).

The distinction between public and private women—between 'bitches' and 'wives'—is of significance largely as ideology. It was, therefore, more an attitude of mind than of interaction in many cases. At the level of ideology, the distinction was un-equivocal; as Shane put it, 'It says in the Bible, seven women to one man . . . just one serious one—concubines the rest' (Interview, 5 Apr. 1991). This was supposedly lived out through the attribution of greater respect and commitment to the 'wives'; while the 'bitches' received less time and less consideration. In practice, however, the distinction was by no means as clear-cut. Clive, for example, spent a considerable amount of time with his casual girlfriends in a domestic setting, only visiting his 'wife' and child two or three times a week. The position of the 'wives', by contrast, was undercut by the ambiguous nature of the power relations. Indeed, it can perhaps be argued that the two categories are inextricably linked, each defining itself in opposition to the other. To be a 'wife', therefore, is simply not to be a 'bitch', and vice versa. The existence of these two 'types' of women facilitates the control of both: thus, the existence of 'bitches' offsets the perceived domination of the 'wives', while the position of 'wives' precludes the possibility of commitment to the 'bitches'. It would be misleading, therefore, to regard the spheres as distinct, with activities in one being unaffected by those in the other.

The conflation of these categories and the confusion over boundaries was a common feature of the boys' relationships with women, despite this ideology. The background to the confrontation between Dion and Satish described at the beginning of the last chapter illustrates this clearly. Satish had been seeing a black woman, Juliet, whom he had met in a West End club, for several months. Dion had been alerted to this by Malcolm and Clive, who, as friends of Dion's, had felt it their duty to hint at this deceit. She began checking on Satish's movements, and finally caught him after he had used the telephone to call Juliet, by pushing the memory recall button. Despite her accusations, Satish went out to meet Juliet, and Dion told him not to return. According to Clive, he and Satish then spent the evening at Juliet's house, where her mother was holding a birthday party, and Satish then stayed the night—as he had done several times before—returning to Clive's shortly before Dion appeared with her 'gift'. After several days, during which Satish spent much time with Juliet, he returned to Dion. Dion, as Satish's 'wife' and the mother of his two children, then telephoned Juliet, as a result of which Juliet and Satish separated.

This incident brought to light a number of attitudes surrounding and transgressing the public/private division. First, all the boys had met and liked Juliet; they also thought that she was a 'nice' girl, which rendered her status as a 'bitch' rather ambiguous. Secondly, they felt that Dion was partly responsible for Satish's behaviour, because she was a 'tyrant' and failed to provide a suitable domestic environment in which to keep 'her man'. Dion was thus felt to be both unable to control Satish and uncontrollable; this meant that her status as 'wife' was also open to question. Nevertheless, she and Satish had been together for seven years, had two children, and shared a home, which the boys felt demanded respect. This required that Satish be able to keep his affairs within the public sphere and not allow them to affect his home life. Satish had transgressed these rules by staying with Juliet overnight: this not only brought suspicion into the home, but it also failed to keep Juliet within the appropriate arena. In the many discussions during and after these incidents, it was generally agreed that Satish had been careless in allowing Dion to find out about the affair; more than this, however, it was felt that this had been inevitable because Satish had failed to observe the boundaries between spheres. It was in this failure that his fault lay, rather than in the act of infidelity itself. Surprisingly, much of the boys' sympathy lay with Juliet, who, they claimed, had been misled into thinking that Satish was more serious about her than he really was. He had entered her home, stayed over-night, and met her mother; he had thus entered into the private sphere of interaction. He had, moreover, bought Juliet a gold ring for her birthday, which was a symbol of a commitment he was unprepared to fulfil.

It is interesting to consider the roles of the boys themselves in this series of events. First, they had been instrumental in the initiation of the affair: indeed, Satish's initial reaction upon dis-covery was to deny the truth of the accusations, claiming that he had made up the stories of his exploits in order to keep up with peer group expectations. They had also lied and covered up for Satish while the affair was conducted. Nevertheless, when the affair dragged on and became more serious, threatening the domestic sphere, Clive and Malcolm felt it was their duty to warn Dion, and help maintain the family unit. Indeed, all of the boys felt that the domestic environment should be maintained at all costs, especially if there were children involved. Their prim-ary concern was, however, that the two spheres remain distinct. If Satish were going to stay with Juliet, all felt that he should make a clean break with Dion: there could only be one wife.

A further complicating factor in this incident was the racial component. Satish is Asian, and both Dion and Juliet are black. For the boys, this meant a division of loyalties. As men, they supported Satish in his behaviour; as black men, however, their support remained ambiguous. Juliet, as a black woman, de-manded more respect than she was given in her role as 'bitch' because she represented 'the community'. Satish, as an Asian, was outside this community and therefore a threat: his action was a symbol of disrespect. Were Dion not also black, the choice would have been simpler: the boys would have urged Satish to drop Dion and commit himself to Juliet. The sympathy the boys expressed for Juliet was largely based upon a feeling of commun-ity solidarity. Frank told me that if Juliet had been his sister, he would have happily killed Satish for his behaviour. Angelina once told me, with some cynicism, that the reason black men protected their mothers, sisters, wives, and daughters was because they knew what they were doing to other men's mothers, sisters, wives, and daughters. What this illustrates, however, is that there is a community of women which is considered exempt from exploitation, and that this is articulated at its broadest in terms of belonging and possession. Thus, 'our' women are to be protected and 'their' women to be exploited; it is in this distinction that masculine power between groups is most clearly contested. Amongst the boys, this distinction was usually, though not necessarily, articulated in terms of 'race'.

BLACK WOMEN, WHITE WOMEN: 'RACE' AND CONTROL

To a large extent, though not exclusively, the perceived division between black women and white women corresponded to the public and private divide. Black women were generally considered to be 'our' women and were exempt from the ideology of exploitation which dominated the public arena. It is significant that, when the boys encountered black women in the West End or other mainly white environments, they rarely entered into any interaction with them. Similarly, within black social environments, which were associated with community, the boys never attempted to pick girls up—an activity which was the central feature of their excursions into the West End. White women, by contrast, were perceived as legitimate targets for exploitation and were rarely considered for long-term relationships—at least in theory. They were thus closely associated with the public arena, and with wider society, although this did not prevent the boys from accepting white women involved with black men as 'wives'. This was largely dependent upon the man's presentation of his relationship as one in which exploitation was not an element, although this was not always easily defensible. It should be noted that, in the following discussion, the term 'black women' is taken to include 'mixed-race' women, but to exclude Asian women, who were conceptualized differently and remained largely outside this debate. The position of Asian women will be considered later.

Black women were thus associated with notions of family and the community. Integral to this association was the concept of 'respect'; that black women were to be revered in their roles as mothers and culture-bearers. This meant that black women were to be treated differently from 'other' women in relationships. As Shane told me: 'You tend to be more careful with a black girl, because you handle them with so much care—you don't care about the other races' (Interview, 5 Apr. 1991). Black women were seen as much 'stronger' than white women, and as less open to sexual exploitation. This was partly because of the image that most of my informants had of black women as more aggressive and more knowledgeable in their interaction with black men. Darnell explained:

Maybe they're not more aggressive, but you treat them differently because you think they are. So you don't take as much liberties as you would if it was a white girl. To a white girl, you'd go 'I'm going out', she'd go 'No, you're not'; I'd go 'Well, watch me and see'. Whereas a black girl would go 'you ain't going nowhere' and you'd go 'oh boy, it's a hard night tonight, boy' (Interview, 24 Mar. 1991).

Black women were also regarded as sexually inaccessible, at least for casual encounters. The boys felt that they would have to work harder to meet black women and would have to commit themselves to them before any sexual interaction could take place. Darnell confided to me:

It must be true because I'm finding it hard at the moment. . . . Yeah, a lot of them are harder to get. Like with a white girl, you can go and whisper two things in their ears and within a week you're regular every night, right? With a black girl, you have to say 'Praise Allah and everything', and then they *might* give it up (ibid.).

It should be noted that Darnell, who had never dated a white girl, was not speaking from personal experience here, but from a generalized stereotype and from observing his friends. The boys generally agreed, however, that they never looked to black girls for casual sex. On one occasion, Frank brought a black girl, Paula, to the flat; they had been seeing each other for several months before they had sex, and Frank told me at the time that he had rarely worked so hard to get anything. During their visit, Frank told me that he had been trying to persuade Paula to cook for him, but that she had refused. Frank's insistence was a token of his supposed commitment to the relationship; her refusal was a sign that he would have to provide more evidence before she could be won over. Ricky told me later that Frank's apparent devotion, which I had never witnessed in his dealings with other women, was a ploy to overcome Paula's resistance, and that this was the only way he could ever get a black woman into bed. He also told me that, having succeeded, Frank would lose interest—which he did. This reinforced the image of black women as less promiscuous, but also undermined the assertion that they should be treated differently. As Shane told me, 'I know black girls are a bit of a handful—or dark-skinned girls generally—but if you go about it the right way, you should get it' (Interview, 5 Apr. 1991). 'Respect' at an ideological level, therefore, became merely another obstacle at the level of experience.

The position of black women within the overarching ideology was not, however, unambiguous. Just as the 'wives' were also seen as 'tyrants', black women were viewed with some trepidation by my informants. This was partly due to their role as representatives of the 'community'; they were thus seen both as symbols of solidarity and of constraint. When meeting black women of my acquaintance, therefore, the boys often felt that they were being judged, particularly in their role as provider. This was consolidated by their view of black women as financially independent and therefore in economic control within the relationship. This was not necessarily articulated by the boys; they would more often refer to black women as 'feisty', 'aggressive', or simply 'ignorant'. What these terms indicated, however, was a perception of black women as strong and outside the control of the black man, and thus threatening to his masculinity. This was inevitably denied by the boys themselves. Shane assured me: 'I know that black girls, some of them are quite mouthy, but they really—I'm not being a chauvinist—they want a man to take control; they do like that superior aura from their men' (Interview, 5 Apr. 1991).

Shane's very assertion of the control of black men over black women seems to deny its certainty. Indeed, in his relationship with Marion, his last girlfriend, he admitted that she had been in control; this was also reflected in the way the boys perceived their 'wives'. It is revealing to compare the way the boys

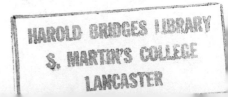

regarded black female–white male relationships in this context. Shane told me:

Black women aren't really attracted to white men . . . but a white man will do anything for a black girl. A black girl can feel in control with a white man. With a black man, it's a different story—those [women] are the ones that won't be in control (ibid.).

Shane places control as the central feature of these relationships; black women go out with white men because they have power over them. Similarly, black men go out with white women because 'the white woman don't [*sic*] argue with him, does everything he says' (ibid.); again, the main attraction is seen as the establishment of control. In black male–black female relationships, this control is seen as contested; it is something that is constantly sought and reasserted.

It is significant that the boys did not seek to establish this control through public interaction as they did with non-black women. Their interactions with black women were thus not marked by the group ridicule and insults which characterized their contact with other women. When the boys met Angelina and Eleanor on two separate occasions, the women were treated with a respect and deference I had rarely witnessed before. Nevertheless, the boys sought to establish control in a number of ways. First, they asked what the women did, seemingly hoping to establish control at the level of occupational superiority. When they discovered both were in Higher Education, the boys changed tactic. They proceeded to ask about the women's personal lives and 'accused' them of dating white men. This would have allowed the boys to dismiss the women as 'traitors', and as being somehow no longer 'black'. This would have enabled them to establish a sense of personal superiority. As Shane explained, 'the black girls that go out with white men are the ones we consider as the ones we don't want. They're not good enough' (ibid.). Eleanor, who did have a white boyfriend, was dismissed with a smug 'Yes, she looks the type' from Ricky. Angelina's boyfriend, however, was not only black, but from Ladbroke Grove—a 'black' area—and the boys could not dismiss her as a 'sell-out'. They thus retreated, literally and in some confusion, from the kitchen where we were sitting, and left the flat.

As with 'wives' and 'bitches', black and white women are

defined against each other. If black women are regarded as objects of respect and non-exploitation, sexually inaccessible and strong, white women are generally held to be the opposite of this. In addition, the association of white women with the public sphere allies them more closely to the power relations reflected in wider society. White women, at least at the level of ideology, are objectified in their role as representatives of 'the other', and the control sought is the enactment of power within these wider structures.

It should be noted that all the boys had been involved, either in the past or presently, with white women. These were mainly women they had met in the leisure sphere, and they were largely confined to this arena. None of the boys had white 'wives', although some had been involved in long-term relationships with white women. Frank, for example, had dated Stephanie, an air hostess, for about two years, while the majority of Ricky's long-term women friends were white. Both denied, however, that they had ever considered taking these women seriously. Frank had dated other women while seeing Stephanie and finally split up with her when she started to demand long-term commitment; Ricky always told me that he would simply never consider marrying a white woman.

The reluctance to commit themselves to a white woman has at least as much to do with ideology as personal preference. As mentioned earlier, the ideology of exploitation surrounding white women meant that black male–white female relationships were almost inevitably defined in these terms. To escape from this definition meant adopting a stance against notions of 'community' which most of the boys were reluctant to undertake. Black male–white female relationships were viewed generally as undermining community solidarity; Shane told me, 'It's weakening my race' (Interview, 5 Apr. 1991). White women were thus perceived as 'their' women; any involvement was seen in terms of the wider social position of black people. I was often told by men I knew that they would not date a white woman because 'the first thing she'll call you in any argument is a black bastard'. The woman is seen in relation to wider power structures, which use of the term 'black bastard' is seen to evoke. The objectification and manipulation of white women can be seen, therefore, as a response to wider social forces. This is not, I would stress, to lay claim to an Eldridge Cleaver-style argument which sees white women as legitimate objects for attack; but that the powerlessness of black men in white society is rearticulated and contested at a street level to empower black men through the use of white women.

White women were thus conceptualized—in opposition to black women—as weak and sexually available. Black male–white female relationships were projected primarily in terms of exploitation, either financial or sexual. Shane insisted: 'I think the black guy goes out with the white girl because it's easiest; things are much more easy. Sometimes the white girl might have money to spend on me more. . . . And it's easy sex' (Interview, 5 Apr. 1991). White women were generally perceived as sexually more active and more adventurous; the boys often insisted—as did some black women I knew—that white women would do things in bed that a black woman would never do. This attitude was reinforced by a group mythology in which the vices of white women they had known were constantly replayed. This included the woman Ricky had sex with in the toilets of the Hippodrome; one of his ex-girlfriends who had agreed to a threesome with Shane; the girl Clive had had intercourse with on a pavement outside a party; the nurse who had done unspeakable things to Satish. 'Wives' were never discussed in these terms, and although black women were discussed, they were never taken as representative of 'black women' in the same way.

It is important to distinguish between this ideology and the realities of such relationships; a distinction of which my informants were fully aware. Darnell told me that black men often dated white women for reasons of genuine affection, 'It's probably because they think she looks nice and they love her off' (Interview, 24 Mar. 1991). Nevertheless, at a collective level, these images persisted and dictated the articulation of attitudes at an interpersonal level. Thus, Darnell also told me that the only reason he would accept for dating a white woman was 'One; if she's got money, that's all' (ibid.). This was, it should be noted, a reason, but not an excuse. At a collective level, amongst the black men and women I knew, such relationships were regarded as unacceptable. White women, or, indeed, white partners in general, were regarded as threatening to 'the community', and were rejected. One of the reasons the boys often told me that they did not date white women on a serious basis was that it was impossible to take them into black environments without attracting scorn and hostility. None would take them to black clubs, and few to houseparties, unless the relationship were long-standing and committed. Most felt that they would have to choose between black and white arenas, and were loath to surrender their contact with 'the community'.

Thus, Darnell told me that to date a white woman would make a black man a 'social misfit in your area' (ibid.).[2] He explained:

If you saw a black guy going out with a white girl, you hear these people calling 'traitor' or 'sell-out'. . . and why you having all that hassle? . . . My friend did—this guy Stewart—and it was like such hypocrisy. He was like a *black* guy, *black* guy through and through; but then he would go up to Sudbury, where this white girl lived and he used to go out with her. He never brought her to a party in Harlesden, never brought her to no houseparties which people from our area would be at. . . . Because he would get run, wouldn't he? People start to cuss him (ibid.).

Shane similarly talked of the community pressure against mixed-race dating: 'Walking down the streets with them; holding hands and all that—I don't like that. I get dirty looks from black people and white people—you get remarks shouted out sometimes' (Interview, 5 Apr. 1991). Ricky also claimed that it was impossible to take white partners to black social environments because the girl would be harassed by black women present, who considered them to be stealing 'their men'. Moreover, should trouble occur over her presence, it would be impossible for him, as a black man, to defend her, a white woman, against other black people. It is interesting that this hostility was often articulated by denying the individual's status as a 'black man'; at least if the relationship was seen as more than purely exploitative.

This attitude was intensified in the minds of my male informants if the relationship involved a black woman dating a white man. These women were often perceived as not only no longer black, but as permanently outside the bounds of the 'black

[2] Some of my informants have also assured me, however, that mixed-race relationships are both more common and more acceptable in South London. The extent to which this is the case is impossible for me to assess and could reflect either the creation of territorially-based community images discussed in Ch. 2 or a different enactment of 'community' in these areas.

community'. Darnell told me that neither he nor Rommell would allow Angelina to date a white man, 'She's going to have to move outside of London' (Interview, 24 Mar. 1991). He even claimed that he would call on one of their uncles, who would disapprove, to help them prevent such a liaison; this was despite the fact that the uncle involved was living with a white woman. Darnell was less vehement about Angelina's friends, Eleanor and Fenella, both of whom had white boyfriends; he told me that they had always been 'white-minded' (ibid.). Although his relationship with these women remained amicable, he refused to be seen out with their boyfriends, and once told me that if he ever saw either talking to a black man, he would feel obliged to 'warn' him of her involvement, even if it had ended. Frank, who almost exclusively dated white women and was the only one of my informants who considered marriage a possibility, similarly told me that he would never let his sister get involved with a white man.

If the boys were guilty of the objectification of white women, it is also true that this was how they saw themselves within this sphere of interaction. Most defined the relationships with 'race' as the central feature. The women thus became objectifications of 'white', and the men of 'black'. The interaction was structured, therefore, by overarching racial and sexual stereotypes, which were implemented on both sides, and created something of a self-fulfilling prophecy. White women were cast primarily within a sexual role; as Darnell once told me: 'White girls are for practice'. Similarly, the attraction of black men for white women was seen as dominated by the myth of black male sexuality; or, as Rommell called it, 'the *legend* of black male sexuality'. Shane commented: 'We're well-toned, we're physical, we're funny, we're rhythmic. . . . We have nice bodies, we look good. Just look at a white man—look at a 25-year-old white man to a 25-year-old black man' (Interview, 5 Apr. 1991).

Shane's insistence is on physical attraction and supposed sensual satisfaction. Although, in other arenas, the boys were keen to move away from such stereotyping, in this sphere, it remained paramount. Indeed, the boys were insistent on the 'reality' of such stereotypes; as Shane said: 'Of course it's true. Ask a white woman who's been with a black man' (ibid.). It is revealing that Shane does not use black women as a measure of his sexual prowess. It was these images, focused on strength and power, that the boys enacted in the leisure sphere when trying to attract women. Darnell similarly testified to the mystique of the black male: 'I've been asked plenty of times, "Is it true that the black man has a twelve-inch dick?" I go, "There's only one way to find out"' (Interview, 24 Mar. 1991). Darnell was aware that this emphasis on black sexuality has been intensified through popular culture, in which black men are portrayed with physicality as their defining characteristic. He continued:

Boy, they don't even have to use that [sexual stereotype] now; just because they're black—that's enough. Before, like maybe a couple of years ago, they'd say 'oh yeah, the black man's well endowed, I want to go out with him'. But now it's not even that, it's that going out with a black guy is very trendy (ibid.).

The mutual objectification involved in these interactions and the alliance of white women with the wider power structure did, however, render the image more ambiguous than the ideology suggests. Several of the boys expressed frustration to me at various times during my fieldwork that they were unable to escape the roles that these interactions created. Nathan, for example, who often told me that he was ready to settle down, found himself consistently cast as a sex object; a role his size and physical presence made it difficult to escape. Ricky told me, 'women look at N[athan] and think, sex!' (Interview, 9 Dec. 1990).

The experience of Frank, who was almost exclusively attracted to white women, exemplifies these tensions and conflicts. He told me that he rarely found black women attractive; this was mainly because, for Frank, they were associated with a negative image of community, and thus with downward mobility. White women, on the other hand, were seen as a symbol of individual success. This does not mean that Frank used white women because he felt it would help him to achieve or 'integrate'; more that the association of white women with the wider power structure allied them with an *image* of success that he found irresistible. He told me: 'Some black men look on it as a big image thing. . . . It's a status thing, I think. Most black men see it as a big status thing, to go out with a white girl' (Interview, 5 Apr. 1991). For Frank, white women were more in keeping with his self-image of success; indeed, this can be seen as a corollary to the attitude of 'successful' black women cited by Kogbara, who do not want to go out with bus drivers. Even Shane, who was the most hostile of all the boys to white women—in theory, if not in practice—was forced to concede that white women did confer status, at least in the eyes of white society; thus, he said, 'They think, "he's more whitified, he's going out with one of us"' (Interview, 5 Apr. 1991).

This association with social success was considered by the boys the only legitimate reason for being committed to a white woman. Shane told me: 'If a black man goes out with a white woman, she has to be *better* than the average white woman before he could even consider going out with her' (ibid.). With the exception of Clive, whose lack of discernment with women was legendary within the group, the boys were only interested in meeting middle-class white women. This was defined by the boys as a woman who dressed well, had well-paid employment, a car, and a flat. Frank, for example, told me that he would never consider dating a woman, black or white, he felt to be 'working-class':

I prefer a woman who's got something about her going, not just 'hi, coming down my mother's on Sunday, come down the pub on Friday, we'll have a laugh. We'll get Sharon and Tracy to come down'. I'll have none of that, *please* (Interview, 5 Apr. 1991).

Frank preferred meeting women in winebars because he felt these attracted a 'better' class of women. One evening, he met an air hostess, Shirley, at Corks in Bond Street. He started talking to her, gave her his telephone number and they met up the following week. Frank was very enthusiastic about Shirley; told us all over and over again about how she was a member of String-fellow's nightclub and had taken him there, paid all night, and driven him home in her new sports car. She was, he insisted, a 'nice' girl—someone he could get attached to, someone who shared his interests and looked good on his arm. Despite her 'image' compatibility, Frank insisted that he was very much 'in control' and that Shirley was in danger of being too demanding of his time and attention. This was, it later transpired, more an imagined than real danger; it is significant, however, because Frank used his supposed indifference, and her enthusiasm, as a means of establishing control—if only in his mind and the minds of his friends. The next Friday, he met Shirley again, this time taking Anne and Ricky with him, probably to impress them. Shirley was very rude to all of them, danced with other, older white men all evening and behaved, they agreed, 'like a whore'. Although this was typical behaviour by the boys, Frank was furious and they never met again.

This encounter was replicated on a number of occasions with Frank. He would meet a 'nice', middle-class white woman, they would meet two or three times, have sex, and then the woman would dump him. What this pattern illustrated was a conflict of perceived roles. Frank, on the one hand, was interested in the women because he considered them to be in keeping with his image of upward mobility and social success. This meant that he was prepared to be committed to them, although this was partly offset by the overarching ideology which cast these women as 'bitches' by virtue of race and environment. This latter aspect led him to articulate the relationship in terms of exploitation on his part, although he was clearly impressed by the status these women represented. The women, on the other hand, seemed not to see Frank in any other role than that of 'black stud'. The myth of black male sexuality does *not* cast the man in a role of which long-term commitment and equality is a part—indeed, its sexual objectification of black men precludes any equality by definition. Shirley's action on the second occasion called into being the white social power structure with which she was allied, and turned this against Frank, to deny his control and his existence beyond the stereotype.

The interaction between race and gender thus proved complex. Frank's primary purpose was to establish male control over Shirley in her role as a woman; Shirley, however, was able to assert the primacy of 'race' over gender. It would be too simplistic, then, to regard the boys' attitude to white women as purely exploitative. Within the wider social arena in which these encounters took place, a number of other pressures and role constraints were brought to bear, which rendered the whole concept of control ambiguous and shifting. It would be misleading, moreover, to regard the ideology which surrounded women and 'race' as in any way inevitable or unique. Indeed, it should be noted that the same discourses were employed internally to the black community, in which 'race' was not a defining characteristic. Darnell, for example, divided his black female friends into 'nice' and 'not nice' women, and treated them accordingly, although with less stress on financial exploitation.

A NOTE ON BEING AN ASIAN FEMALE RESEARCHER

Inevitably, my position as a woman within an almost exclusively male environment made me a focus for much of the discussion about the role and position of women. Although my purpose with the group was known and accepted, and the boys themselves were mainly co-operative, I was never considered to be the 'honorary male' so beloved of women anthropologists. My position within the overarching discourse was, however, ambivalent; a status which both facilitated and constrained aspects of my research.

Thus, I was considered to be part of both the public and private spheres. I lived with Ricky and spent much time with the boys in their domestic environments; I also went with them into the public leisure arena. Therefore, I was neither 'bitch' nor 'wife'. Had I been the latter, the risks of taking me with them to the West End would have been too great and their interaction with women there would have been severely constrained. Had I been considered merely a 'bitch', the boys would have refused to discuss their private relationships, and would have been concerned more to exploit than to assist me. The only other woman who was in a similar position was Anne, Ricky's girlfriend, who was always with Ricky on the boys' nights out. Anne was considered to be a 'nice' girl, who knew and accepted her role on these occasions and never interfered with the other boys' activities. She was seen very much as Ricky's 'wife' and appendage and was thus irrelevant to the rest of the group. To an extent, both of us were seen as ornaments and were expected to act as such. Ricky would tell Anne what clothes to wear before they went out; the boys would also often try to prescribe my mode of dress. This had to be short, tight, and sexy. However, where Anne was seen as Ricky's possession and thus subject to his control, my status as an unattached woman was undefined. I thus became a group possession and was subject to group control.

This was manifested in a number of ways. While we were out,

no other man was allowed to come within about ten feet of me, even though I was often left alone in a corner. On one occasion, Frank spotted another man winking at me and smiling, and he went over and 'warned' the man to leave me alone. On another occasion, Ricky came close to hitting a white man who had been harassing me. Ricky told me more than once that while I was on my fieldwork and living in his flat, I would be expected to date only one of the group; outsiders would not be tolerated. However, as a group possession, and not a 'wife', the boys were not enjoined to show me any of the usual respect; they would often display their ownership in public by trying to 'sell' me to people they met. The usual price was about £2.50, although I never discovered what they would have done had anyone accepted. The boys generally felt that they should have full knowledge of my movements at all times and be able to sanction these if they disapproved.

The ambiguity of my position became clear during my friendship with Dion. Although I met Dion through Clive and Satish, my continued relationship with her proved a source of great anxiety for all the boys. Although the 'wives' all knew each other, the boys ensured that contact between them remained erratic. This meant that none of the women could rely on the others for information about her partner and discover infidelities. The boys often used each other for alibis during their affairs, and their position would have been seriously undermined by close friendships between the women. My friendship with Dion threatened the internal security of the group because I knew how the boys conducted themselves in the public arena, and was not bound to secrecy by the masculine norms of the group. When Dion and Satish split up, my position came under immediate fire from Satish, although the other boys assured him that I had said nothing.

My position, which transcended public/private divisions, was facilitated by my perceived ethnicity. As an Asian woman, I was not subject to the racialized ideologies and ambiguities which marked the boys' relationships with both white and black women. As a member of a minority group, I was not allied to white social power and escaped sexual censure; as a non-black woman, I avoided the ambiguities of community identification and judgement. Asian women were generally outside the ideology which circumscribed male–female relationships, although there is some evidence that, as the number of black–Asian relationships increase, this ideology is also changing.

CONCLUSION

The attitude to women expressed by the boys can thus be seen as complex and shifting. Even in 'ideal' mode, there are a number of ambiguities, focusing around issues of race, economic status, and a perception of 'community' and 'the other'. These attitudes suggest that black masculinity must be envisioned as more than a 'cultural' expression of black misogyny and must take into account the position of black men within society. This chapter maintains that black men articulate power within a wider social structure as control at a street level, formed and contested in interaction with women. This should be regarded, as with peer group formation and action, more as an *extension* of male societal power than a substitute for it. Control is enacted through the discourse of exploitation, although this is seen to be less clearly applied at the level of experience. In 'real' mode, therefore, issues of power and control conflict and are displaced in a continual process of negotiation and contestation. In interaction, ideological ambiguities and structural constraints provide the material for a constant slippage in the 'living out' of black male experience, which renders generalization and certainty an illusion.

7

Conclusion

they could deal with the Negro as a symbol or a victim but
had no sense of him as a man.

(James Baldwin 1963)

to become a Negro man . . . one had to make oneself up as
one went along.

(James Baldwin 1961)

I HAD been in 'the field' less than a month when I was taken on
my first expedition with 'the boys' into the West End for their
usual Friday night outing. Outside a pub in Covent Garden, I
was introduced to two new members of the group, Nathan and
Arif: 'This is Claire; she's an anthropologist and she's studying
black men. She wants to know why we all hang around on street
corners with ghetto blasters, mugging old white women.' Nathan,
who is about 6'2", and very fierce looking, fixed me with a steely
glare and said, 'We don't all do that, you know.' After a dramatic
pause he added, 'Any white woman will do.'

What this episode showed, and what became a recurrent theme
throughout my fieldwork, was what might be described as a
kind of double consciousness. In 1903, W. E. B. DuBois described
this as the 'sense of always looking at one's self through the eyes
of others, of measuring one's soul by the tape of a world that
looks on in amused contempt and pity' (1969: 3). For DuBois,
double consciousness was a gift of 'second sight' (ibid.), in
which self-consciousness was inseparable from the gaze of others
and yet not wholly determined by it. Amongst my informants in
London, this consciousness yielded at once a knowledge of the
external image of black youth, and a recognition of the imaginative hiatus between this image and the individual, which allowed
for the creation and manipulation of identity on a day to day
basis. All were aware of the stereotypes and expectations surrounding black youth; all had at some stage been constrained

and restricted by the spectre of the black 'folk devil'; and all had at times used this to their own advantage. One of their major concerns was that this image should not be regarded as the *sole* definition of black identity.

It is the articulation of this concern that has formed the major aim of this research. It contends that external ascriptions of identity have consistently attempted to impose definitions of what it is to 'be black'; definitions rooted in a long-standing equation of black identity with 'race', and a belief in the cultural vacuity of black life which precludes identity choice and individual action. To 'be black' is therefore portrayed as something inherent, essential and inescapable, rather than a created category with socially ascribed meanings and features. Black youth, in particular, have been transfixed in the popular imagination as the ultimate 'Other'; an unchanging and implacable 'stranger'.

This study has attempted to challenge these dominant ascriptions of Black British youth identity and illustrate the fluidity and dynamism of its created alternatives. It should not, however, be regarded as definitive in intent or exhaustive in its portrayal. My informants represent a limited range of responses, generated as much from their stance as individuals as from the constraints of their social position. The study is, then, not of an alternative Black British identity, but of alternative identities, which contest both the possibility and desirability of a unitary definition.

In exploring the multifarious imaginings of Black British youth identities, this research hopes both to challenge and to complement existing macro-level studies of the black communities of Britain. In focusing on a small number of young people in an intensive and intensely personal micro-level account, the research has sought to reveal the complexity and richness of black youth experience and expression. I have deliberately chosen not to dwell excessively on the obvious structural constraints on black Britons, but on the ways in which, in everyday experience, these constraints are encountered. I have not dealt with police harassment and racial attacks, partly because these features of Black British life have been researched more fully elsewhere and partly because their existence is here assumed as an already acknowledged backdrop to the research. I have not talked about drugs, street crime, and violence—the usual markers of 'studies' of 'black culture'—because these elements were simply not a significant part of the lives of my informants. More than this, this study has aimed to examine the ways in which these constraints and im-ages are translated and transformed—or not—in interaction. By focusing on black 'culture' as it is created, enacted, and experi-enced, I have hoped to reinstate black youth as actors.

As was argued in Chapter 1, the imagination of a homo-genized and unified black social identity has led to the consistent denial of 'culture' and of agency. In placing black communities at the margins, defined only in their relation to the dominant im-agination, black people have been objectified and dehumanized—their experiences rendered opaque and mysterious: they have become, in effect, invisible. As Cornel West has written:

The modern Black diaspora problematic of invisibility and namelessness can be understood as the condition of *relative lack of Black power to present themselves and others as complex human beings, and thereby to contest the bombardment of negative, degrading stereotypes put forward by White supremacist ideologies* (1993: 210; emphasis in original).

This invisibility has been consistently and persuasively chal-lenged by academics, writers, and artists in the arena of 'Culture'. Taking 'Culture' in its more narrowly defined sense of expres-sive and plastic art forms, workers in the domain of cultural production have sought to deconstruct and reimagine the 'rifts and crevices' (Gilroy 1992: 112) of black life and experience. West thus calls for a recognition of human agency and cultural crea-tivity as the foundation of transformative political praxis (1993: 213):

Black cultural workers must constitute and sustain discursive and insti-tutional networks that deconstruct earlier modern Black strategies for identity formation, demystify power relations that incorporate class, patriarchal and homophobic biases, and construct more multivalent and multi-dimensional responses that articulate the complexity and diver-sity of Black practices in the modern and postmodern world (ibid. 212).

It is significant that West, along with others (hooks 1990; Hall 1992*b*; Gilroy 1993), places 'Culture' as the primary arena for contestation and political transformation. It is also significant that West places the onus on 'black cultural workers'; on those artists and writers in the realm of 'Culture'. Such workers are, in a very real sense, faced with the 'burden of representation'—with the ability and responsibility to re-create and re-present, in all its forms, 'The Race'. There exists, then, some ambiguity in even the new theoretical approaches to black culture, in which 'culture' as a way of life becomes inextricable from 'Culture' in its expressive forms: Black 'Culture' becomes emblematic of—and in many cases, substitutes for—black life. Despite equivocations on the relationship between 'art' and 'life' (Gilroy 1993), it is nevertheless true that black cultural theorists have largely focused on precisely those expressive forms as an indicator of lived experience. Such accounts have, to date, largely overlooked the strategies for identity creation at a 'street level'. However, it is the new cultural theory that provides the most appropriate framework for the observations of the present study: perhaps a case of life reflecting art, after all.

CULTURE WARS II: THE NEW CULTURAL POLITICS OF DIFFERENCE

In *Local Knowledge*, Clifford Geertz asserts, 'The Sociology is not About to Begin. . . . It is scattering into frameworks' (1983: 4). Critiquing a holistic and organic approach to 'culture', he writes further:

anthropologists have traditionally taken the old city for their province, wandering around its haphazard alleys trying to work up some sort of rough map of it, and have only lately begun to wonder how the suburbs, which seem to be crowding in more closely all the time, got built (ibid. 73).

Geertz's image is not only of a bounded 'traditional' core surrounded by new creations, but of a landscape radically transformed by constant incursions and reconstructions. 'Culture' then becomes interpretive rather than objective, transient rather than determined, observable but inseparable from the context within which action takes place (1973, 1983). Geertz writes: 'Culture is not a power, something to which social events, behaviors, institutions, or processes can be causally attributed; it is a context within which they can be intelligibly . . . described' (1973: 14).

The perception of 'culture' as a context recognizes both the structures of meaning through which experience is shaped and constrained, and the indeterminacy of the outcome of individual

decisions and actions. 'Culture' is thus at once 'essentially con-
testable' (ibid. 29), and inseparable from the 'hard surfaces' of
political, economic, and social stratifications (ibid. 30).

As Hall (1990, 1992*a*, 1992*b*) and West (1994) have argued further, 'culture' is itself constitutive of 'structure'. West notes, 'Culture is as much a structure as the economy or politics' (1994: 19).
'Culture' becomes inseparable from ideology, which creates
hegemonic structures and which is embodied in collective, communal modes of living, 'Structures and behaviour are inseparable
. . . institutions and values go hand in hand' (ibid. 18). 'Culture'
also becomes the primary terrain for counter-hegemonic movements, which are enacted in the arena of 'civil society' (Simon
1991). It thus becomes inextricably linked to the relations of power
at the centre of social organization; both coercive and resistive,
constantly re-enacted and contested.

Rather than the autonomous and benign 'bubbles' of ethnicist
absolutism, then, 'culture' becomes a site of struggle over meaning, constructed through the relations of power, in which identities are created, negotiated, and contested as part of an ongoing
search for control. The emphasis therefore lies not on the explo-
ration of natural 'difference', but the ways in which 'difference'
is structured, lived out, and fought over; what Hall has termed
'the relations of representation'. As West has noted: 'Distinctive
features of the new cultural politics of difference are to trash the
monolithic and homogeneous in the name of diversity, multiplicity and heterogeneity' (1993: 204).

The 'politics of difference' thus focuses on the interdependent
nature of identity construction (Rutherford 1990), in which social
formations and individual agents interact in a dynamic and
unfinished process. Hall writes:

Perhaps rather than thinking of identity as an already accomplished
fact, which the new cultural practices then represent, we should think,
instead, of identity as a 'production', which is never complete, always
in process and always constituted within, not outside, representation
(1990: 222).

The sense of self becomes 'Not an essence, but a positioning'
(ibid. 226). Moreover, the recognition of the interactive nature
of identity at once opposes and deconstructs dominant notions
about the essentialist nature of racial or gender categories. 'Race'

192   *Conclusion*

becomes one in a complex of factors through which identities are formulated and contested; part of the interplay of disparate elements in a 'process of hybridity' (Bhabha 1990: 211), through which culture and identity are continually reworked and re-created.[1]

These elements of identity are combined through 'articulation' (Rutherford 1990; Bhabha 1990), which Hall has described as the politics of 'no necessary or essential correspondence of anything with anything' (cited by Rutherford 1990: 20). Constructions of 'race'—as of class, gender, sexuality, ethnicity—interact, fusing with or displacing each other in an ongoing process of confrontation and negotiation (Hall 1992b). Identity is constituted through the intersection of political, social, cultural, and historical contingency; it therefore 'has no guarantees in Nature' (ibid. 254). Thus, Hall proclaims ' "the end of innocence", or the end of the innocent notion of the essential black subject' (ibid.).

While acknowledging the constructedness of essentialized 'racial' categories, it would, of course, be naïve and misleading to claim a complete freedom of creative expression for those groups and individuals so defined. That social formations, functioning as ideology, do have tangible, 'lived' effects is indisputable. That these effects are not absolutely determined and determining has proved a source of greater disagreement (Sivanandan 1990).[2] However, the assertion of a cultural 'free-for-all' denies the structures of dominance and subordination through which culture is created and experienced (Harvey 1990; Hall, forthcoming). It also ignores the specificities of historical positioning in the enactment of cultural choice (hooks 1990). Hall writes: 'Cultural identities come from somewhere, have histories . . . identities are the names we give to the different ways we are positioned by, and position ourselves within, the narratives of the past' (1990: 225).

What the 'politics of difference' demands finally is an uprooting of certainty surrounding traditional approaches to identity formation, which allows for both freedom and control within the

[1] Bhabha thus argues that the notion of identity should be replaced with 'identification', which incorporates a non-sovereign sense of self (1990).

[2] Sivanandan asserts: 'Black youth in the inner cities know only the blunt force of the state' (1990: 43). While not denying the structural forces that restrict and oppress black youth in Britain, it is, however, reductive and equally oppressive to deny the creativity with which black young people seek to empower themselves, within, through, and because of these circumstances.

social structure, and places 'culture' at the centre of struggle. Although these forms of struggle are by no means always, or of necessity, coherent, commensurate or 'progressive', as Hall claims:

It is never a zero-sum cultural game; it is always about shifting the balance of power in the relations of culture; it is always about changing the dispositions and the configurations of cultural power, not getting out of it (1992*b*: 24).

The arenas of this 'cultural game' are, however, as this study has shown, often inescapably local and transitory—the living out of constraints, resistance, and emergence in momentary encounters. Within and between such moments, meanings and structures shift and reconfigure, the results indeterminate, often contradictory and sometimes reactionary. There exists within this analysis, therefore, a tension between the actions and intentions of the individual or group, and the 'political' interests of the collective. Bhabha has recently called for a recognition of the possibility of 'agency without intentionality',[3] which rejects the insistence on a collective political consciousness, while allowing for the constrained freedom of individual action.

The question of intentionality, with regard to my informants, proves somewhat vexed. Their self-inventions were often consciously constructed and manipulated to create and maintain control of any given situation; on the other hand, they were often inconsistent, short-lived, and somewhat indeterminate in outcome. This was particularly the case in confrontation with other foci of power, such as in employment situations (Chapter 3) or, indeed, in their interaction with women (Chapter 6). The issue of control within such a shifting matrix of power and hierarchy must inevitably remain unresolved. More than this, these self-constructions were rarely aimed, at least with those young men I knew, at any collective 'political' mobilization, although they were crucially founded upon a series of collective images. That is, they were centred upon stock images and stereotypes of 'the black community', although these could be used as a means of identification or distinction, fusion or fission, as the occasion required. As the examples in Chapter 2 clearly illustrate, the

---

[3] Ethnic Relations Seminar, St Antony's College, Oxford University, 16 June 1994.

meanings and values attached to these images are fluid and constantly shifting, almost from one moment to the next.

There remains, then, a degree of ambiguity around the creation of identities amongst my informants: as Ricky once pointed out to me, 'you have to be able to adapt, or you're fucked'. At the same time, the self-inventions pivoted crucially on the assertion of images that were held to be, at any given moment, relatively fixed; any perceived inappropriacy was immediately cast as an aspersion on the individual's 'racial' (or, indeed, gender or class) identity (Chapter 2). 'Being black' was, then, at once fluid and transiently rigid: Avtar Brah's description of identity formation as a 'kaleidoscope' provides an appropriate metaphor (1992). Furthermore, although my informants were aware of the mutability of their attitudes and behaviour, this was usually regarded with general disinterest. There is little doubt that the boys themselves would not have regarded their actions as the expression of fractured self-representations structured through dominance; they were, simply, a way of—as Frank would say—'passing through'.[4] In this respect, many of the constructions enacted by the boys were accommodations to the expectations of those around them; this is clear, for example, in their social life (Chapter 4). Perhaps partly because of this, the fluidity and sometimes ambiguity of the stances they adopted were not considered unusual or problematic—they were a way of being. More than this, they were a way of being with those around them, often as much an expression of community as of individuality, of solidarity as of contestation.

It is neither the intention, nor within the capabilities, of the present study to seek to resolve these contradictions. Acknowledging that my informants constructed their identities according to the situation and to the immediate aim they were trying to achieve also requires a recognition that these identities were often regarded as the only 'really black' ones—whatever that may mean at any moment in time. Identities were thus both fluid and transiently essentialized, a product of individual choice and of wider circumscriptions. However, what may seem from an external standpoint an impossibly contradictory stance was one

[4] Bhabha terms this, though rather more dramatically, as 'survival' (Ethnic Relations Seminar, 16 June 1994); the ways in which people seek resolutions, however temporary, within situations which are not of their own choosing.

inhabited without reservation by the people I knew. While refusing any easy resolution, therefore, this study also refuses to problematize these self-inventions.

To some extent, it can be argued that it would be both distorting and unfair to reduce the complexities of my informants' lives to the vagaries of theory. The present work has some doubts about casting the boys in any neatly constructed and carefully delineated theoretical mould. In asserting their freedom to create their identities, the constraints must also be acknowledged; in portraying their creativity, the conventions of their circumstances cannot be overlooked. My informants both eschewed essentialism and enacted it, constructed themselves and were constructed, won and lost imaginative space—sometimes at the same time. The dichotomous clarity of theory becomes inescapably blurred when related to lived experience, even when told at second hand.

Nevertheless, it would be equally misleading to deny the significance of theory in contextualizing the actions of my informants. If their identity choices were not as predictable in performance or outcome as one might wish, or as obviously directed at wider societal transformations, neither were they random, egocentric, and insignificant. The strength of theoretical developments in the 'Cultural' (rather than 'cultural') politics of difference for the present work is its refusal of predictability, of easy definitions and solutions, and its recognition of the role of individual and collective agency. Furthermore, the deconstruction of organicist approaches to 'culture' and the recognition of the relations of power in the production of 'culture' are crucial to an understanding of the ways in which the boys strove to create themselves. This new 'culture', then, is not the bounded and organic 'bubble' of ethnicity theory, nor the reified oppositional weapon of early identity politics: this 'culture' is actively and self-consciously made and remade, heterogeneous and often conflicted, unbounded and fractured, imagined, contested, and sometimes reactionary—the product and terrain of 'representation'.

'WRITING CULTURE': THE LIMITS OF ANALYSIS

A study of identity constitutes something of a chimera: it reifies a momentary transaction, fixes what is constantly in flux; it creates, almost by default, the very essence it claims to deny. If, as Hall claims, 'Cultural identity . . . is as much a matter of "becoming" as well as of "being"' (1990: 225), such a study cannot but represent an artificial foreclosure of an ongoing and constantly transforming process (Harvey 1990).

The present study is, then, subject to a number of constraints, in its scope and enunciation. First, it makes no claims to 'objectivity', or to what Shelby Steele has termed 'innocence' (Duneier 1992: 138), 'a feeling of essential goodness in relation to others and, therefore, superiority to others' (ibid.). Rather, the work recognizes and accepts that the accounts presented here are, to some extent, the result of a negotiated and unequal encounter between a number of constructed Subjects and myself. The selections and interpretations offered here are my own, from a range of self-constructions presented to me by my informants: to this extent, they are 'fiction' (Clifford 1986). Secondly, the study recognizes that, in the act of writing, these selections are further mediated and distorted; Harvey thus quotes Baudelaire, 'Writing tears practice and discourse out of the flow of time' (1990: 206). In denying claims to 'Truth', the research offers no alternative; it merely acknowledges its implication in the process of ethnographic creation.

Thirdly, it bears repetition here that the study makes no pretence of, or claims to, representativeness. By seeking to reveal some of the complexities of Black British youth identities, the study lays emphasis more on process than content. It does not, therefore, contend that the encounters, experiences, and reactions recounted should be taken as a general statement about all black youth: indeed, that would be replacing one definition of 'being black' merely with another. On the other hand, however, the process of negotiation and search for control that marked out all of my informants' interactions should not be regarded as unique or unusual. I would argue further that the processes of self-invention described here are not specific to Black British youth, but are applicable to other 'minority' groups, as well as, of course, to the dominant hegemonic group.[5]

---

[5] Work on the constructions of 'whiteness' has been undertaken, for example, by Catherine Hall (ed.), *White, Male and Middle Class* (1992) and 'Nation, Empire, Gender: The White Brotherhood of Britain in the 1860s', presented to the Ethnic Relations Seminar, Oxford, Feb. 1994; Ware (1992).

What this study has attempted to show is the creation of identities amongst a small group of black youth at a particular moment in time. It is a snapshot of the lives I witnessed and shared for twelve months between 1990 and 1991. The study is thus necessarily bound by time and circumstance: it does not aim to provide a historical overview and is wary of making sweeping generalizations. More than this, it acknowledges that since the fieldwork was completed, the lives of my informants have moved on and their identity construction has accordingly undergone transformations beyond the scope of this study.

THE STORY SO FAR . . .

I left London in July 1991. Since then, Angelina successfully completed her teaching course at the London Institute of Education: she is now teaching history and religious studies at a secondary school in South London. Her brothers, Rommell and Darnell, have recently completed their BA degrees in Accounting Studies. Darnell has started a job as a credit controller in a large design firm in North London. Rommell, as yet, has been unable to find a suitable job. Eleanor has been working in the haematology department in a hospital in South London for the past two years. She separated from her boyfriend, Kevin, soon after leaving college and has been seeing a Black British man, Paul, for over a year. Fenella has recently completed a PGCE course in English and Drama at the London Institute of Education, having obtained an upper second class degree in Humanities. She is currently working as a secretary, while she decides on her future plans. She is still with her English boyfriend, Nick, whom she met towards the end of my fieldwork.

'The boys', as I came to know them, no longer exist. Towards the end of my time in London, a number of obvious fissures appeared in the group's structure and have since dissipated much of its internal cohesion. Although they still keep in contact, they rarely meet as a group and operate in the public sphere only infrequently. Ricky, my erstwhile flatmate, undertook a trainee manager's course for a shoe retail company and has been working in their stores for some time. He and Anne got married in January 1993 and have moved to a new flat in Tower Hill. Anne

completed her nursing degree and has started a computer training course. Clive has been unable to find comparable employment since his 'redundancy' from the stockbrokers. He has been
working in Marks and Spencer as a sales assistant—in, he informed me, the ladies' underwear department—for the past eight-
een months. He is also taking night classes in accountancy and
remains optimistic about his chances for career development. He
has finally separated from his long-time girlfriend, Pat, but still
sees their son regularly. Frank has returned to university in London to study aeronautic engineering and is seen only rarely by
the others; Edgar has also started university, studying psychology. Shane has become a father and married last year. His wife
is continuing with her nursing career and is pregnant again; Shane
stays at home to look after their son. He continues with his musical
ambitions and has a weekly spot as a singer in a nightclub in
East London. Nathan lost his job at the advertising company in
Covent Garden, but has since found employment in the same
field—though at a lower salary. He is currently living with his
English girlfriend at his mother's house in South London. Arif
has found a new flatmate and has allied himself with an all-
white group, in which, Ricky told me, he is the epitome of 'black'
style. Satish and Dion separated, but, after spending a year apart,
have recently reunited. Satish is working as an electrical engineer
and Dion works nights as a carer at an old people's home. She
is hoping to have another child in the near future. Malcolm is
believed to be living with his girlfriend, Veronica, but his life
remains otherwise relatively unchanged.

Black British youth identity can best be understood, therefore, as
a momentary configuration of images and attitudes, formed in
interaction with others and encapsulating a multiplicity of shifting definitions and interpretations. The interaction between these
multiple images is complex and alters with both the context and
the individual concerned: perhaps inevitably, then, a study such
as this raises more questions than it answers. What is clear, however, is that the creation of black youth identity cannot be encapsulated within any simple paradigm centred around assumptions
based on 'race'. It thus transcends the role of symbol or victim,
combining disparate and sometimes contradictory elements,
external definitions and internal redefinitions, in what Gates has

termed 'constrained contestation'.[6] This recognizes both the salience of power in restricting identity choice and of the ability to
confront and challenge such limitations. Black British youth identity is, then, necessarily incomplete, in a state of constant flux
and reinvention, engaged in a continual process of 'becoming'.

Black British youth identity is thus something of an 'art'. It is
an 'imagined' construction, which is constantly reinvented and
challenges traditional notions of essentialized cultural or racial
entities. Although the belief in an essentialized 'black' identity
forms an integral part both of British society and of parts of
black youth culture—for example, with some branches of the
Black Moslem movement—such reifications are being continually contested by the experiences, actions, and attitudes of Black
British youth themselves. 'Being black' is at once a demand for
inclusion within the bounds of 'British' identity and a celebration
of 'hybridity'—

'I am not, really, a stranger any longer' (Baldwin 1985).

---

[6] Clarendon Lectures, Oxford University, 1992.

BIBLIOGRAPHY

ADEBAYO, D. (1990), 'Bigot MP in New Race Row', *Voice* (6 Nov.).
ALEXANDER, J. (1991), 'Flying Colours', *Guardian* (June).
ANDERSON, B. (1983), *Imagined Communities* (London: Verso).
ANDERSON, E. (1978), *A Place on the Corner* (Chicago: University of Chicago Press).
—— (1990), *Streetwise: Race, Class and Change in an Urban Community* (Chicago: University of Chicago Press).
—— (1994), 'The Code of the Streets', *Atlantic Monthly* (May), 80–94.
ANTHIAS, F., and YUVAL-DAVIS, N. (1993), *Racialized Boundaries* (London: Routledge).
ARDENER, E. (1987), 'Remote Areas', in A. Jackson (ed.), *Anthropology at Home* (London: Tavistock).
BAKER, L. (1989), 'Funki like a Dred', *Face* (Apr.).
BALDWIN, J. (1961), *Nobody Knows My Name* (New York: Dial).
—— (1963), *The Fire Next Time* (New York: Dial).
—— (1985), *Notes of a Native Son* (London: Pluto).
BARKER, M. (1981), *The New Racism* (London: Junction Books).
BARTH, F. (1969), Introduction in F. Barth (ed.), *Ethnic Groups and Boundaries* (Bergen: Universitetsforlaget).
BAUMANN, Z. (1988), 'Strangers: The Social Construction of Universality and Particularity', *Telos*, 78: 7–42.
BENSON, S. (1981), *Ambiguous Ethnicity* (Cambridge: Cambridge University Press).
—— (forthcoming), 'Asians Have Culture, West Indians Have Problems: Discourses on Race Inside and Outside Anthropology', in Y. Samad, O. Stuart, and T. O. Ranger (eds.), *Culture, Identity and Politics* (Aldershot: Avebury Press).
BEN-TOVIM, G., GABRIEL, J., LAW, I., and STREDDER, K. (1986), 'A Political Analysis of Local Struggles for Racial Equality', in J. Rex and D. Mason (eds.), *Theories of Race and Ethnic Relations* (Cambridge: Cambridge University Press).
BHABHA, H. (1990), 'Interview with Homi Bhabha: The Third Space', in J. Rutherford (ed.), *Identity: Community, Culture, Difference* (London: Lawrence & Wishart).
—— (1994), *The Location of Culture* (London and New York: Routledge).
BHAT, A., CARR-HILL, R., and OHRI, S. (1988), *Britain's Black Population* (Aldershot: Gower).
BOTT, E. (1971), *Family and Social Network* (London: Tavistock).

BRAH, A. (1992), 'Difference, Diversity and Differentiation', in J. Donald and A. Rattansi (eds.), *'Race', Culture and Difference* (London: Sage).

BRAKE, M. (1980), *The Sociology of Youth and Youth Subcultures* (London: Routledge & Kegan Paul).

BROWN, C. (1984), *Black and White Britain: The Third PSI Survey* (Policy Studies Institute: Heinemann Educational).

—— (1992), ' "Same Difference": The Persistence of Racial Disadvantage in the British Employment Market', in P. Braham, A. Rattansi, and R. Skellington (eds.), *Racism and Antiracism* (London: Sage).

CASHMORE, E. E. (1979), *Rastaman: The Rastafarian Movement in England* (London: Allen & Unwin).

—— and Troyna, B. (1982) (eds.), *Black Youth in Crisis* (London: Allen & Unwin).

CCCS (Centre for Contemporary Cultural Studies) (1982), *The Empire Strikes Back* (London: Hutchinson).

CLIFFORD, J. (1986), 'Partial Truths', in J. Clifford and G. Marcus (eds.), *Writing Culture: The Poetics and Politics of Ethnography* (Berkeley and Los Angeles: University of California).

—— (1988), *The Predicament of Culture* (Cambridge, Mass.: Harvard University Press).

COHEN, A. (1974) (ed.), *Urban Ethnicity* (ASA Monograph, 12; London: Tavistock).

—— (1993), *Masquerade Politics* (Oxford: Berg).

COHEN, A. K. (1955), *Delinquent Boys* (Chicago: Free Press).

COHEN, S. (1980), *Folk Devils and Moral Panics* (Oxford: Basil Blackwell).

CROSS, M., and JOHNSON, M. (1988), 'Mobility Denied: Afro-Caribbean Labour and the British Economy', in M. Cross and H. Entzinger (eds.), *Lost Illusions: Caribbean Minorities in Britain and the Netherlands* (London: Routledge).

—— and ENTZINGER, H. (1988), *Lost Illusions: Caribbean Minorities in Britain and the Netherlands* (London: Routledge).

CULLER, J. (1988), *Framing the Sign* (Oxford: Blackwell).

DANNATT, A. (1989), 'Cut and Strut', *Guardian* (11 Sept.).

DENT, G. (1992), 'Black Pleasure, Black Joy: An Introduction', in *Black Popular Culture* (Seattle: Bay Press).

DONALD, J., and RATTANSI, A. (1992) (eds.), *'Race', Culture and Difference* (London: Sage).

DOWNES, D. M. (1966), *The Delinquent Solution* (London: Routledge & Kegan Paul).

DuBOIS, W. E. B. (1969), *The Souls of Black Folk* (New York: Signet).

DUNEIER, M. (1992), *Slim's Table* (Chicago: University of Chicago Press).

EADE, J. (forthcoming), 'Ethnicity and the Politics of Cultural Difference: An Agenda for the 1990s?', in Y. Samad, O. Stuart, and T. O. Ranger (eds.), *Culture, Identity and Politics* (Aldershot: Avebury Press).

EGGLESTONE, J., *et al.* (1986), *Education for Some* (London: Trentham).

ELY, M., *et al.* (1991), *Doing Qualitative Research: Circles within Circles* (New York: Falmer Press).

ENLOE, C. (1989), 'Nationalism and Masculinity', in *Bananas, Beaches and Bases* (London: Pandora).

FISHER, G., and JOSHUA, H. (1982), 'Social Policy and Black Youth', in E. E. Cashmore and B. Troyna (eds.), *Black Youth in Crisis* (London: Allen & Unwin).

FITZGERALD, M. (1988), 'Afro-Caribbeans in British Politics', in M. Cross and H. Entzinger (eds.), *Lost Illusions: Caribbean Minorities in Britain and the Netherlands* (London: Routledge).

FOLB, E. (1980), *Runnin' Down Some Lines: The Language and Culture of Black Teenagers* (Cambridge, Mass.: Harvard University Press).

FRYER, P. (1984), *Staying Power* (London: Pluto Press).

GASKELL, C., and SMITH, P. (1981), ' "Alienated" Black Youth: An Investigation of "Conventional Wisdom" Explanations', *New Community*, 9/2 (Autumn): 182–93.

GATES, Jr., H. L. (1992), *Loose Canons: Notes on the Culture Wars* (New York: Oxford University Press).

GEERTZ, C. (1973), *The Interpretation of Cultures* (New York: Basic Books).

—— (1983), *Local Knowledge* (New York: Basic Books).

GILLESPIE, M. A. (1993), 'What's Good for the Race?', *Ms. Magazine* (Jan./Feb., 80–1).

GILROY, P. (1982a), 'Police and Thieves', in Centre for Contemporary Cultural Studies, *The Empire Strikes Back* (London: Hutchinson).

—— (1982b), 'Steppin' Out of Babylon: Race, Class and Autonomy', in Centre for Contemporary Cultural Studies, *The Empire Strikes Back* (London: Hutchinson).

—— (1987), *There Ain't No Black in the Union Jack* (London: Hutchinson).

—— (1992), 'The End of Anti-Racism', in A. Rattansi and J. Donald (eds.), *'Race', Culture and Difference* (London: Sage).

—— (1993), *Small Acts* (London: Serpent's Tail).

GLAZER, N., and MOYNIHAN, D. P. (1963), *Beyond the Melting Pot* (Cambridge, Mass.: MIT Press).

GUTZMORE, C. (1983), 'Capital, Black Youth and Crime', *Race and Class*, 25/2: 13–30.

HALL, C. (1992) (ed.), *White, Male and Middle-Class: Explorations in Feminism and History* (Cambridge: Polity Press).

HALL, S. (1980), 'Race, Articulation and Societies Structured in Dominance', in UNESCO, *Sociological Theories: Race and Colonialism* (Paris: UNESCO).

—— (1990), 'Cultural Identity and Diaspora', in J. Rutherford (ed.), *Identity: Community, Culture, Difference* (London: Lawrence & Wishart).

—— (1992a), 'New Ethnicities', in J. Donald and A. Rattansi (eds.), *'Race', Culture and Difference* (London: Sage).

—— (1992*b*), 'What is this "Black" in Black Popular Culture?', in G. Dent (ed.), *Black Popular Culture* (Seattle: Bay Press).

—— (forthcoming), 'Political Mobilization and Identity', in Y. Samad, O. Stuart, and T. O. Ranger (eds.), *Culture, Identity and Politics* (Aldershot: Avebury Press).

—— and JEFFERSON, T. (1976) (eds.), *Resistance through Ritual* (London: Hutchinson).

—— *et al.* (1978), *Policing the Crisis* (London: Macmillan).

HANNERZ, U. (1969), *Soulside: Enquiries into Ghetto Culture and Community* (New York: Columbia University Press).

—— (1974), 'Ethnicity and Opportunity in Urban America', in A. Cohen (ed.), *Urban Ethnicity* (London: Tavistock).

—— (1977), 'Growing Up Male', in D. Y. Wilkinson and R. Taylor (eds.), *The Black Male in America* (Chicago: Nelson Hall).

HARVEY, D. (1990), *The Condition of Postmodernity* (Oxford: Basil Blackwell).

HEBDIGE, D. (1976), 'Reggae, Rastas and Rudies', in S. Hall and T. Jefferson (eds.), *Resistance through Rituals* (London: Hutchinson).

—— (1979), *Subculture: The Meaning of Style* (London: Methuen).

HENNESSY, A. (1988), 'Workers of the Night: West Indians in Britain', in M. Cross and H. Entzinger (eds.), *Lost Illusions: Caribbean Minorities in Britain and the Netherlands* (London: Routledge).

HEWITT, R. (1986), *White Talk, Black Talk* (Cambridge: Cambridge University Press).

HOOKS, B. (1990), *Yearning: Race, Gender and Cultural Politics* (Boston: South End Press).

—— (1992), *Black Looks* (London: Turnaround Press).

HOWE, D. (1982), 'From Bobby to Babylon, Part 3: Brixton before the Uprising', *Race Today*, 14/2: 61–9.

ISAACS, H. R. (1975), *Idols of the Tribe* (Cambridge, Mass.: Harvard University Press).

JACOBS, B. D. (1988), *Racism in Britain* (London: Christopher Helm).

JAMES, W. (1986), 'A Long Way from Home: On Black Identity in Britain', *Immigrants and Minorities*, 5/3: 258–84.

JENCKS, C. (1992), *Rethinking Social Policy* (Cambridge, Mass.: Harvard University Press).

JENKINS, R. (1986), 'Social-Anthropological Models of Inter-Ethnic Relations', in J. Rex and D. Mason (eds.), *Theories of Race and Ethnic Relations* (Cambridge: Cambridge University Press).

—— (1992), 'Black Workers in the Labour Market: The Price of Recession', in P. Braham, A. Rattansi, and R. Skellington (eds.), *Racism and Antiracism* (London: Sage).

JONES, J. (1992), 'The Accusatory Space', in G. Dent (ed.), *Black Popular Culture* (Seattle: Bay Press).

JONES, S. (1988), *Black Culture, White Youth* (London: Macmillan Education).

KOGBARA, D. (1992), *The Sunday Times* (24 May).

LAWRENCE, E. (1982*a*), 'Just Plain Commonsense: The "Roots of Racism" ', in Centre for Contemporary Cultural Studies, *The Empire Strikes Back* (London: Hutchinson).

—— (1982*b*), ' "In the Abundance of Water the Fool is Thirsty": Sociology and Black "Pathology" ', in Centre for Contemporary Cultural Studies, *The Empire Strikes Back* (London: Hutchinson).

LIEBOW, E. (1967), *Tally's Corner: A Study of Negro Street-Corner Men* (Boston: Little, Brown & Co.).

MATZA, D. (1964), *Delinquency and Drift* (New York: John Wiley).

MERCER, K. (1988), 'Racism and the Politics of Masculinity', in R. Chapman and J. Rutherford (eds.), *Male Order: Unwrapping Masculinity* (London: Lawrence & Wishart).

MILES, R. (1982), *Racism and Migrant Labour* (London: Routledge).

MIRZA, H. S. (1992), *Young, Female and Black* (London: Routledge).

MUNGHAM, G., and PEARSON, G. (1976) (eds.), *Working Class Youth Cultures* (London: Routledge & Kegan Paul).

PATRON, E. J. (1989), 'By Any Means Necessary?', *Sky Magazine* (Sept.).

PATTERSON, S. (1965), *Dark Strangers* (Harmondsworth: Penguin).

PEACH, C. (1984), 'The Force of West Indian Island Identity in Britain', in C. Clarke, J. Ley, and C. Peach (eds.), *Geography and Ethnic Pluralism* (London: Allen & Unwin).

—— (1986), 'Patterns of Afro-Caribbean Migration and Settlement in Great Britain, 1945–81', in C. Brock (ed.), *The Caribbean in Europe* (London: Frank Cass).

POPHAM, P. (1993), 'Now in your Back Yard', *Independent Magazine* (30 Nov.).

PRYCE, K. (1967), *Endless Pressure* (Harmondsworth: Penguin).

RAMDIN, R. (1987), *The Making of the Black Working Class in Britain* (Aldershot: Gower).

REX, J. (1983), *Race Relations in Sociological Theory* (London: Routledge & Kegan Paul).

—— (1986), *Race and Ethnicity* (Milton Keynes: Open University Press).

—— and MOORE, R. (1967), *Race, Community, and Conflict* (London: Oxford University Press).

—— and MASON, D. (1986) (eds.), *Theories of Race and Ethnic Relations* (Cambridge: Cambridge University Press).

ROCK, P. (1979), *The Making of Symbolic Interactionism* (London: Macmillan).

RUTHERFORD, J. (1990), 'A Place Called Home: Identity and the Cultural Politics of Difference', in J. Rutherford (ed.), *Identity: Community, Culture, Difference* (London: Lawrence & Wishart).

SAMAD, Y. (1992), 'Book Burning and Race Relations: The Political Mobilisation of Bradford Muslims', *New Community*, 18/4: 507–19.

SCARMAN, Lord Justice (1986), *The Scarman Report* (Harmondsworth: Penguin).

SCHULZ, D. (1977), 'Growing Up as a Boy in the Ghetto', in D. Y. Wilkinson and R. Taylor (eds.), *The Black Male in America* (Chicago: Nelson Hall).

SEGAL, L. (1990), *Slow Motion: Changing Masculinities, Changing Men* (London: Virago).

SIMON, R. (1991), *Gramsci's Political Thought: An Introduction* (London: Lawrence & Wishart).

SIVANANDAN, A. (1981/2), 'From Resistance to Rebellion: Asian and Afro-Caribbean Struggles in Britain', *Race and Class*, 23/2–3: 111–51.

—— (1982), *A Different Hunger* (London: Pluto Press).

—— (1990), 'All that Melts into Air is Solid: The Hokum of New Times', in *Communities of Resistance* (London: Verso).

Sky Magazine (Sept. 1989).

SMALL, S. (1991), 'A Critique of Research on "Race Relations" in Britain', *Charles Wootton News* (June), 11–13.

—— (1994), *Racialized Barriers: The Black Experience in the United States and England in the 1980s* (London and New York: Routledge).

SOLOMOS, J. (1986), 'Varieties of Marxist Conceptions of "Race", Class and the State: A Critical Analysis', in J. Rex and D. Mason (eds.), *Theories of Race and Ethnic Relations* (Cambridge: Cambridge University Press).

—— (1988), *Black Youth, Racism and the State* (Cambridge: Cambridge University Press).

—— (1992), 'The Politics of Immigration since 1945', in P. Braham, A. Rattansi, and R. Skellington (eds.), *Racism and Antiracism* (London: Sage).

—— (1993), *Race and Racism in Britain*, 2nd edn. (Basingstoke: Macmillan).

—— et al. (1982), 'The Organic Crisis of British Capitalism and Race: The Experience of the Seventies', in CCCS, *The Empire Strikes Back* (London: Hutchinson).

STOLCKE, V. (1993), 'Is Sex to Gender as Race is to Ethnicity?', in T. del Valle (ed.), *Gendered Anthropology* (London: Routledge).

TAYLOR, R. L. (1977), 'Socialization to the Black Male Role', in D. Y. Wilkinson and R. Taylor (eds.), *The Black Male in America* (Chicago: Nelson Hall).

TONKIN, E., MCDONALD, M., and CHAPMAN, M. (1989) (eds.), *History and Ethnicity* (London: Routledge).

TROYNA, B. (1979), 'Differential Commitment to Ethnic Identity by Black Youths in Britain', *New Community*, 7/3 (Winter): 406–14.

Voice, (1992), 'Raga Girls are in Town' (21 Apr.).

WALLACE, M. (1990), *Black Macho and the Myth of the Superwoman* (London: Verso).

WALLMAN, S. (1986), 'Ethnicity and the Boundary Process in Context', in J. Rex and D. Mason (eds.), *Theories of Race and Ethnic Relations* (Cambridge: Cambridge University Press).

WARE, VRON (1992), *Beyond the Pale: White Women, Racism and History* (London: Verso).

WATERS, M. C. (1990), *Ethnic Options: Choosing Identities in America* (Berkeley and Los Angeles: University of California Press).

WEEKS, J. (1990), 'The Value of Difference', in J. Rutherford (ed.), *Identity: Community, Culture, Difference* (London: Lawrence & Wishart).

WEST, C. (1993), 'The New Cultural Politics of Difference', in S. During (ed.), *The Cultural Studies Reader* (London: Routledge).

—— (1994), *Race Matters* (New York: Vintage).

WESTERN, J. (1992), *A Passage to England: Barbadian Londoners Speak of Home* (Minneapolis: University of Minnesota).

WILLIS, P. (1977), *Learning to Labour* (Farnborough: Saxon House).

—— (1978), *Profane Culture* (London: Routledge & Kegan Paul).

WILMOTT, P. (1966), *Adolescent Boys of East London* (London: Routledge & Kegan Paul).

WRENCH, J. (1992), 'New Vocationalism, Old Racism and the Careers Service', in P. Braham, A. Rattansi, and R. Skellington (eds.), *Racism and Antiracism* (London: Sage).

INDEX